Hebrew Academy of West Queens

*To give every Jewish child a Torah education,
no matter what their background,
and make them and their families* שומרי תורה ומצות

A lofty goal, no doubt, yet critical to the survival of the Jewish nation in these turbulent and rapidly changing times.

Since opening its doors in 1965, the Hebrew Academy of West Queens has provided thousands of children with a Torah-true education.

In addition to a full Yeshiva curriculum featuring superior Jewish and secular studies divisions, the Hebrew Academy operates a specialized and highly successful outreach program. Remedial classes, private tutoring and social services are offered to former public school students, as well as to Soviet, Iranian and Israeli emigres.

Unique in its approach, the program blends the new with the old, the recently arrived with the veteran yeshiva student, to facilitate a quick and effective transition into the school's mainstream classes.

Each year, hundreds of foreign children find new life within the Yeshiva's caring environment. Its dedicated staff members have inspired many to embrace our beautiful heritage and become outstanding members of the American Jewish community.

88-01 102nd Street / Richmond Hill

2

In memory of

Rabbi Michael Scholar

הרב ירחמיאל יח׳אל מיכל בן אברהם אבא סקאלער

A dedicated Rebbe and Marbitz Torah
who brought Torah and its values
to the children of the
Hebrew Academy of West Queens
with his exemplary generosity and kindness.

Bernard Zynlewski, President
Rabbi Moshe Stahler, Dean
Rabbi Aaron Scholar, Administrator

In Memory of

Mr. Herschel Walfish

Our beloved Husband, Brother, Father,
Grandfather, and Gread-Grandfather

לזכר ולעלוי נשמת האי גברא יקירא, איש תם וישר
ר' צבי בן שלמה זלמן הלוי ע"ה
נפטר בשם טוב ח' ניסן תשס"א

His selfless devotion and guidance
will never be forgotten

Miriam Walfish
Oscar Walfish and Bernie
Jack and Chani Walfish
Frances and Pinchas Shalit
Ari and Alyson Walfish
Avi and Gila Tashman
Menachem and Michelle Walfish
Moshe Walfish
Doron, Tzippy, Anat, and Chen Shalit
Avi, Uri, Naomi, Shmuli, Rifkie, and Yonah

In Memory of
Mr. Abraham Feldstein

לזכר נשמת

ר' אברהם ב"ר זאב הכ"מ

י"ד אלול תשנ"ח

Whose experiences and accomplishments
could fill several lifetimes.
Whose חסד was done with all his heart.
Whose love for his family knew no bounds.

His irreplaceable presence is sorely missed.

The Feldstein Family

ישראל אשר

The kindness that you bestowed
upon our family
will never be forgotten.
Your generosity and your soft words
you said to us about Gregory
will remain in our hearts forever.
We will find the strength we need
in each other as time stands still.

Cary and Madeline Schwartz
Amanda and Alyson

Dedicated in Cherished Memory of our
Dear Son and Brother

Michael Ross Feurman

A loving heart and Ben Torah
and a complete joy
to all who were privileged to know him.
During his brief lifetime he brought us
only nachas and happiness.

The Feurman Family

כי אם בתורת ה' חפצו ובתורתו יהגה יומם ולילה

His desire is in the Torah of Hashem
and in His Torah he meditates day and night.

In Memory of

David Gordon

Florence Gordon

Hy Fein

Leonard Steiner

Evelyn Herzog

Hy Herzog

Martin Schultz

Milton Steiner

Rochel Leah Schnabel

Chaim Schnabel

Iris Gordon Fein and Morris Schnabel

לזכר נשמות

ר' שלמה רפאל בן חיים סראלאוויטש

חיה בת ר' אליעזר הלוי סראלאוויטש

ר' נפתלי בן ר' רפאל פרוידינבערגער

אסתר בת ר' יחיאל מיכל ווינקלער

May their exemplary lives of devotion to Torah
and chesed be an inspiration to their children,
grandchildren and great grandchildren

Mr. and Mrs. Allen Szrolovits
and Family

In Memory of
our beloved parents
Mr. Joseph Leitner ע״ה
Mrs. Fanny Leitner ע״ה
Mr. Ernest Prager ע״ה
Mrs. Edith Prager ע״ה
Who taught us, guided us,
and inspired us בדרך התורה
so that we could do the same
for our children

Shmuel and Yocheved Prager

לזכר נשמת

In memory of
our beloved and esteemed
friend and colleague

Paul Mittel

ר' יששכר ב"ר דניאל הלוי

שנלב"ע בערב שבת נחמו נחמו עמי

ט"ו באב תשנ"ב

Who served as Vice President
of our Yeshiva for may years
with dedication, total commitment,
personal involvement and sacrifice.

Hebrew Academy of West Queens
Mr. Bernard Zynlewski, President
Mr. Ludwig Katz, Vice President
Mr. Jerry Ornstein, Treasurer
Mrs. Iris Fein, Secretary
Rabbi Moshe Stahler, Dean
Rabbi Aaron Scholar, Administrator

In Memory of Our Beloved Sister and Aunt

Ethel Somerstein

עטיל סערקא בת יוסף ע"ה

Whose sudden and untimely *petirah* has
left us all with a tremendous emptiness and loss.
Her acts of *chesed,* her friendliness and ever
ready smile, her words of sound advice, her
graciousness and true beauty have created for
us wonderful memories, which with Hashem's
help, will be a constant and everlasting source
of *chizuk* for us.

Miriam and Moshe Stahler and Family
Hinda and Shlomo Orbach and Family
Yocheved and Shmuel Prager and Family
Shoshana and Harry Kaplovitz and Family

In Memory of

Morris and Anna Hulkower

Louis and Rose Zyniewski

Lee Zyniewski

Libby Alperowitz

Helen Goodman

Sarah Schurman

לזכר נשמות

ר' יוסף בן ר' יעקב ע"ה
מרת פייגא בת ר' יעקב ע"ה
ר' חיים יהושע בן ר' דוד ע"ה
מרת חנה בת ר' משה הכהן ע"ה
מרת שרה פייגא בת ר' חיים יהושע ע"ה
מרת עטיל סערקא בת ר' יוסף ע"ה

In Loving Memory of

Joseph and Fanny Leitner
Hyman and Anna Stahler
Sandra Fay Stahler
Ethel Somerstein

Their lifelong dedication to Torah education
continues to be an inspiration to us
their children and grandchildren

Rabbi and Mrs. Moshe Stahler
and Yosefa
Rabbi and Mrs. David Zharnest
and Family
Mr. and Mrs. Yaakov Stahler
and Family

ArtScroll Series®

Rabbi Nosson Scherman / Rabbi Meir Zlotowitz

General Editors

Rabbi Frand

Published by

Mesorah Publications, ltd

on the Parashah

Insights, stories and observations
by Rabbi Yissocher Frand
on the weekly Torah reading

FIRST EDITION
First Impression ... August 2001

Published and Distributed by
MESORAH PUBLICATIONS, LTD.
4401 Second Avenue / Brooklyn, N.Y 11232

Distributed in Europe by
LEHMANNS
Unit E, Viking Industrial Park
Rolling Mill Road
Jarow, Tyne & Wear, NE32 3DP
England

Distributed in Australia and New Zealand by
GOLDS WORLDS OF JUDAICA
3-13 William Street
Balaclava, Melbourne 3183
Victoria, Australia

Distributed in Israel by
SIFRIATI / A. GITLER — BOOKS
6 Hayarkon Street
Bnei Brak 51127

Distributed in South Africa by
KOLLEL BOOKSHOP
Shop 8A Norwood Hypermarket
Norwood 2196, Johannesburg, South Africa

ARTSCROLL SERIES®
RABBI FRAND ON THE PARASHAH
© Copyright 2001, by MESORAH PUBLICATIONS, Ltd.
4401 Second Avenue / Brooklyn, N.Y. 11232 / (718) 921-9000 / www.artscroll.com

ISBN:
1-57819-594-2 (hard cover)
1-57819-595-0 (paperback)

Typography by CompuScribe at ArtScroll Studios, Ltd.

Printed in the United States of America by Noble Book Press Corp.
Bound by Sefercraft, Quality Bookbinders, Ltd., Brooklyn N.Y. 11232

This book is dedicated to our grandfather and
great-grandfather,

BERNARD MARGOLIUS

who has always instilled in us the importance
of Judaism and a passion for knowledge.

Michael, Ann, Benjamin, and Rose Karlin

Dedicated in honor and appreciation
to our parents,

MARSHALL AND SYLVIA LAVINE,
HAROLD AND DOLORES ARNOVITZ

From their children,
David and Andi Arnovitz

הרב אהרן פלדמן
רח' הפסגה 71
ירושלים

בס"ד ירושלים ת"ו טז באב תשס"א

הן הראני הרה"ג הרב ר' יששכר דוב פראנד שליט"א ר"מ בישיבת
נר ישראל גליונות מספר שהולך ומוציא לאור, הכולל מאמרים
שנשא בפני קהל שומעי לקחו, המיוסדים על אדני פז של דברי
חז"ל ומפרשיהם הראשונים והאחרונים, והמסודרים בשפה
האנגלית בכתיבה נאותה ובצורה המושכת את הלב כדי שהספר
יהי' שוה לכל נפש.

והרב הנ"ל ידוע זה רבות בשנים כמרביץ תורה מובהק וכאחד
מהנואמים הגדולים של דורנו ששמעו הולך בכל הארץ ע"י
קלטות לרבבות המופצות בכל קצוות תבל. ומכיון דאיתמחי גברא
ואיתמחי קמיע אני מברכו שבקרוב יצא ספרו לאור עולם ואין לי
ספק שרבים יהנו לאורו ויתקדש שם שמים על ידו, והנני גם מברכו
שיצליח ד' את דרכו בהמשך העמדת תלמידים ובהמשך השפעתו
הגדולה על העם.

החותם לכבוד התורה ולומדיה,

אהרן פלדמן

Table of Contents

Shemos

Vayikra

Bamidbar

Preface

PREFACES USUALLY CONTAIN A PARAGRAPH OR TWO IN which the author thanks those individuals who contributed to the preparation and publication of the book. In this present volume, the entire preface must be devoted to acknowledgments, because this book is really the joint effort of many individuals. Let me explain by giving some background of the genesis of this book.

Just about twenty years ago, I started giving a weekly *shiur* at the Agudas Yisroel of Baltimore, Maryland. The format of the *shiur* was to explore some *halachic* issue with a loose connection (which became looser and looser as the years went by) to the *parashah* for about forty-five minutes and then to complete the hour with fifteen minutes of *divrei Torah* on the *parashah* itself. As it turned out, this weekly hour has changed my life in a profound way, for these *shiurim* were eventually taped and distributed, on a scale I never could have imagined.

About five or six years ago, one of the regulars at the weekly *shiur*, Mr. Hillel Markowitz, asked if he could write them up for distribution via e-mail. At the time, I had no clue about e-mail, but I figured if it could reach more people there would be more *harbatzas Torah*. And so, almost ad hoc, the concept of distributing the *shiur* via e-mail began.

Mr. Markowitz took it upon himself to take notes during the *shiur*, rewrite them and then send them out. Since the *shiur* was given on Thursday and people had to receive it before Shabbos, he was working with a window of a few hours at best. The time pressure and the logistical demands made the task too difficult, and we sought a better way of doing it. We settled on the idea of taking tapes from previous years so that they could be transcribed, reviewed and edited properly and without tight time constraints. The vehicle of distribution became an organization called Project Genesis, which had begun to do electronic Torah distribution.

The biggest challenge was finding someone who could undertake the arduous task of listening to the tapes and turning them into readable essays. My lifelong friend Rabbi David Twersky of Seattle, Washington, eagerly accepted this tremendous task. Fortunate is the person who still maintains a close friendship with a kindergarten mate, especially when separated by an entire continent.

Working in obscurity, almost anonymously, David diligently and brilliantly turned the spoken word into the written word. And now, more than five years later, there are more than 13,000 people who download these *divrei Torah* every week.

The journey from David's keyboard to someone's computer screen sometimes took a circuitous route. A *talmid* of mine, Rabbi Dovid Hoffman, was the relay person to get David's work to Project Genesis. Dovid was learning in *kollel* in Yerushalayim at the time. Consequently, the words traveled from Seattle to Yerushalayim and then back to the offices of Project Genesis in Baltimore, Maryland. Given the time differences among all these venues and the pressure of Shabbos, you can well imagine the difficulties involved. For this, I give my great thanks to both Rabbi Dovid Hoffman and Rabbi Yaakov Menken of Project Genesis.

After speaking about the *parashas hashavua* for more than twenty years, I've learned that you can go through the *parashah* again and again year after year and discover new insights all the time. I've also found that just about all people love to hear a nice *vort* on the *parashah*. In fact, the *parashah* seems to unify the entire spectrum of Klal Yisroel like no other area of Torah study, even more so than the wonderful Daf Yomi does. All people, old and young, men, women and children, and people from all walks of life and all backgrounds share the *parashah*. It is the same for all of them; everyone is "holding" in the same place at the same time. I can speak about the *parashah* with my three-year-old granddaughter as well as with *rabbanim* and *roshei yeshivah*.

This book is a compilation of several years' worth of Chumash *shiurim* previously available on tape or through electronic distribution. I have tried to choose those thoughts that in addition to the basic comment of one of the commentators contain some additional material — sometimes a story, an analogy or an application to a different area of Torah or to life and every so often an insight of my own. That is why this book is a collective effort, not only by the people I have mentioned, but from the thousands of years of Jewish thought on the *parashah*, from Chazal to the Rishonim to the likes of the Chasam Sofer, Meshech Chachmah and Sfas Emes. I apologize in advance if I have not given proper credit to the original authors. It was certainly not intentional.

This project required a fair amount of work in selecting and then recasting those pieces I thought appropriate. For this I am indebted to my son Baruch Yair, who spent a considerable amount of time going through several years of *shiurim*. Since this *sefer* is not unique or original in the essays I present, I very much wanted them to read easily and cogently, while at the same time maintaining the tone and style in which they were originally said. For this I turned to Rabbi Yaakov Yosef Reinman whose beautiful pen and delicate ear have captured how I wanted these *shiurim* presented. It has been a pleasure working with him, and to him I say, "*Yasher koach.*"

They talk about the global village, or for us, the global shtetl. Through the technology of e-mail, I have come into contact with people all over the world who send me comments and questions on the *shiurim*. I have never met most of these people and probably never will. And yet a bond is created via e-mail exchanges, and sometimes a chance encounter through my travels. Two such people are Michael Karlin and David Arnovitz who graciously and generously dedicated this present volume. Their motivation was one thing and one thing only — *harbatzas Torah*, spreading the light of Torah. May the Almighty grant them *nachas* from their families and continued success in all their endeavors.

This match between Michael, David and myself required, as all good matches do, a matchmaker, and he is Rabbi David Silverman of Atlanta. To him I say, "*Gadol hame'aseh yoseir min ha'oseh. Yasher koach ve'tizkeh lemitzvos.*"

This is my third book published by ArtScroll, a wonderful organization with which to be associated. Rabbi Meir Zlotowitz and Rabbi Nosson Scherman have built a truly world-class organization and surrounded themselves with talented, dedicated people, like Rabbi Avrohom Biderman, who have helped bring this book to publication. Special thanks to Rabbi Zlotowitz for the special efforts he made on my behalf. I consider him more than just my publisher; he is my friend.

Writing a book is not something one does very often, and at least for me, it is a milestone at which to stop and reflect. On the eve of publication of this volume, I cannot help but think back over the six years since the appearance of my first ArtScroll book. It was the summer of 1995, and in the midst of getting the manuscripts ready for press, my mother ע"ה had to undergo emergency open-heart surgery. I dedicated that book to her *refuah sheleimah* and speedy recovery, and for the most part she did indeed recover from that ordeal. The Almighty granted her five more precious years of life. Now six years later, almost to the day, I will observe her first *yahrzeit* on 28 Tammuz.

My mother, among all her other fine attributes, loved to read. She would often say that she was content as long as she had her mind and eyes and could read. Unfortunately, the Parkinson's disease that robbed her of all of her physical abilities took from her that ability as well, for eventually she could not even turn the pages of a book. Nevertheless, her attendant would read to her from my other books. I think she enjoyed them almost to the end, and I hope she will enjoy this book from her deserved place in Gan Eden.

At this mile marker, in the spirit of that beautiful *berachah* of Shehechianu, I humbly give thanks and praise to the One Above for all the kindness He has showered on me. The list would fill a book of its own, but in this preface, I will mention only two.

First, I want to thank Him for the ability to learn and teach Torah in Yeshivah Ner Yisroel. May the Yeshivah continue to grow and prosper under the leadership and guidance of its revered Menahel, Rabbi Naftali Neuberger, and its new Rosh Yeshivah, Rabbi Aharon Feldman, whom I thank for the his letter of *berachah*.

And I also want to thank the Almighty for the wonderful family with which He has blessed me. May He continue to grant us *nachas* from our expanding family: our son Yakov, his wife Shuli and their son Dovid; our daughter Avigayil, her husband Yisroel Rapps and their two daughters, Malka and Sora; and from our son Baruch Yair, who has recently become engaged to Miss Toby Harrar, daughter of Mr. & Mrs. Baruch Harrar.

And *achronah achronah chavivah*, for my wife Nechama. Happy is the man whose wife is his best friend.

Yissocher Frand
28 Tammuz 5761
Baltimore, Maryland

Bereishis

Parashas Bereishis
פרשת בראשית

Adam: A Work in Progress

וַיִּקְרָא הָאָדָם שֵׁמוֹת לְכָל הַבְּהֵמָה וּלְעוֹף הַשָּׁמַיִם
וּלְכֹל חַיַּת הַשָּׂדֶה וּלְאָדָם לֹא מָצָא עֵזֶר כְּנֶגְדּוֹ׃

And Adam gave names to all the animals
and all the birds of the sky
and all the beasts of the fields. (2:20)

ADAM WAS A MAN OF ASTONISHING INSIGHT. HE COULD take one look at any of the myriad creatures of the earth and recognize its essence, its function, its very *raison d'être*. Even the angels in Heaven did not have this uncanny ability.

The Midrash relates (*Bereishis Rabbah* 17:4) that God challenged the angels to assign Hebrew names to all the animals, but they were unable to do so. Then He commanded Adam to assign names to the animals, which he did with perfect accuracy, demonstrating the superiority of man over the angels.

In other languages, words do not have any special connection to the things they represent. They are simply arbitrary sounds that have become associated with those things over a period of time. If you analyze the words cat or elephant or fire, you will not find any hint to the particular characteristics of those things. In Hebrew, however, the names of things reflect what they are all about. Since the angels could not discern the essence of all the animals, they could not assign names to them. Only Adam, with his extraordinary insight and perception, could pair each animal with its correct name.

Nonetheless, when it came to choosing a name for himself, Adam seems to have been strangely uninspired. He chose the name Adam, because he had been formed from the *adamah*, the earth. A human being is the pinnacle of creation, the highest form of living being, spiritual, intellectual, creative, complex, profound, a *tzelem Elohim*, formed, as it were, in "the image of the Lord." How then can it be that Adam, with all his insight and perception, could find no better definition of a human being than that he had been formed from the earth?

The Alter of Slobodka explains that, quite to the contrary, Adam's choice of a name for himself showed his greatest insight. Man represents the ultimate paradox in creation. On the one hand, he is such a sublime creature, higher than the angels, capable of reaching the most transcendent levels of spirituality. And yet, at the same time, he is so painfully human, so incredibly frail. With one slight misstep, he can plummet from the highest pinnacle to the abyss. He can easily fall to the level of the humble dust from which he was originally formed.

This is a critical aspect of the human condition, one that man must always keep in sight and mind if he is to be successful on this earth. Therefore, the choice of the name Adam to recall the *adamah* from which he was taken touches on the very essence of a human being. He had the wisdom to recognize that man can never declare, "I am beyond temptation." No matter how high he has risen, man is never far from the earth from which he was formed. Until the very end, man can always plunge to rock bottom. Ultimately, this lifelong struggle defines the greatness of mankind.

We find the same dichotomy on Yom Kippur. For the morning Torah reading, *Chazal* chose selections describing the divine service of the *Kohein Gadol* in the Sanctuary and the Holy of Holies. As we read these words, we are transported to the holiest place in the universe on the holiest day of the year. And yet, a few hours later, the Torah reading during Minchah enumerates the prohibitions against illicit libidinous encounters.

Is this what we need to hear on Yom Kippur after spending so many hours in fasting and prayer? Is this what we need to contemplate in our exalted condition during the waning hours of the day as Yom Kippur draws to a close? Why did *Chazal* choose this particular reading for us on the holiest afternoon of the year?

The answer is that Yom Kippur of all days is exactly when we need to hear this. On Yom Kippur, we allow neither food nor water to pass our lips, and we ascend into the heavens on wings of prayer. Ethereal spirits with but a tentative connection to the physical world, we reach for the heights, soaring above the angels of Heaven. And so we can easily lose perspective and delude ourselves that we are indeed like the angels, creatures of pure spirit. Therefore, *Chazal* remind us that even in our moments of greatest inspiration we are never far from the carnal desires of the flesh. They make us aware that we invite disaster if we ever lose sight of the abyss that stretches before us.

Along the same lines, we can perhaps resolve another anomaly in the creation story. With regard to the creation of all the species, the Torah tells us, "*Vayar Elokim ki tov*. The Lord saw that it was good." The insect gets a *ki tov*. The elephant gets a *ki tov*. Every creature gets a *ki tov*. But the creation of man does not get a *ki tov*. Hashem examines His handiwork after each step of creation and pronounces it "good." But He makes no such pronouncement after the creation of man.

Rav Yosef Albo, in his *Sefer Ha'ikrim*, explains that every element of creation is a finished product. When Hashem forms an insect or an elephant or an apple tree, it becomes what it is. It will never rise in stature nor will it ever fall. Therefore, it can be evaluated and declared "good."

Man, however, is a work in progress. He is a vast bundle of potential whose final form is as yet undetermined. Will he blossom? Will he flourish? Will he rise to the exalted spiritual levels of which he is capable? Or will he languish in mediocrity or worse? These unresolved questions must be answered by each and every individual human being throughout a lifetime of struggle. There is, therefore, never a time when he can be considered a finished product and declared "good." Man is always in a state of potential.

The Talmud states (*Berachos* 17a) that when the Sages took leave of each other they would say, "*Olamecha tir'eh bechayecha*. May you see your world during your lifetime." What exactly does this mean?

Rav Shimon Schwab offers a beautiful interpretation. The word *olamecha*, your world, is cognate with *he'elamecha*, the part of you that is concealed. A person's world is the part of him that has not yet seen the light of day, the part that is still potential. That is the arena where he works and struggles and strives to achieve. Realizing the full potential is the work of a lifetime.

This was the blessing the Sages wished each other. May you see your world during your lifetime. May you achieve during your sojourn in this world the full realization of all the potential Hashem has invested in you.

Parashas Noach
פרשת נח

The Fruits of Indulgence

וַתִּשָּׁחֵת הָאָרֶץ לִפְנֵי הָאֱלֹקִים וַתִּמָּלֵא הָאָרֶץ חָמָס

And the earth was degenerate before the Lord,
and the earth was filled with violence. (6:11)

WHAT EXACTLY DID THE PEOPLE OF THE Generation of the Flood (*Dor Hamabul*) do to deserve such a dreadful fate? The Torah is quite explicit on this point. They were corrupt, degenerate, violent. They reached the outer limits of perversion, affecting even the animals and the land itself. We can well understand when society becomes so depraved and incorrigible, it is time to wipe the slate clean and make a fresh start.

But the Midrash tells us something entirely different (*Bereishis Rabbah* 32:2). The men of the Generation of the Flood used to take two wives. One was designated to bear children, the other to keep her husband company. The first was forced to live in seclusion, in a state of virtual widowhood while her husband was still alive. The second was given medications that would make her barren. She would sit beside her husband, heavily made up, and entertain him. This is inferred from the verse in *Iyov* (24:21), "He encourages the barren woman that does not give birth, but he gives no benefit to the widow." Rashi quotes this Midrash in *Bereishis* (4:19).

Now, we would certainly not argue that this sort of practice reflected the highest levels of spirituality. In fact, it was certainly an indication of a high level of self-indulgence. But was this such a terrible sin that virtually the entire human race had to be wiped out? Was this such an abysmal level of human corruption that the world had to be inundated and obliterated by the Flood?

The answer is that this Midrash is not providing a picture of antediluvian society in its final degenerate form. Rather, it is revealing to us the root cause of the precipitous decline of society. How does society fall so low that it is defined by pervasive degeneracy, theft and violence? By making the unchecked pursuit of personal pleasure the ultimate value.

Eat, drink and be merry. Have a good time. Enjoy yourself. Live for today. Self-indulgence. Gratification. When these are the values of society, when the moral compass goes haywire, the road leads straight down. Today, people may limit themselves to made-up, barren pleasure wives, but tomorrow they will inevitably expand their horizons. Eventually, they will turn their greedy eyes to unexplored illicit indulgences and all sorts of other acts of perversion and immorality. It is only a matter of time before it happens. The two-wife system led to the "degenerate world filled with violence" that triggered the Flood.

Unfortunately, we have a vivid illustration of this process in our own times. Look at what has happened in the past few decades. As soon as the society opened the door to permissiveness and self-indulgence, it went into a sharp downward spiral. Morality has become a thing of the past. Family life is disintegrating. Respect for authority and civic responsibility are just about nonexistent. Drugs and alcohol take over at a very young age. All that matters is a good time. People measure the value of their lives by the number of pleasure buttons they have managed to push.

This insight allows us to understand a rather puzzling passage in the Midrash (*Bereishis Rabbah* 36:3). The Torah tells us (9:20) that after the Flood, "Noach, the man of the earth, profaned himself and planted a vineyard." The Sages observe that Noach, who had originally been described (6:9) as "a righteous and perfect man in his generations," was now described as a lowly "man of the earth." In contrast, Moshe was originally described (2:19) as "an Egyptian man" and is eventually described (*Devarim* 33:2) as "a man of the Lord." Moshe went up, while Noach went down. And all because he planted a vineyard.

What is so terrible about planting a vineyard? All right, it would have been better to plant some wheat or string beans to provide some basic levels of nourishment. Noach was probably off the mark in choosing to start with a vineyard. But how did Noach "profane himself"? Was planting a vineyard such a dreadful crime?

Indeed it was. By planting a vineyard before anything else, Noach showed that he had not fully learned the lesson of the Flood. He saw the end result of many long years of degeneracy — the perversion, the immorality, the violence — but he did not penetrate to the root causes. He failed to see the whole picture. He did not recognize that it had all begun with some supposedly harmless self-indulgence. He did not recognize that the vineyard, the self-indulgence of intoxicating wines, was the symbol for the downward spiral that led to the Flood.

If there was one thing he should not have done after such a Flood, it was to plant a vineyard.

A Touch of Paranoia

וַיְשַׁלַּח אֶת הָעֹרֵב וַיֵּצֵא יָצוֹא וָשׁוֹב

And he sent off the raven, and it went out,
flying back and forth. (8:7)

THE RAVEN WAS A RELUCTANT MESSENGER, TO SAY THE least. After many months of confinement in the ark, Noach opened the window and looked out on a water-covered earth. Was this the end of the Flood? Were the waters finally receding? Was life finally going to return to a semblance of normalcy? Noach had to find out, and he decided to send out the raven to investigate.

But the raven refused to go. He kept "flying back and forth," hovering over the ark and refusing to let it out of his sight. What was the reason for this strange behavior? Rashi, based on the Talmud (*Sanhedrin* 108b), explains that the raven suspected Noach of improper designs on his mate. Somehow, he got the idea into his head that Noach was sending him away from the ark on this special mission because he wanted to be alone with the female raven. And so he circled endlessly over the ark, keeping an eagle eye on Noach.

This is certainly a strange *Agadeta*, especially for someone unfamiliar with the style of the Sages. A new student of Ohr Somayach in Israel in the process of returning to Torah had just been through this Rashi when he met a member of the faculty.

"So how is it going?" asked the *rebbi*.

"Pretty good," the young fellow replied.

"And what are you learning?"

"I'm learning *Chumash*," he replied. "Noach, specifically."

"And it's going well?" asked the *rebbi*.

"Just great. But there's one problem. I've just learned a Rashi today that is ridiculous, pardon the expression."

"Really? And which Rashi is that?"

"The one about the raven that's worried about Noach starting up with his mate. What's with this sick raven? C'mon. Give me a break."

The Rebbi smiled and placed his arm around the young man's shoulders. "You need to become more familiar with the style of the *Agadah*, my young friend. You need to find the keys to the code. Our Sages did not come to teach us here about ravens. They are teaching us about human beings. The fears of the raven were, of course, ridiculous as you correctly pointed out. That's the whole point. Our Sages are teaching us about paranoia!"

Paranoia makes no sense. It is ridiculous. When a general sends a soldier on a mission, should he assume he was chosen because he was qualified and could be expected to succeed? Or should he suspect that the general has it in for him and wants to get rid of him by placing him in a precarious situation? Sanity chooses the first, paranoia the second.

Has it ever happened to you that you see two people conversing at a wedding on the other side of the room and their conversation comes to an abrupt end as soon as you approach? Do you wonder if they were talking about you? Do you begin to wonder what you ever did to these people and why they would bear a grudge against you?

These are paranoid thoughts. Most likely, they were gossiping about some insignificant topic, and they were embarrassed to have you hear what nonsense occupies their minds. This is certainly the more logical explanation for what has happened. But for some reason, it is not the one that comes to your mind. Why is this so? Because we all suffer from a touch of paranoia.

At the root of this type of paranoia lies egocentrism. We tend to view everything around us in terms of how it affects us, because in our eyes, we are the center of the universe. If someone is muttering under his breath when he passes by, it must be that he is an anti-Semite or a general misanthrope. It does not occur to us so easily that he may have been chewed out by his boss just minutes before. We do not easily interpret anything we experience as being unrelated to ourselves. And so we suffer from paranoia.

I once heard that until the age of 20 we are completely obsessed by what others are thinking about us. From the age of *twenty* until the age of *forty*, we develop the self-confidence to disregard what others are thinking about us. After the age of *forty*, we develop the wisdom to see that others are not thinking about us. They are thinking about themselves.

Noach had plenty to think about besides the raven's mate. Had the raven had the wisdom to understand this, he would have spared himself a lot of endless circling over the ark.

The Technological Delusion

וַיֹּאמְרוּ הָבָה נִבְנֶה לָּנוּ עִיר וּמִגְדָּל וְרֹאשׁוֹ בַשָּׁמַיִם
וְנַעֲשֶׂה לָּנוּ שֵׁם

*Come, let us build us a city and a tower
with its top reaching in the heavens,
and let us make a name for ourselves. (11:4)*

LATER ON IN THE PARASHAH, WE READ ABOUT THE Generation of the Dispersal (*Dor Hahaflagah*) that built a tower and prepared to do battle with Hashem. Let us follow the sequence of events.

The Torah relates (11:3), "And they said to one another, 'Come, let us make bricks and fire them in the flames,' and the bricks served them as stone, and the lime as mortar." Rashi offers an interesting bit of information. He explains that they needed bricks because there are no stones for building in Babylon.

In the very next verse, the Torah tells us (11:4), "And they said, 'Come, let us build us a city and a tower with its top reaching in the heavens, and let us make a name for ourselves.'"

Since the Torah mentions that they made bricks, a seemingly insignificant point, it would appear that this was somehow important in the sequence of events. They make bricks. They built a tower to do battle with Hashem. Where is the cause and effect? What is the connection?

Rav Yosef Chaim Sonnenfeld explains that the manufacture of bricks was a technological breakthrough of major proportions. For the first time, people were able to manufacture their own building materials, even if nothing was readily available from nature. And thus, people fell into the self-delusion of saying (Devarim 8:17), "Kochi v'otzem yadi asah li es hachayil hazeh. My strength and the power of my hands made all this wealth." They became drunk with the idea that they were the masters of their own destiny, and they decided that the sky was the limit. Literally. And all because of a few bricks.

Parashas Lech Lecha
פרשת לך לך

Small Deeds, Great Rewards

וַיָּבֹא הַפָּלִיט וַיַּגֵּד לְאַבְרָם הָעִבְרִי

*And the refugee came and reported
to Avram the Hebrew. (14:13)*

WHEN THE KINGS OF MESOPOTAMIA OVERRAN Sodom and Amorrah, the Torah tells us (14:13) that "the refugee came and reported to Avram" that his nephew Lot and his family had been taken captive. Avram quickly marshaled his forces, gave chase and liberated the captives.

Who was this mysterious escapee? Our Sages identify him as Og, king of the Bashan, who escaped death during the Flood by holding on to Noach's ark. His timely report from the battlefield enabled Avram to rescue his captive nephew.

Many years later, when the Jewish people prepared to launch the conquest of Canaan, Og's kingdom stood in the way. The Torah tells us (21:34), "And God said to Moshe, 'Do not fear him, for I have delivered him into your hands.'" From this, we can infer that Moshe was afraid. Why was he afraid?

The Talmud explains (*Nidah* 61a) that Moshe was afraid that the merit of saving Lot's life would protect Og against the invading Jewish people.

But let us dig a little deeper. Why indeed did Og bring the battlefield report to Avram? What were his motives? Was he concerned for Lot's safety and welfare? Hardly. Rashi explains that he was hoping Avram would rush into battle with the Mesopotamia kings, as he actually did, and that he would perish on the battlefield. This would leave Sarah a widow, and he, Og, would marry her.

Not very noble motives. Og was certainly not thinking of *chessed*, of performing an act of kindness. And yet, despite the glaring lack of altruism, the act itself was considered such a powerful merit for Og that Moshe was afraid to engage him in battle so many years later without specific Divine reassurance. Rav Leib Chasman points out that this shows us the incredible power and reward of a *mitzvah*, no matter how small and imperfect.

A similar story took place during the Holocaust, where a relatively minor good deed was, according to the Bluzhever Rebbe, repaid with immense reward.

A Jewish family by the name of Hiller — a husband, wife and a 6-year-old boy named Shachne — were living in the Krakow ghetto in 1942. Prospects for survival were extremely dim. People were being deported to Auschwitz almost daily. Only those capable of working for the German war effort had any hope of survival. A little boy didn't stand a chance.

As time passed, the situation grew ever more desperate. The Hillers despaired of keeping little Shachne alive in the ghetto. There was only one chance. The Hillers were friends with a Polish couple named Jakovicz, who had no children of their own. They felt that these people were trustworthy and that they would take good care of little Shachne until the war was over.

On the night of November 15, 1942, Mrs. Hiller and little Shachne, at the risk of being shot on sight, slipped past the guardposts of the ghetto and into the city. Hearts pounding, they ran through the streets under cover of darkness, two shadows in the misty night, until they reached the Jakovicz house.

"Who knows if we will ever survive this horrible war?" Mrs. Hiller told her Polish friend. "If my husband and I survive, or even one of us, we will come back for our precious Shachne. But if we do not survive, Heaven forbid, I am relying on you to deliver him to our relatives." She slipped her hand into her pocket and brought out two envelopes addressed in a spidery handwriting. The ink was smudged as if by falling tears. "Here are two letters. One is to our relatives in Montreal, the other to our relatives in Washington. Either of them will take him and raise him as a Jew. Even if we die, at least Shachne will carry on as a Jew. I am relying on you, my dear friend, to see this through. God bless you, my friend."

Unfortunately, the Hillers' trust in the Jakovicz family was misplaced. The Hillers perished in the Holocaust, but they had not left their precious Shachne in good hands. Mrs. Jakovicz, a devout Catholic, loved the boy, and he loved her in return. She took him to mass regularly and taught him all the Catholic hymns and prayers. Within a few years, he was just like a Christian child.

In 1946, when it became clear that Shachne's parents were not coming back for him, Mrs. Jakovicz approached the young parish priest to discuss having the boy baptized as a Christian. During their discussion, the priest discerned that the boy in question was already 10 years old so he asked Mrs. Jakovicz why he had not been brought for baptism in all the preceding years. Mrs. Jakovicz was evasive, and the priest grew more curious. Finally, she told him the entire story.

The young priest urged Mrs. Jakovicz to fulfill her promise to the boy's dead parents and honor their wishes for their son. Mrs. Jakovicz relented and sent off the letters to the relatives in America. In June 1949, through the efforts of the Canadian Jewish Congress, fourteen Jewish orphans from Poland,

Shachne among them, were allowed into Canada. In February 1951, by a special act of Congress signed by President Truman, Shachne was allowed into the United States, and he went to live with his family in Washington.

Shachne grew up as a religious Jew in the United States unaware of his close call with baptism. He was successful in the business world, rising to the level of vice president of an important corporation. Throughout the years, he retained close bonds of love and gratitude with Mrs. Jakovicz. He kept in touch with her and sent her letters, gifts and money. She never mentioned that she had almost had him baptized.

Finally, in 1978, Mrs. Jakovicz felt she had to clear her conscience. She wrote a letter to Shachne in which she admitted the entire story to him. She wrote about the parish priest who had urged her to do the right thing. His name was Karol Wojtyla, better known to the world as Pope John Paul II.

"Who can know why Hashem does what He does?" observed the Bluzhever Rebbe. "But it seems reasonable to me that for that one word of good advice the young priest gave this Polish woman he was rewarded with the greatest award possible for a priest. He became the pope."

Count the Stars

הַבֶּט נָא הַשָּׁמַיְמָה וּסְפֹר הַכּוֹכָבִים אִם תּוּכַל לִסְפֹּר
אֹתָם וַיֹּאמֶר לוֹ כֹּה יִהְיֶה זַרְעֶךָ

"Look up at the sky and count the stars,
can you count them?" And he said to him,
"So shall your children be." (15:5)

WHAT ARE YOU SUPPOSED TO DO WHEN YOU ARE asked to do the impossible? Most people would simply shrug their shoulders and forget about it. After all, doing the impossible is impossible, isn't it? Not necessarily.

The Torah tells us that Hashem promised Avram that he would have children (15:3-5). "And Avram said, 'O my Master, Lord, what can you give me if I am childless?' . . . And He brought him outside, and He said, 'Look up at the sky and count the stars, can you count them?' And he said to him, 'So shall your children be.'"

Rav Meir Shapiro asks what a person would do if he were told to count the stars. One look at the myriad stars in the heavens would tell what an impossible task this was, and he would not even bother to attempt it. But that is not what Avram did. When Hashem told him to "look up at the sky and count the stars," that is exactly what he did. He began to count the stars even though doing so appeared to be impossible.

"*Koh yihyeh zarecha,*" Hashem responded. "So shall your children be." Avram's extraordinary trait of eternal optimism, his refusal to acknowledge the impossibility of any task, will characterize his descendants. This will be the hallmark of the Jewish people. No matter how difficult a task may seem, the Jew will not despair. He will try and try and try again.

And when we try, amazing things often happen. Even if we think something is entirely beyond our meager abilities, when we try persistently we discover strengths and abilities that we never knew we possessed. We find in ourselves new reservoirs of capability, new potential that we never knew existed. We learn we can go beyond all the limits and restrictions that we had considered impenetrable boundaries.

A blind Jew once brought a volume of his *chiddushei Torah* to Rav Isser Zalman Meltzer. He asked Rav Isser Zalman to take a look at one particular piece. "That piece," he remarked, "was the last piece I wrote, and then I went blind."

"What happened?"

"I worked on my *sefer* for many years," the man explained. "I toiled over the Gemara and Rishonim and Poskim with every fiber of my being, and my labors were blessed with some success. Some of the pieces are really very good. But they took so much effort, and I was getting older. One day, after finishing work on a *chiddush*, I decided that I had had enough. I just didn't have the strength to keep this up. From now on, I decided, I would continue to learn, but I would not put in the effort necessary to come up with *chiddushei Torah*. I wrote down my *chiddush*, and there and then," he paused and took a deep breath, "I became blind!"

"Did you go to doctors?" asked Rav Isser Zalman.

"Of course I went to doctors," the man replied. "And you know what they told me? They said that based on the condition of my eyes I should have been blind ten years earlier. They simply could not understand why I hadn't gone blind before."

For ten years, this man had done the impossible. He had studied and written *chiddushei Torah*, using eyes that should not have been functioning. But "so shall your children be." Jewish people, the descendants of Avraham, can accomplish the impossible.

Parashas Vayeira
פרשת וירא

Refinement Without Fear

וַיֹּאמֶר אַבְרָהָם כִּי אָמַרְתִּי רַק אֵין יִרְאַת אֱלֹקִים
בַּמָּקוֹם הַזֶּה

*And Avraham said, "For I thought, only
there is no fear of the Lord in this place." (20:11)*

HE TROUBLE BEGAN WHEN AVRAHAM INTRODUCED HIS
wife Sarah to the people of Gerar as his sister. One
thing led to another, and she was taken to the palace
of Avimelech, king of Gerar, as a prospective new wife.
Avimelech came very close to sinning with Sarah, but
Hashem revealed her true identity to him.

Avimelech was upset. "You almost got me into terrible
trouble," he said to Avraham. "You told me she was your sister when she was really your wife. Why didn't you tell me the
truth? Why did you do this to me?"

"For I thought," said Avraham, "only there is no fear of the
Lord in this place (20:11)".

The word "only" in this verse seems to be out of place.
What is it supposed to imply?

Rav Elchanan Wasserman raised this question when he
addressed a group of rabbis in Germany during the 1930's.

Then he shocked them with the Malbim's explanation.

"Your city is wonderful," Avraham was telling the people of Gerar, according to the Malbim's interpretation. "It is a place of culture and refinement, of exemplary citizens. There is only one thing wrong with it. The Lord is not feared in your city. And if the Lord is not feared, then all your other refinements and accomplishments are meaningless. If you are not governed by fear of the Lord but by your own human standards, there is no hope for you. You cannot be trusted not to kill a man with a desirable wife. Your civilized ways mean nothing. They will not be allowed to get in the way of your passions and ambitions, because you do not fear the Lord."

The implications of what Rav Elchanan was saying were clear. Germany was a civilized country, but there was no fear of the Lord. Therefore, it was a dangerous place. Anything could happen there.

"Not so," some of the German rabbis objected. "Germany is a land of laws, culture, civilization, high moral standing, science, technology. We are not some backward backwater from the Middle Ages. Jews are not at risk here. We are protected by the law."

Germany was indeed a country of laws, but what were those laws? Rabbi Reuven Bulka of Ottawa, Canada, recalls attending *cheder* in Germany during Kristallnacht. One of the children ran into the classroom and informed the *rebbi* that his house was on fire. The *rebbi* immediately telephoned the fire department and reported the fire, but his pleas for assistance fell on deaf ears. He got through to the fire chief, but to no avail.

"We are sorry," said the fire chief, "but we cannot put out the fire. It is against the law."

It was now against the law to put out fires in Jewish homes. Germany was still a land of laws. That had not changed. Only the laws had changed. All the culture and the civilization meant nothing. When there is no fear of God in a place, the laws mean nothing.

When Rav Yitzchak Hutner was learning in Slobodka, Rav Avraham Elya Kaplan came back to the *yeshivah* after spending some time in Germany. The Alter of Slobodka invited Rav Avraham Elya to convey to the *yeshivah* his impressions of the German people. What were they like?

"It seems to me that the Germans are a kind and refined people," he replied. "When you ask directions from someone, he will give you very precise instructions for getting there, and then he will say to you, '*Nicht wahr*? Isn't that so?' Now, he knows that you have absolutely no idea about how to get there. In fact, that's why you're asking directions. He also knows perfectly well that he doesn't need nor can he expect any confirmation from you. And still he says in such a deferential tone, '*Nicht wahr*?' I see this as a sign of refinement. The Germans are a refined people."

At this point, an argument broke out among the *bachurim* of the Slobodka Yeshivah. Some argued, Rav Hutner among them, that we should seek to learn good *midos* only from the holy Torah, the repository of all desirable ethics and values, and not from the Germans or any other gentile communities. Besides, if they were not rooted in the Torah, it was quite possible that refined manners were no more than a superficial cloak for a dark interior.

"I disagree," declared one *bachur*. "A wise person learns from everyone. If we see something admirable among the gentiles, we should give credit where credit is due and adopt it for ourselves as well. I think the practice of saying *nicht wahr* is a sign of politeness, refinement and a very becoming modesty. We should learn from the virtues of the Germans."

Nearly 50 years later, Rav Hutner was saying a *shiur* in Yeshivah Rabbeinu Chaim Berlin when an old man walked in. He sat in the back and waited until the *shiur* was over. Then he approached Rav Hutner.

"You don't remember me, do you?" he said. "I am the *bachur* in Slobodka who argued with you about admiring the refined manners of the Germans."

"Ah, of course I remember you," said Rav Hutner. "Ah, it is good to see you again after all these years.

He reached out to take the old man's hand, but there was only a hook where the hand should have been. Rav Hutner's hand remained suspended in midair.

"I lost it in the concentration camps," the old man explained. "When the Nazi was sawing off my right hand, he kept saying, 'This is hurting you, *nicht wahr*? The pain is intense, *nicht wahr*? And even as I was screaming as if my lungs would burst, he was smiling all the time. Such a gentle, refined smile. Reb Yitzchak, you were right, and I was wrong."

When "there is no fear of the Lord in this place," when people live by their own rules, all the culture and refined manners mean nothing. It was true in Gerar. It was true in Germany. It is true everywhere.

The Roots of Trust

וַיֵּלְכוּ שְׁנֵיהֶם יַחְדָּו

And the two of them went together. (22:6)

THE NARRATIVES OF THE TORAH ARE FAR MORE THAN stories or even lessons in morality. They are a description and an account of the formation of the national Jewish character. Our Sages tells us that "*maaseh avos siman l'vanim*, the deeds of the father are signs for the sons."

Rav Chaim Volozhiner, in his commentary to *Pirkei Avos*, points out that the Jewish ability to submit to martyrdom with faith and courage derives from Avraham, who allowed himself to be thrown into the fiery furnace rather than deny Hashem. The same is true of the historical preparedness of the Jewish people to make great sacrifices and endure great hardships in order to fulfill the *mitzvah* of living in Eretz Yisrael. Today, this is a relatively simple thing to do, but it was not always so. Nonetheless, during the 19th century, thousands of Jews emigrated from Europe and other countries in the Middle East and settled in Eretz Yisrael. Where did they get that fortitude and intense devotion to living in the Land? Rav Chaim Volozhiner contends that they inherited it from our forefather Avraham, who obeyed Hashem's command to forsake everything, leave his home behind and journey to Eretz Yisrael. He instilled this trait in the national character, and now it is in our blood.

Another outstanding and crucial feature of the Jewish character is our *emunas chachamim*, our confident trust in our sages. Where does it come from? How was this trust instilled in the national character?

The Chasam Sofer gives the credit to our forefather Yitzchak. We are accustomed to viewing the ordeal of the *Akeidah* from Avraham's perspective. Hashem put Avraham to the test by telling him to sacrifice the son on whom he had pinned all his hopes for the future. But there was also a second aspect to the *Akeidah*, the ordeal from Yitzchak's perspective.

Yitzchak had not heard firsthand Hashem's command that he be sacrificed. In fact, it certainly must have seemed bizarre to him that the Almighty, Who valued life and justice so highly, would command his faithful follower Avraham to sacrifice his own son on the altar. Could such a thing be true? All he had was his father's word. And yet, he accepted it without question. He father was his *chacham*, his sage, whose word had to be accepted faithfully.

This powerful *emunas chachamim*, which Yitzchak so magnificently exemplified, forms the backbone of the Jewish people, the source of its indomitable strength. We live by the *mesorah*, the oral transmission of our tradition from sage to honored sage for centuries, the hallowed chain of transmission that renders our Torah immune to the interpretations and reinterpretations of alien ideologies. And the *mesorah* lives by the *emunas chachamim* of our people, our trust and confidence in our sages, the revered guardians of our tradition.

Where did we get such powerful *emunas chachamim*? From Yitzchak.

Parashas Chayei Sarah
פרשת חיי שרה

The Golden Years

גֵּר וְתוֹשָׁב אָנֹכִי עִמָּכֶם תְּנוּ לִי אֲחֻזַּת קֶבֶר עִמָּכֶם
וְאֶקְבְּרָה מֵתִי

I am an alien resident among you,
give me a burial ground among you
that I may bury my dead. (23:4)

CCORDING TO TRADITION (*AVOS* 5:3), HASHEM PUT
Avraham to the test ten times, and he passed them all
with flying colors. It is generally accepted that the ten
tests were progressively harder, that once he proved himself in
a lesser test, Hashem presented him with a more difficult test
until he proved himself to have the highest level of faith. It is
also generally accepted that the tenth and most difficult test
was the *Akeidah*. After all, what could be more challenging
than to be commanded to sacrifice the treasured child born to
him in his old age?

Rabbeinu Yonah in *Avos* (ibid.), however, lists the
Akeidah as the ninth test. What was the tenth? When
Avraham could not find a place to bury Sarah, he was forced
to buy a plot from Ephron for an exorbitant sum.

The question springs out from the pages. True, it must have
been exceedingly frustrating for Avraham to be forced to pay

anything at all, let alone an exorbitant sum, for land Hashem had promised him as an everlasting birthright. True, it must have been difficult to deal with this frustration in his bereavement over the death of his wife Sarah. But still, is this at all comparable to the test of the *Akeidah*? Does this even begin to come close to being asked to sacrifice a son on the altar?

There is tendency among people to look forward to the golden years of retirement. They work very hard. They struggle to be successful, to build a reputation for themselves and to provide their families with a good standard of living. Then there comes a point in a person's life when he steps back and surveys all he has accomplished, and he says, "Enough! I've done all that could be expected of me and more. It's time to stop, to ease up on the pace, to sit back and enjoy life. After all, I've earned it!" And indeed, he has. There is no reason he should not enjoy his golden years of retirement.

But in the realm of spirituality, it is not so. There is never a point when a person can sit back and say, "I've done enough!" In the realm of spirituality, a person either moves up or he moves down; he never remains in one spot. If he "retires," he immediately goes into decline. The struggle for spiritual growth does not end until a person draws his very last breath.

When Avraham came back from the *Akeidah*, he had reached a level of achievement so exalted that the Jewish people throughout history are sustained by its merit. It undoubtedly took every last ounce of spiritual courage and fortitude he could muster to withstand such a horrific ordeal. And he did it! Avraham found those hidden reservoirs of strength and faith, and he showed himself ready to sacrifice his son if Hashem so commanded. And in the end, everything had worked out for the best. He had proved himself, and his son's life had been spared. Avraham returned home with a sense of boundless relief, ready to share his experience with his wife. One can imagine his shock when he found her dead, and his frustration when he encountered so many difficulties in bringing her to eternal rest.

Avraham could easily have raised his voice in righteous indignation and complained. "Enough already! How much do I have to go through? Isn't it enough that I have just gone through the ordeal of the *Akeidah*? Do I have to go through this as well? I have put in so many years of effort. I have glorified Hashem's Name in so many places for so many years. I have made so much *kiddush Hashem*. Don't I deserve a little respite to sit back and enjoy the golden years of my life?"

This was a very subtle test, the ultimate test, and Avraham could easily have reacted instinctively, as most people would. But he did not. He realized that he had one more important lesson to teach the world. By his example, he could demonstrate that there is no retirement from *avodah*, that being a faithful *eved Hashem* is literally the work of a lifetime. There is no retirement. But the years are certainly golden.

Rav Eliahu Dessler, in *Michtav m'Eliahu*, offer a different explanation. He sees in this tenth and final test the demonstration of two of the most critical aspects of Avraham's personality.

Consider the situation. Avraham finds himself forced to conduct business dealings with the wily and duplicitous Ephron. He is exceedingly frustrated both by his own circumstances and by Ephron's opportunistic behavior. How does he conduct himself?

Imagine you set out to purchase a used car, or perhaps we should say a pre-owned car, and you run into the proverbial used-car salesman. He is wearing a loud checked suit and a fluorescent smile, and he bombards you with an incessant stream of high-pressure sales pitch. He turns a deaf ear to your stated preferences in price and model and does his best to persuade to buy the high-priced clunker that you absolutely do not want. After five minutes, you are gnashing your teeth and clenching your fists.

How do you speak to this man? Do you treat him with the respect and deference due any human being formed in the image of the Lord, the *tzelem Elokim*? Or do you respond to his crudeness with a crudeness of your own? Do you allow external frustrations get the better of you?

And how about internal frustrations?

I was recently at a supermarket, and I asked the person bagging my groceries not to make the bags too heavy.

"If you don't like the way I do it," he barked at me, "do it yourself!"

I was taken aback, to say the least. "Excuse me," I said. "Did I say something nasty to you? Why did I deserve such a response?"

The man gave me a sheepish grin. "Sorry. I had a hard day."

I guess that explains it all. He had a hard day, which gives him the right to give me a hard time, I suppose.

Having a "hard day" is obviously not a justification for rude behavior. But how about something that goes beyond your ordinary "hard day"? Imagine you have just come off an overseas flight. You have spent a solid hour watching the luggage circulate around the carousel until you have each piece memorized down to its smallest details, but your own luggage seems to have disappeared into thin air. You go to the ticket office to report your loss. Are you justified in snapping at the agent because of what you are going through?

Let us take this a little further. You are in the hospital attending a relative who is in serious condition, perhaps even in mortal danger. A doctor or nurse or some other hospital functionary gives you a hard time, and you respond with a sharp retort. Does your anxiety about the health of your relative justify such behavior?

Now let us consider Avraham's circumstances. He has just come back from the *Akeidah*, where he narrowly escaped slaughtering his own son. Can you imagine his mental and emotional state? Then he comes home to discover that Sarah, his wife of a century, has died and that he has to go through some difficult negotiations in order to secure a burial plot for her. I suppose one could safely say that Avraham was having a rather "hard day." To top it all off, he must contend with Ephron, who may not have been wearing a checked suit but was certainly no better than the sleaziest used-car salesman.

This was Avraham's test. He could have played hardball with Ephron. He could have wiped the floor with him. But he didn't. He treated him with the respect and deference due every human being. Just because he was having a hard day, he did not have to make Ephron suffer.

On the night Rav Shlomo Zalman Auerbach's *rebbetzin* died, he was standing in the hall of the hospital trying to deal with his profound grief. A *talmid* of his, whose wife had just given birth, was also in the hospital at the time. The *talmid* noticed Rav Shlomo Zalman in the hallway, and he ran over to give him the wonderful news. He was so excited that it did not even occur to him to ask what his *rosh yeshivah* was doing in the hospital at that time of the night.

Rav Shlomo Zalman gave the *talmid* his warmest blessing and graced him with his famous smile, so full of love and sheer joy. The *talmid* walked away with his heart singing, completely unaware that his *rosh yeshivah* had been told just a few minutes earlier that his wife had passed away.

Following the example of his forefather Avraham, Rav Shlomo Zalman saw no reason to diminish his *talmid's* joy in the very least just because he himself was suffering.

Parashas Toldos
פרשת תולדות

Past and Present Love

וַיֶּאֱהַב יִצְחָק אֶת עֵשָׂו כִּי צַיִד בְּפִיו וְרִבְקָה אֹהֶבֶת
אֶת יַעֲקֹב

And Yitzchak loved Eisav,
for the game he put in his mouth,
but Rivkah loves Yaakov. (25:28)

EVEN PEOPLE NOT NORMALLY ATTUNED TO GRAMMAR
are struck by the Torah's strange use of tenses to
describe the relationship of Yitzchak and Rivkah with
their children. Yitzchak "loved" Eisav, in the past tense, while
Rivkah "loves" Yaakov, in the present tense. What is this
meant to teach us?

The Dubno Maggid suggests a solution based on a keen
observation of the world. In non-Jewish society, people define
themselves and are defined by others according to what they
do. In Jewish society, people are defined by what they are.

Eisav represented non-Jewish values. He defined himself
and expected other to define him by what he did. He wanted
to be seen as the athlete, the warrior, the storied hunter. The
basis for the admiration and love of other people was what he

had accomplished in the past. Should he cease to be a hunter, the admiration would cease as well. Therefore, Yitzchak "loved" Eisav, in the past tense, *"for the game he put in his mouth,"* the things he had done in the past. But Yaakov represented Jewish values. He was defined by what he was rather than by what he did. Therefore, Rivkah "loves" Yaakov, in the present tense, a love that continues uninterrupted and is not dependent on his latest feat and achievement.

This is particularly true in our own times. Ask a non-Jewish child what he wants to be when he grows up and he will inevitably tell you he wants to be a doctor or a lawyer or a Silicon Valley entrepreneur or perhaps a rock star. Ask a Jewish child, and hopefully he will tell you he wants to be a *tzaddik*, a *talmid chacham*, a *baal chessed*, and *oveid Hashem*. Hopefully.

The Jewish child answers the question directly. He tells you what he wants to "be." The non-Jewish child, however, is not giving a direct answer to the question. He is telling what he will "do" rather than what he will "be." He has been conditioned to believe that a person's entire value is dependent on his profession or vocation. If he is a doctor he is important. If he is a mailman he is not important.

A columnist here in Baltimore recently wrote a piece decrying this tendency in society. Whenever he meets someone new at a function or party, it takes no more than fifteen seconds before he is asked, "So what do you do?" Sometimes, he is so annoyed he identifies himself as an auditor for the Internal Revenue Service, which is a guaranteed conversation stopper. Obviously, he concludes, in America "you are what you do," and what you really are — your character, your interests, your thoughts, your feelings, your opinions — do not really matter that much.

In America, you are measured by your performance, by what you do. Therefore, you may be idolized and adored one day and despised the next. If the level of your performance falls off, if you go through a stretch when you strike out instead of hitting, your fickle admirers will turn on you. After all, it was not what you are that they never admired but what you do, and when you no longer do it, there is no longer any basis for the admiration.

This is not the perspective of Judaism. In fact, it is the exact opposite. Judaism values all people for what they are, for their *tzelem Elokim*, for their character, their integrity, their goodness, their ethical standards, their *menschlichkeit*, their spiritual accomplishments. What they do for a living or for professional fulfillment is only secondary.

A Dose of Holiness

וַיָּרַח אֶת רֵיחַ בְּגָדָיו וַיְבָרְכֵהוּ

And he inhaled the scent of his garments,
and he blessed him. (27:27)

YITZCHAK LOST HIS SIGHT IN HIS OLD AGE, BUT HIS SENSE of smell was just fine. Yaakov was counting on that. He put on Eisav's garments, brought Yitzchak delicacies and asked for the blessing. Yitzchak "inhaled the scent of his garments" and gave him the blessing. And the rest is history.

The Midrash offers a completely different homiletic interpretation of these words. The word used here for "his garments" is *begadav*. With alternate vowelization, it can be read as *bogdav*, which means his renegades. In other words, when

Yitzchak "inhaled the scent of his renegades," when he sensed prophetically the descendants of Yaakov who would become renegades to the Jewish people, he was inspired to give him the blessings. What exactly does this mean?

Let us consider the renegade the Midrash holds up as an example. His name was Yosef Meshisa, and he was an awful Jew. When the Romans mounted their assault on the *Beis Hamikdash*, this Yosef Meshisa served as their native guide. As a reward, the Roman officer gave him permission to take for himself any of the valuables he wanted. He went into the *Heichal* and took the golden *menorah*, but the Roman decided it was too extravagant a treasure for a mere commoner.

"Go back and take something else," the Roman told him.

"I cannot go back in," Yosef Meshisa replied.

"No, you must go back," said the Roman.

"But I simply cannot," said Yosef Meshisa. "Isn't it enough that I defiled the Lord's Temple once? Must I do it again?"

"Aha! What have we here all of a sudden?" said the Roman. "A pious man, no less. Well, I absolutely insist that you go back in."

But Yosef Meshisa would not budge from his resolution. The Roman beat and tortured him mercilessly, but still he refused to go back into the *Heichal*. In his agony, he cried out, "Woe is me, for I have angered my Creator!" Finally, he died.

What had transformed this renegade Jew into a holy martyr in a matter of minutes? One minute, he was prepared to loot the *Beis Hamikdash* and carry off the golden *menorah*, and the next, he allows himself to be tortured to death rather than violate the sanctity of the *Heichal*. What, asks the Ponovezher Rav, brought about this amazing change?

The answer is simple, says the Ponovezher Rav. Stepping into a holy place transformed him. He may have entered the *Heichal* with the worst of motives. But once there, he was exposed to the aura of holiness, and he emerged a changed man.

This, according to the Midrash, is what Yitzchak saw in Yaakov's future that convinced him to give him the blessings.

He saw that even the lowest of the low among Yaakov's descendants, even the most despicable renegades such as Yosef Meshisa, would have such strong spiritual fortitude that they could be turned around by exposure to holiness. As low as they would fall, they would be one mere step from transformation into righteous people willing to die *al kiddush Hashem*. This was the lineage that was truly deserving of the blessings.

History has shown us that these kinds of transformations are not limited to the Inner Sanctum of the *Beis Hamikdash*. In the early 20th century, a Jew named Franz Rosenzweig told his story in a book entitled *The Star of Redemption*.

Franz was a successful author, a respected philosopher and a totally secular Jew. At one point, he was engaged to a gentile woman and was seriously considering baptism. It was during the First World War, and he served as a captain of cavalry in the German army on the Eastern front.

On the night of Yom Kippur, he found himself stationed in a small Polish town. As he made his rounds, he saw the light in the *shul* and heard the voices of the congregants, and out of curiosity, he stopped in to see what was going on. When he walked out a little while later, he writes, he was a religious Jew, a sincere *baal teshuvah*. He broke off his engagement to the gentile woman and led a life of observance from that point on.

In Germany of 1915, the idea of a *baal teshuvah* was virtually unheard of, unlike today when it such a common phenomenon. What brought about his incredible transformation? One thing: exposure to holiness. When he stepped into the *shul* and experienced the aura of Yom Kippur, he became a different person.

Such is the power of holiness, not just the holiness of the *Shechinah* in the *Beis Hamikdash*, but the holiness of just a handful of sincere Jews praying together in a small village *shul*. They too have the power to change a man forever.

Parashas Vayeitzei
פרשת ויצא

The Up-and-Down Ladder

וְהִנֵּה סֻלָּם מֻצָּב אַרְצָה וְרֹאשׁוֹ מַגִּיעַ הַשָּׁמָיְמָה

*And behold, there was a ladder,
planted on the ground, its top
reached into the heavens. (28:12)*

AMONG PROPHETIC SYMBOLS, YAAKOV'S LADDER IS probably one of the most memorable. In his dream, he has a vision of an immensely tall ladder "planted on the ground, its top reaching into the heavens." What is the significance of this ladder? The Midrash and the Rishonim provide innumerable answers.

One of the interpretations of the Midrash is particularly curious. Hashem was showing Yaakov two of his descendants. One of these was Moshe, who ascended into Heaven, as symbolized by the top of the ladder, which "reached into the heavens." The other was Korach, who was swallowed up by the earth, as symbolized by the ladder "planted on the ground." What was the point of showing Yaakov these two individuals?

The Baal Haturim points out that the *gematria*, the numerical value, of the word *sulam*, ladder, is equal to the numerical of the word *mamon*, money, and of the word *oni*, poverty. They all total up to 136.

A ladder, according to the Baal Haturim, is a metaphor both for money and for poverty. A ladder can bring a person up to the greatest heights, and it can also bring him down to the lowest depths. Money has the same ability to either elevate or degrade a person. When Hashem entrusts a person with money, he can use it to promote his own and his family's spiritual growth. He can give charity and do acts of *chessed* with other people. He can support community institutions. If these are the paths he chooses, the money will raise him up to the highest levels of spiritual achievement. But if he decides to use the money to indulge his drives and appetites, to push as many pleasure buttons as he can, it will bring him down to the lowest levels of debasement.

This concept may explain why Yaakov was shown Moshe and Korach. Our Sages tell us that both of these men were wealthy. Korach was so wealthy, in fact, that he lacked nothing in the world. His wealth corrupted him, and he developed such a hunger for power that he dared challenge Moshe's authority. His money ladder led him to the abyss — literally. The earth opened its mouth, and Korach descended to a depth no man had even experienced before or since. Moshe was also a wealthy man, but he went on to become the father of all prophets, the teacher of all the Jewish people. His money ladder led him only upwards.

Poverty also has this ambivalent power. On the one hand, it is a terrible ordeal. According to the Talmud (*Eruvin* 41b), a person afflicted by poverty is vulnerable to sinfulness. On the other hand, a person who passes the "test of poverty" is freed from the restrictions of money. His happiness comes from within and is not dependent on the size of his bank account. People who can adjust to a simpler life, who can successfully trim down their needs and lower their expectations, who have only a little but need even less, these people are truly free, rich and fortunate. They can use their acceptance of poverty to focus on Torah, spirituality and personal growth.

I heard a story that took place right here in Baltimore. A woman went shopping for a *sheitel*, a wig, and she brought along her 12-year-old daughter for company. They spent some time considering different style and shades. Finally, the woman found a *sheitel* that really appealed to her.

"This is the one I like," she said to the saleslady.

The saleslady fidgeted uncomfortably. She knew that the woman was very far from being wealthy. The *sheitel* she had chosen was out of her range. "I don't think that *sheitel* suits you," said the saleslady.

"But it's perfect," said the woman. "I like it. How much is it?"

"Let me show some other styles that are more suited for you."

"What's the point?" the woman persisted. "I like this one. Why do we have to bother looking any further?"

The saleslady cleared her throat. "Well, you see. The *sheitel* you've chosen is rather expensive. I don't think you can afford it."

The woman smiled. "Look, I can't afford any of them. So let me at least take the one that I like."

The saleslady shrugged and walked away.

Just then, the woman's young daughter, who had sat by silently during the entire exchange, spoke up. "Mommy," she said, "why can't we afford any *sheitel*? Are we poor? I never knew we were poor!"

I suppose we can fault the woman's lack of discretion for having this conversation in front of her daughter, but we have to admire her ability to raise her children in poverty with happiness and contentment and never feeling deprived. One thing we know for sure. The focus in that home, its source of happiness, is not on material things but on riches of the mind, the heart and the soul. That family's poverty is a ladder reaching into the heavens.

av Mordechai Ilan offers another interpretation to this Midrash. The Talmud states (*Megillah* 16a), "This [Jewish] nation is compared to dust and to the stars. When they are in decline, they descend to the level of dust; but when they rise, they ascend to the stars."

A ladder is, therefore, the perfect metaphor for the Jewish people. No one ever remains standing on a ladder. He either goes up, or he goes down. Chairs, sofas, beds can symbolize a static existence, but a ladder clearly symbolizes change. The Jewish ladder spans the entire spectrum of the people, from Moshe at the very top to Korach at the very bottom. Jewish people are always in a state of change, either progressing or regressing. There is no standing still. They either go down to the dust or up to the stars.

What's in a Name

וַיִּקְחוּ אֲבָנִים וַיַּעֲשׂוּ גָל . . . וַיִּקְרָא לוֹ לָבָן יְגַר
שָׂהֲדוּתָא וְיַעֲקֹב קָרָא לוֹ גַּלְעֵד

They took stones and made a mound . . .
Lavan named it Yegar Sehadusa,
but Yaakov named it Gal-Ed. (31:46-47)

FTER YAAKOV AND LAVAN SETTLE THEIR DIFFERENCES, they erect a monument to memorialize the event. Then the Torah tells us a seemingly insignificant point of information. Lavan gives the pile of stones the

Aramaic name Yegar Sehadusa, the pile that bears witness. Yaakov calls it Gal-Ed, the Hebrew version of the same name.

Sforno sees in this yet another facet of the dominant theme of the Book of *Bereishis* — the statement of the Sages that "*maaseh avos siman l'vanim,* the deeds of the father are signs for the sons." According to our Sages, one of the safeguards of the identity of the Jewish people in Egypt was their insistence on speaking their own language. Where did they get the fortitude to adhere to their own language despite the pressure to assimilate with the dominant culture of the Egyptians? Sforno contends that it came from this seemingly insignificant act of Yaakov's. When he insisted on spurning the Aramaic name Lavan had given the monument and identifying it instead by its Hebrew name, he implanted in the Jewish people a strong devotion to their own language and identity.

Taking this line of thought a step further, it appears that the entire *Parashas Vayeitzei* is a paradigm for the future exile and return of the Jewish people. It begins with Yaakov being driven into exile with a promise from Hashem that he will one day return triumphant. And ultimately he does.

Let us listen to the dialogue between Lavan and Yaakov at the point of separation, when Yaakov finally breaks away from his state of exile and returns home. At the end, Lavan does not accuse Yaakov of being overly religious. He accuses him of dishonesty (31:30).

"What is my transgression?" Yaakov replies. "What is my sin that you have so hotly pursued me? When you rummaged through all my possessions, what did you find of all your household objects? Set it before my kinsmen and yours, and let them decide between us. These twenty years I have been with you, your ewes and she-goats never miscarried, nor have I eaten the rams of your flock. I never brought you the mangled — I bore the loss myself, you would exact it from me, whether it was stolen by day or by night. This is how I was, scorching heat consumed me by day and frost by night. My sleep was dispelled from my eyes . . ."

If "*maaseh avos siman l'vanim*, the deeds of the father are signs for the sons," then this speech foreshadows the argument we will have to offer in our own defense when the end of the exile draws near. And what is its theme? Honesty. Integrity. We did not cheat in business. We did not rob the gentiles. We were *ehrliche Yidden*. That is what will bring us out of exile.

Parashas Vayishlach
פרשת וישלח

Observant But Not Religious

כֹּה אָמַר עַבְדְּךָ יַעֲקֹב עִם לָבָן גַּרְתִּי וָאֵחַר עַד עָתָּה

*So said Yaakov, "I lived with Lavan,
and I have lingered until now." (32:5)*

RASHI, QUOTING FROM THE MIDRASH, OFFERS A FAMOUS insight into Yaakov's declaration that "I lived with Lavan." The Hebrew word for "I lived" is *garti*, which is also an anagram for *taryag*, the numerical expression of the six hundred and thirteen *mitzvos* of the Torah. Yaakov was saying, "Although I lived with Lavan, I observed all six hundred and thirteen *mitzvos* and did not learn from his evil ways."

My *Rosh Yeshivah*, Rav Yaakov Ruderman pointed out that there seems to be a redundancy in Yaakov's words. If he indeed fulfilled all six hundred and thirteen *mitzvos* — the entire Torah! — then he certainly did not learn any of Lavan's evil ways, which would have been in violation of the Torah.

Clearly, observed Rav Ruderman, it is possible for a person to keep the entire Torah, to fulfill every *mitzvah* meticulously, and still emulate the lifestyle of a Lavan.

I would like to expand a little on this crucial point by quoting from Rabbi Emanuel Feldman's response to a popular

Jewish periodical's survey regarding the current state of Orthodoxy in America:

"Can it be truly said that today's Orthodox individual is any less self-indulgent, less hedonistic, less undisciplined than those who do not perform *mitzvos*? The authors of those crudely worded wedding invitations that condescendingly remind us to dress modestly 'in accordance with Orthodox tradition' frequently forget that Jewish tradition requires modesty not only in sleeve length, but in Viennese tables, flowers and other vulgar excesses which mark the typical contemporary Orthodox wedding. Disagreements within the Torah community are not always models of civility and restraint. *Tznius* in dress is not always extended to *tznius* in words. Is it quite possible in this day of resurgent Orthodoxy to have a synagogue with a proper *mechitzah* but yet whose noise volume on Shabbos is so high that one cannot hear the reading of the Torah? Is it quite possible in effect to be a secular Jew with a *yarmulke*, to eat kosher but to think *treif*, to be fully observant but to adopt the worst attitude and values of the society around us and still claim to be Orthodox? Is it possible to be observant and yet never think about what God wants of us, only of what we want from God?"

Strong words. We have much cause for gratification in the Orthodox community. Forty years ago, the death of Orthodoxy in America was widely predicted, but the opposite has come to pass. These last forty years have seen an incredible resurgence of Orthodox growth, of Torah study and *mitzvah* observance. But does more observant necessarily mean more religious? Does our greater observance bring us closer to Hashem or does our fascination with American materialism drive us further away?

This is what Yaakov was saying. I have kept all six hundred and thirteen *mitzvos*. I have been perfectly observant. I have also remained perfectly religious. Moreover, I did not learn from his evil ways. I kept my values intact. What I am, the way I live, the way I act, the way I think, the goals to which I aspire, all these are informed by my connection to Hashem and His Torah. They were not influenced by Lavan's evil ways.

The Name of the Angel

וַיִּשְׁאַל יַעֲקֹב וַיֹּאמֶר הַגִּידָה נָּא שְׁמֶךָ וַיֹּאמֶר לָמָּה זֶּה תִּשְׁאַל לִשְׁמִי

And Yaakov asked, and said, "What is your name please?" and [the angel] replied, "Why do you ask my name?"
(32:30)

HROUGHOUT THE NIGHT, YAAKOV STRUGGLED WITH THE angel of Eisav, and he was victorious. Toward morning, the angel asks Yaakov to release him, but Yaakov refuses unless the angel blesses him. The angel informs Yaakov that his name will be changed to Yisrael. "And what is your name?" Yaakov asks the angel. But the angel's only response is a cryptic question, "Why do you ask my name?"

What is the implication of this dialogue?

According to our Sages, this angel was the guardian angel of Eisav, also known as Satan, also known as the *yetzer hara*, the evil inclination. Rav Leib Chasman explains that, since the name of a person or being reflects his essence, when Yaakov asked the angel for his name he was actually trying to discover his essence. He was actually saying, "What are you all about, *yetzer hara*? What makes you tick? What is the secret of your power over people?"

And the angel replied, "Why do you ask my name?" In other words, explains Rav Leib Chasman, there is no point in asking this question. The *yetzer hara* is not a reality, only a figment of the imagination. It is an image that is conjured in the mind when a person is consumed by desire. But in reality, there is no separate entity called the *yetzer hara*. It is the person himself.

Sometimes, a person lies in the dark and sees huge shadows forming on the wall. He is terrified. Perhaps it is a bear, or an intruder. But then he flicks on the light and sees that it was nothing, only his own overactive imagination. This is the *yetzer hara*, a shadow in the night, a figure of fantasy, without reality, without essence. And when you flick on the light, you discover that nothing was there in the first place.

Rav Chaim Dov Keller offers a different interpretation of the dialogue between Yaakov and the angel. He interprets Yaakov's question along the same lines as does Rav Chasman. Yaakov wanted to know the essence of the *yetzer hara*, because he wanted to forewarn his descendants and fortify them against this formidable foe.

"Why do you ask my name?" the angel replied. "It is a pointless endeavor to prepare your descendants for their encounters with me. My mission is to test people, and in order to do this, I change form in every generation. The situations change, the temptations change, and I change. In one generation, the temptation may be idol worship, and that is where I concentrate my efforts. In another generation, it may be the heresies of so-called enlightenment, and that is where I concentrate my efforts. I am always taking on a different form and changing my essence. Telling what my name is now would not help your descendants in the future."

In our own times, it seems to me, the changed form of the *yetzer hara* is the pursuit of wealth and worldly pleasures. Materialism is the bane of our generation. And that chameleon known as the *yetzer hara* is working actively to promote it.

Parashas Vayeishev
פרשת וישב

In The Spotlight

וַיִּשְׁמַע רְאוּבֵן וַיַּצִּלֵהוּ מִיָּדָם וַיֹּאמֶר לֹא נַכֶּנּוּ נָפֶשׁ

Reuven heard, and he rescued [Yosef] from them, and he said, "Let us not murder him." (37:21)

THE ISSUES WERE COMPLEX. YOSEF'S BROTHERS HAD sat in judgment and decided that he posed a mortal threat to them. They deemed him a *rodef*, a stalker bent on destruction, and they condemned him to death. But Reuven wanted no part of it. When he heard what they intended to do, he objected and suggested they toss Yosef into a pit instead. His intention was to come back later and spirit Yosef out of the pit and bring him back safely to Yaakov. But it did not work out that way.

The Midrash comments (*Rus Rabbah* 5:6), "Had Reuven known that Hashem would write in the Torah, 'Reuven heard and rescued [Yosef] from them,' he would have snatched Yosef and carried him back to his father on his shoulders." The Midrash also makes a similar comment about Aharon. "Had Aharon known that Hashem would write in the Torah, 'Behold, he will come out to welcome you,' he would have greeted Moshe with music and dancing." And Boaz also merits such a comment, "Had Boaz known that Hashem would write in the Torah, 'And he tossed [Rus] roasted grains, and she ate her fill and left some over,' he would have served her a feast of fatted calves."

What exactly is the Midrash saying here? At first glance, Reuven, Aharon and Boaz seem to be portrayed as publicity hounds. If they had known how much press coverage and exposure they could receive, they would have done things differently. As it was, however, unaware that the public would scrutinize their acts so closely, they did not overextend themselves.

But this cannot be the intent of the Midrash, which clearly comes to praise them, not to bury them. But if so, why didn't these three righteous people do the right thing even without the additional publicity?

The issue in all three cases, apparently, was not one of publicity but of clarity. None of them was certain he was doing the right thing. However, had he known Hashem would endorse his decision and emblazon it in the Torah for all eternity, he would have acted in a much more decisive and resolute way.

Reuven had to contend with his brothers, the future tribal patriarchs of the Jewish people, men of great scholarship, righteousness and character. They had sat in judgment and condemned Yosef to death. As much as Reuven objected to the decision of the majority, could he be absolutely certain that he was right and they were wrong? And so Reuven acted tentatively. He persuaded them to toss Yosef into the pit, hoping to sneak back later and pull him out to safety. Had he known Hashem would write in the Torah, "And Reuven heard, and he rescued Yosef," had he known Hashem would endorse his view rather than that of his brothers, he would have acted more decisively. He would have hoisted Yosef onto his shoulders and carried him back to his father.

When Aharon went out to greet Moshe, he also had his doubts. After all, he was the older son, the acknowledged leader of the Jewish people in captivity, a man who enjoyed the gift of prophecy. How would people look at it if he stepped aside in favor of his younger brother? Wasn't the younger brother obliged to honor his older brother? If so, how could he assume a superior position? And so Aharon, who was prepared to accept Moshe as the leader with the least bit of resentment, whose heart was filled to bursting with joy at the prospect of seeing his brother, went forth to greet Moshe, but he suppressed his natural urge to bring musicians and dancers. He did not have the confidence to make such a public spectacle of their reunion. Had he known Hashem would write in the Torah, "Behold, he will come out to welcome you," he would have brought the music and the dancers.

Boaz was afraid of the appearance of impropriety. He was concerned that people seeing him give food to the young maiden Rus would raise an arch eyebrow and snicker, "Hey, what's going on with Boaz and Rus? Isn't she a little too young for him?" Had he known Hashem would endorse his actions, he would have laid out a lavish feast for her.

The Midrash concludes, "In days gone by, a person would do a *mitzvah* and the prophet would record it. But now, when a person does a *mitzvah* and people mock him, who records who was right? Eliahu and Mashiach write it down and the Holy One, Blessed is He, signs in affirmation, as it is written (*Malachi* 3:16), 'Then those who fear Hashem spoke to one another and Hashem listened . . .'"

The problem of hesitation in the face of criticism and scorn plagues us in every generation. The prophet Malachi foretells a time, just prior to the Messianic era, when people will ridicule those who do *mitzvos*, but Eliahu, Mashiach and Hashem Himself will give the seal of approval to those with the courage to do what is right. The prophet encourages us not to hesitate, not to act tentatively when others accuse us of not being "modern" enough or "progressive" enough. We need not worry that we are in the minority and our detractors are in the majority. We need to act according to the conviction of our beliefs, and in the end, we will surely be vindicated.

Outside Influence

וַתִּתְפְּשֵׂהוּ בְּבִגְדוֹ לֵאמֹר שִׁכְבָה עִמִּי . . . וַיָּנָס וַיֵּצֵא הַחוּצָה

And she grabbed him by his garment,
saying, "Lie with me,"…
and he fled and ran outside. (39:12)

YOSEF DID ALL HE COULD TO RESIST THE ADVANCES OF Potiphar's wife. He pleaded with her, saying (39:9), "How can I do this evil thing?" But she persisted. One day, she grabbed him by his garment, and he "fled and ran outside."

There is a well-known Midrash on the verse in *Tehillim* (114:3), "The sea saw and fled." What did the sea see that caused it to flee? It saw Yosef's coffin. The sea "fled" when it saw the one who "fled." The Midrash makes a connection between these two instances of flight. What is this connection?

There is another remarkable word in the verse describing Yosef's flight. He runs *hachutzah*, "outside." Significantly, this word appears four times in the story of Yosef's ordeal. This word is strongly reminiscent of the *Bris Bein Habesarim*, the Covenant between the Pieces, in which Hashem takes Avraham *hachutzah*, outside, and shows him the stars (15:5). The Midrash comments that Hashem was telling Avraham to step out of his normal sphere of experience and rise above the restrictions of the laws of nature. Henceforth, Avraham would no longer be under the power of natural law. Even if in the natural course of events he could not have children, he would father great nations.

The word *hachutzah*, "outside," therefore, indicates the ability to rise above nature. This was exactly what Yosef did when he fled "outside." He overcame his natural tendency to succumb to her advances. He broke away and overcame his nature.

When the Jewish people came to the Sea of Reeds, the waters were not so ready to split apart and interrupt their flow as dictated by nature. But the appearance of Yosef's coffin at the seashore suspended the laws of nature. The sea "fled" in the merit of the one that overcame his nature and "fled."

Somewhat more kabbalistically, the Shemen Hatov goes a step further. Quoting from the *Sefer Hapardes*, he points out that there are 112 verses in *Parashas Vayeishev*, 104 of which begin with the letter *vav*, which is a conjunction. These eight independent verses, says the Pardes, represent the eight days leading up to *milah*.

The Shemen Hatov explains that all the incidents in the *parashah* are one large continuum connected by the *vav* conjunctions. Everything is cause and effect. But the life of a Jew, symbolized by the eight days of *milah*, is not affected by this continuum. There are no *vavs*, conjunctions, in the verses that represent the Jewish people, because there is no ordinary cause and effect in the lives of Jewish people. The life of a Jew is beyond the control of nature. It is identified with the number eight, which symbolizes the supernatural; seven being the symbol of nature and eight being the supernatural.

The eight days of Chanukah, which always fall during *Parashas Vayeishev*, also fall neatly into this pattern. The eight days signify the supernatural, which is an apt description for the miracle of Chanukah.

Parashas Mikeitz
פרשת מקץ

Chanukah All Over Again

POPULAR WISDOM CONTENDS THAT "THE MORE THINGS change, the more they stay the same." The Talmud recognizes the value of popular wisdom, often remarking, "*Hainu d'amri inshi*, this is what people say." Popular sayings are the product of long experience, and they are usually on target.

The more things change, the more they stay the same. Events change. Conditions change. Styles change. But people do not change. Human nature today is no different from what it was a hundred, a thousand or five thousand years ago. Therefore, sooner or later, people driven by the unchanging drives and ambitions of human nature will manipulate the new events, conditions and styles into forms that help them achieve the same goals people have been pursuing since time immemorial.

A little over two thousand years ago, Alexander the Great, at the head of a Greek and Macedonian army, conquered the entire Middle East and introduced it to Greek philosophy and culture. The Greeks transformed the ancient world by rejecting the worship of a Higher Being and making mankind the focus of the culture. The Greeks promoted the importance of the human intellect and the beauty of the human form as ideals to be held up for admiration and even worship. It was the antithesis of Judaism, which focuses on the Creator and gives man value in proportion to the level of his relationship with the Divine.

The Greeks recognized the power of the Torah. They knew it was the mortal enemy of their culture, the force that threatened Greek civilization more than any other, and they mounted a campaign to eradicate Torah observance among the Jews. They passed laws outlawing fundamental Jewish practices such as *milah* and Shabbos. And they built theaters and gymnasiums throughout Eretz Yisrael to entice the Jews to share in the pleasures and rewards of Greek culture.

Unfortunately, the Greek campaign was very effective. Many Jews, among them High Priests and others holding the highest offices in the land, abandoned the ways of their fathers and assimilated into Greek society. These Jews were known as Hellenizers, since the Greeks referred to Greece as Hellas and themselves as Hellenes. As time went on, it seemed as if the juggernaut of Greek culture and values would completely absorb the tiny Jewish commonwealth and Torah would be forgotten. But then the Chashmonaim, a small band of staunch Jews loyal to the Torah and Jewish tradition, rose up against the Greek oppressors nearly two hundred years after the Greek conquest, and they restored the supremacy of the Torah among the Jewish people. The festival of Chanukah celebrates this triumph every year.

In our own days, we have seen similar events take place. One hundred years ago, a new philosophy called communism appeared on the stage of world history. The appeal of communism was in the simplicity and apparent justice of its ideas. The rich should not exploit the poor. All the people should own all means of production. Everyone should work according to his ability and consume according to his need. In all else, everyone in society would be equal. As you can well imagine, this was an extremely attractive system for the masses in impoverished and exploited societies, and it spread like wildfire. It scored its first victory in Russia and then spread to Eastern Europe, China and countries in Southeast Asia, the Caribbean and Africa, as well as innumerable "liberation movements" across the world.

Sad to say, many Jews were drawn into the communist movement during its early stages. Young men and women chafing under the repressive Czarist and other totalitarian regimes and too restless to adapt to *shtetl* life sought fulfillment of their natural idealism in the communist ranks. For a while, there was even a Jewish section in the Communist Party called the Yevsektzia. This went on until the 30's when Stalin purged the party of its Jews. Afterwards, the Jews were only on the receiving end of communist repression.

Ultimately, communism was discredited by the old nemesis of all starry-eyed systems, the avarice and ambition of human nature. In the end, the communist system engendered more exploitation and less justice than any other system in history. It remained in force for nearly a century by virtue of state terrorism, and then it collapsed. But in the interim, it brought untold devastation and ruin to the world for an entire century.

Hellenism rose, and Hellenism fell. Communism rose and communism fell. All changes are impermanent. The more things change, the more they remain the same. The only constants are Torah and Judaism. The Rambam writes (*Yad, Hilchos Mezuzah* 6:13), "[By affixing a *mezuzah*,] he will be reminded of the Name of the Holy One, Blessed is He, every time he enters or leaves. He will be stirred from his slumber and realize that nothing endures forever other than the knowledge of [Hashem]." All ideologies are like a fleeting shadow, but Torah endures. Many Jewish brothers and sisters forgot this during the times of the Greeks, with disastrous consequences. Many more forgot it in the last century, with consequences that were perhaps even more disastrous.

For those of us that grew up during the Cold War, the fall of communism was a thing of absolute wonder. Among my childhood memories are Khrushchev pounding the lectern in the United Nations with his shoe. I remember listening to the radio during the Soviet invasion of Hungary in 1956. I remember the Prague Spring of 1968, when Soviet tanks crushed the rebirth of democracy in Czechoslovakia. For me, communism was a fact of life, something I expected to prey on my consciousness for the rest of my life.

And then it was gone. Just like that. Poof! The Soviet Union, that dreaded "evil empire," crumbled to dust.

In December of 1989, I was riding in a cab in New York. The driver had a thick Eastern European accent, and I thought he might be a Russian Jew. We began to talk, and it turned out he was a Romanian. By then, Hungary, East Germany and Czechoslovakia had already gone the way of the Soviet Union and I remarked that Romania would be next.

He guffawed. "If you knew that tyrant Ceausescu, [the Romanian president], you would never say such a thing. He is another Stalin!"

Well, it didn't take long before Ceausescu fell and Romania discarded communism. Stalin himself could not have stopped this disintegration of a movement that had once seemed poised to take over the world.

What was happening here?

Why did communism have such phenomenal, almost supernatural success in the beginning, and why did it experience such a phenomenal, almost supernatural collapse in the end?

Rav Shimon Schwab believed that communism enjoyed such great success because the early communists were true believers; they were doing it *lishmah*, for altruistic reasons. They were willing to forgo personal gain and honor for the sake of the greater cause. Altruism can energize any idea, even if it is the greatest falsehood.

Rav Schwab asks a question. The first time Balak's messengers asked Bilam to curse the Jewish people, Heaven forbid, Hashem did not grant him permission to go with them. But when they returned a second time and offered Bilam money and honor, Hashem let him go. What changed?

The first time, Rav Schwab explains, they did not offer Bilam any reward. His curse would have been delivered altruistically. This would have been a dangerous curse. The second time, however, they offered him rewards. Now, his curse would be delivered for self-interest. Such a curse would not have nearly the same power and effectiveness.

The Kotzker Rebbe was once asked why other religions, which are based on *sheker*, falsehood, are so successful, while Judaism, which is the *emes*, the truth, doesn't attract others and even loses many of its own. "True, they serve *sheker*," the Kotzker snapped, "but they serve it as if it were *emes*. True, we serve *emes*, but we do it as if it were *sheker*."

This was the power of the early communists. They were sincere. They were altruistic. They believed in what they were doing. They believed they were creating a utopian society on earth. It was a fantasy, an illusion, a mirage, but their idealism gave it reality for almost a century.

So why did communism fall so precipitously? Granted that the idealism had dissipated over the years, to be replaced by cynicism and corruption, but how do we explain the sudden collapse?

Rav Schwab contends that the only antidotes to falsehood are Torah and *mitzvos*. During the last years before the collapse of world communism, there was a revival of Torah in the Soviet Union. A small group of people returned to Torah with great *mesiras nefesh*, dedication at tremendous personal risk. They underwent circumcision even when there were no anesthetics available. They abstained from family relations when they had no access to a *mikveh*. They studied Torah diligently, even if it meant losing their jobs or being expelled from universities and other institutes of higher learning. They did it because they believed in it, not for personal gain, and their

Torah *lishmah* brought down communism. All the other factors about which one reads in articles and books — economics, finance, geopolitics, military preparedness — are just window dressing. The Torah of the dissidents brought down communism. They are the Chashmonaim of our generation. They wrought the modern miracle of Chanukah.

Parashas Vayigash
פרשת ויגש

Short and Sharp Rebuke

וַיֹּאמֶר יוֹסֵף אֶל אֶחָיו אֲנִי יוֹסֵף הַעוֹד אָבִי חָי וְלֹא
יָכְלוּ אֶחָיו לַעֲנוֹת אֹתוֹ כִּי נִבְהֲלוּ מִפָּנָיו

And Yosef said to his brothers, "I am Yosef.
Is my father still alive?" And the brothers
could not respond to him, for they shrank
from him in shame. (45:3)

FTER A SHARP CONFRONTATION WITH YEHUDAH, WHO
pleads with him to have mercy on his aged father,
Yosef can longer maintain his masquerade. He bursts
into tears and reveals his identity to his brothers. "I am Yosef,"
he cries out. "Is my father still alive?" And the brothers "shrink
from him in shame."

The Midrash comments (*Bereishis Rabbah* 93:10), "*Oy lanu
miyom hadin, oy lanu miyom hatochachah.* Woe is to us on the
day of judgment. Woe is to us on the day of rebuke . . . If the
brothers could not endure Yosef's rebuke [without shrinking
away in shame], each individual will certainly not endure it when
the Holy One, Blessed is He, rebukes him for what he has done."

What connection is the Midrash making? How does Yosef's
rebuke to his brothers foreshadow the rebuke each of us will
face on the final day of reckoning?

Let us consider for a moment. What exactly were Yosef's

words of rebuke? "I am Yosef." Why are these words considered rebuke?

For twenty-two years, the brothers lived under the impression that they had acted justly by selling their brother into slavery. They saw their broken-hearted, inconsolable father, but they still thought they were right. They saw that the *Shechinah* had consequently departed from their home, and still, they were convinced that they had done the right thing.

They suffered through a famine. They went down to Egypt to buy food and found themselves caught in a web of intrigue. They were accused of being spies. Some of them were taken hostage. They were endangered. And now they were falsely accused of robbing the viceroy's cup. They must have wondered why they were being subjected to such trials and tribulations, but they didn't have any answers.

And then Yosef declares, "I am Yosef." And everything is crystal clear! Like a flash of lightning, those words illuminate the landscape of their lives for the previous twenty-two years. Suddenly, they understand everything. All the mysteries are dispelled, and they understand that they have been living a lie for all these years. There could be no stronger rebuke, and they shrink back in shame.

Each of us goes through life distracted by this, distracted by that, puzzled by this, puzzled by that, confused, deluded, and in the process, we wander off in wrong directions and make mistakes. We lose sight of our priorities and pursue the wrong goals. But when the final day of reckoning arrives, all Hashem will say is, "I am Hashem!"

Like a flash of lightning, these three short words will illuminate our lives for us. Suddenly, we will understand everything that has happened to us, and we identify all our mistakes with perfect clarity. And it will be terribly painful. Those three words are all it will take. "I am Hashem!" When we hear those words, woe is to us of the day of judgment, woe is to us on the day of rebuke.

Conclusive Proof

וַיַּרְא אֶת הָעֲגָלוֹת אֲשֶׁר שָׁלַח יוֹסֵף לָשֵׂאת אֹתוֹ
וַתְּחִי רוּחַ יַעֲקֹב אֲבִיהֶם

*And [Yaakov] saw the wagons Yosef had sent
to transport him, and the spirit of
their father Yaakov was revived. (45:27)*

BEFORE YAAKOV WOULD ALLOW HIMSELF TO ACCEPT
the news that his long-lost son Yosef had been found
alive and that he was now the viceroy of Egypt, he
wanted to see some solid proof. Perhaps the whole thing was
some kind of cruel hoax.

Yosef could easily have sent along all sorts of signs that
he was genuine and not an impostor. He could have
described his room or any other intimate details that would
not be known to a stranger. But he did something altogether different. According to the Midrash, the "wagons Yosef
had sent to transport Yaakov to Egypt" were really a hint at
the *sugya*, Talmudic topic, they had discussed in private on
the last day they had seen each other — the topic of *eglah
arufah*, the decapitated calf. (The Hebrew word for wagon is
agalah, which is reminiscent of the word *eglah*.) This sign
convinced Yaakov that this was not a hoax and revived his
spirits.

But why indeed was this such a conclusive proof? Just as
an impostor might have somehow learned other intimate
details about Yosef, why couldn't he have discovered this
information as well?

During the time of the Vilna Gaon, a very strange incident
took place in his city. A young couple had gotten married, and
shortly afterward, the husband vanished without a trace. The

poor wife was left an *agunah*, a living widow unable to remarry because her husband might still be alive.

Thirty years passed, and then, one fine day, a man appeared on her doorstep and declared, "My dear wife, I'm back!" Then he told her a long story about what had kept him from returning for so many years.

The woman looked at the man and did not recognize him as her husband. But then again, she couldn't be sure that he wasn't. Thirty years wreak changes on a person. They also fade the memory, especially in those times when there were no photographs. The man was about the same build and coloring as her husband. His features were not really dissimilar. His face was weathered by time and the elements, and it was difficult to imagine what he might have looked like thirty years earlier. It was not impossible that this was her husband. And yet, he did not seem familiar.

She expressed her reservations to the man, and he was very understanding.

"Test me," he said. "Ask me any question about our life together. See if I know the answers."

So she asked him questions, and he had all the answers. He knew all about their families, their wedding day, their home, including some intimate details that only the two of them could have known.

Still, she remained suspicious, and she decided to seek the advice of the *beis din*. The *dayanim* of the *beis din* interrogated the man extensively, but they could not catch him in a mistake. He was very convincing. And yet, his wife was not convinced, which was certainly cause for suspicion. What should they do? They sought the counsel of the Vilna Gaon.

"Take the man to the *shul*," said the Gaon. "Ask him to point out his *makom kavua*, the place where he normally sat."

They took him to the *shul* and asked him to point to his seat. The man hemmed and hawed, but he could not do it. Then he broke down and admitted that he had learned all his information from the husband whom he had befriended many years earlier.

The Vilna Gaon had put his finger on the flaw in this man's diabolical plan. Assuming that the man was an impostor seeking to move in with another man's wife, he was obviously far from a righteous person. Such a person would seek out all sorts of important details to "prove" his identity, but it would not occur to him to find out about the husband's seat in *shul* or any of the other holy matters in Jewish life.

Similarly, Yaakov knew that if the man who claimed to be Yosef was an impostor he might have extracted all sorts of intimate and obscure information from the real Yosef. But he also knew that it would never occur to an impostor to ask which *sugya* he and Yaakov were discussing when they last saw each other. When Yosef was able to refer to the *sugya* of *eglah arufah*, Yaakov was convinced that he had found his long-lost son.

Serious Jews identify themselves by the holy aspects of their lives. The important information is not the make and color of their cars, not the size of their houses, not the last time they went fishing or played baseball. It is the *mitzvos* they have performed, the *chessed* they have done, the place where they sit in *shul*, the last *sugya* they discussed.

Parashas Vayechi
פרשת ויחי

The Precious Final Moments

וַיֹּאמֶר לְיוֹסֵף הִנֵּה אָבִיךָ חֹלֶה

And [the messenger] said to Yosef,
"Behold, your father is sick." (48:1)

THE MESSENGER CAME FROM GOSHEN AND REPORTED to Yosef, "Behold, your father is sick." It would seem that this was a fairly commonplace message, especially regarding elderly people, but in actuality, it was a very remarkable statement, an unheard-of statement.

According to *Pirkei d'Rabbi Eliezer*, there had never been illness in the world before this time. Death never came as the culmination of a long illness. A person would be fit as a fiddle one moment and dead the next. He would just sneeze, and his soul would depart through his nostrils.

Yaakov, however, prayed to Hashem that people should become ill so that they should have some inkling that death is imminent. "Please do not take my soul," he prayed, "before I have the opportunity to leave instructions for my children and my household."

Hashem accepted Yaakov's prayer. He became sick. And the messenger came to report to Yosef about the amazing thing that had happened in Goshen. "Behold, your father is sick." It was sensational news.

I once heard a radio newscaster comment on an air disaster, "Thank Heaven, they never knew what hit them. When a bomb goes off on an aircraft at thirty thousand feet, there is no time to think. You're just dead in an instant. They never had a chance to think, 'Yikes, I'm abut to die.' They were spared the pain and the anguish of looking death in the face. Boom, and they were dead. Just like that."

Well, I suppose that is one way of looking at it, but it is not the Jewish way. The *Pirkei d'Rabbi Eliezer* describes the Jewish way. Terminal diseases may be painful, but at least they give a person a warning that he is about to depart from this world. He is forewarned that he must tie up the loose ends.

A person leaving this world must make a *cheshbon hanefesh*, taking spiritual stock of his life, what he has accomplished and what he has failed to accomplish. He must do *teshuvah* for his transgressions and shortcomings and prepare his soul for the next world. He must review all his outstanding obligations and make sure he has discharged them properly. He must leave instructions to his children and his household. He must make sure he is not leaving a mess for someone else to clean up. A lifetime of activity calls for a lot of wrapping up. A person who is struck by a bus and never knows what hit him will never have the opportunity to bring his life to a fitting conclusion. He misses out on a very great blessing.

When the *Challenger* shuttle exploded, there was much speculation about whether the crew members were aware that they were about to die. When they finally found the tapes, they heard some of them say, "Uh oh!" This caused a great uproar. Their attorneys wanted to sue NASA for the additional trauma of their having known about the impending disaster.

"Does it necessarily follow," wrote a gentile columnist at the time, "that it would have been more merciful that death come so instantaneously that the final conscious emotion was a sense of exhilaration? Or does such an end rob a person of the right to reflect, even if only for a few precious moments, on those things that make life worth living?"

For those who believe that death is the end, blissful ignorance at the moment of death is perhaps preferable to a few moments of agony. But for those who believe in the immortality of the soul, in punishment and reward in the next world, in an eternal afterlife, a few precious moments of preparation are priceless indeed.

At All Costs

אָבִי הִשְׁבִּיעַנִי לֵאמֹר הִנֵּה אָנֹכִי מֵת בְּקִבְרִי אֲשֶׁר
כָּרִיתִי לִי בְּאֶרֶץ כְּנַעַן שָׁמָּה תִּקְבְּרֵנִי

*"My father made me take an oath, saying,
'Behold, I am about to die, bury me in the grave
I bought in the land of Canaan.'" (50:5)*

YAAKOV WANTED TO BE BURIED IN THE *ME'ARAS Hamachpeilah*, the gravesite he "bought in the land of Canaan." From whom did Yaakov buy his gravesite in the *Me'aras Hamachpeilah*? It must have been from Eisav with whom he shared the inheritance of the burial ground. He bought out Eisav's share so that he would retain exclusive rights to it for always.

The Torah uses the rather unusual Hebrew word *karisi* to convey that he had "bought" the gravesite. Rashi explains that the word *karisi* brings to mind a *kri*, a pile. The implication is that Yaakov piled up all his money, all the gold and silver he had acquired in Paddan Aram, and offered it to Eisav. "Here," he was in effect saying, "take all the money I made outside Canaan. It is yours. All I want is the *Me'aras Hamachpeilah*. Sell it to me, and all this treasure is yours."

This is not exactly the type of negotiating stance we would have expected of Yaakov. During his years with Lavan, he had shown himself to be exceedingly clever and astute when it came to business negotiations. When negotiating to buy Eisav's share of the *Me'aras Hamachpeilah*, we would have expected him to be more conventional and circumspect. He should have begun with a low but respectable offer. Eisav would have countered with a demand for a higher sum. They would have negotiated and met somewhere in the middle. This approach would most probably have worked. Why didn't he take it?

Furthermore, Yaakov was always very careful with his possessions. He even went back for *pachim ketanim*, small jugs, rather than just abandon them unnecessarily (see Rashi in *Vayishlach* 32:25). He understood that Hashem had given him his wealth and he should not squander it. What then was Yaakov thinking when he dumped everything he owned on the table and said, "Here, take everything I own"?

When Yaakov returned from Paddan Aram after an absence of twenty years, as he contemplated his anticipated confrontation with Eisav, the Torah tells us (32:8) that "Yaakov feared greatly." What did he fear? The Midrash explains (*Bereishis Rabbah* 76:2) that he was afraid Eisav exceeded him in merit in two *mitzvos*. Eisav had been living in the Holy Land and honoring his parents all those years Yaakov had been away.

Yaakov felt compelled to demonstrate somehow that he was as intensely dedicated to these *mitzvos* as was Eisav, if not more. How could he show that he loved the Land with every fiber of his being? How could he show how deeply he cared about the honor of his parents?

There was a way to accomplish both of these goals in one fell swoop. By telling Eisav, "Take everything I own. All that is important to me is to own the *Me'aras Hamachpeilah* as my inheritance in the Holy Land. All that is important to me is to be buried next to my revered parents. Compared to this, everything else is meaningless."

True, Yaakov could have driven a better bargain. But he could not have found a better way to show where his heart lay.

Shemos

Parashas Shemos
פרשת שמות

True Greatness

וַיֹּאמֶר מֶלֶךְ מִצְרַיִם לַמְיַלְּדֹת הָעִבְרִיֹּת אֲשֶׁר שֵׁם
הָאַחַת שִׁפְרָה וְשֵׁם הַשֵּׁנִית פּוּעָה

*And the king of Egypt said to the midwives, one of whom
was named Shifrah and the other Puah. (1:15)*

WHEN PHARAOH DECREED THAT ALL NEWBORN Jewish boys should be drowned, two heroic midwives saved the day. One was named Shifrah and the other Puah. Rashi explains that these two women were none other than Yocheved, Moshe's mother, and Miriam, his sister. Why then were they called Shifrah and Puah? Yocheved was called Shifrah because she was *meshaferes es havlad*, she beautified the infants and smoothed their limbs. Miriam was called Puah because she was *poah umedaberes livlad*, she cooed and whispered to the infants.

It seems strange that the special names the Torah gives Yocheved and Miriam memorialize the care they showed to the infants. These women actually saved their lives. If it weren't for them, those infants would have been drowned. Shouldn't they then have been given names that memorialize their heroic rescue of the Jewish children? Wouldn't it have been more appropriate to name them Hatzalah and Teshuah, for example?

My *Rosh Yeshivah*, Rav Yaakov Yitzchak Ruderman, always used to say that true greatness is manifested in the little things, the low-profile actions that reveal the depth of character and commitment. It is not enough to perform heroic acts that grab the headlines, so to speak. People of lesser worth can also find it within themselves to rise to the occasion for that one moment of heroism and perform acts of greatness. But it is a superficial greatness, because after the deed is done, they revert to ordinariness. They pat themselves on the back and say, "All right, I've done my duty. I've risked my life and saved the world, and now it's time to go home and get on with my life." A meteoric rise and a descent to earth. True greatness, however, is expressed in small but extraordinary deeds. These two heroic women, Shifrah and Puah, were pulling Jewish children to safety in a time of mortal danger, yet they had the sensitivity and the presence of mind to take the time to beautify their little bodies and to soothe their little souls with coos and whispers. This was true greatness.

The Talmud reports (*Avodah Zarah* 18a) that Rabbi Yosi ben Kisma taught Torah in public despite a Roman decree forbidding anyone to do so under the penalty of death. One day, Rabbi Chanina ben Teradion visited him.

"Don't you know," asked Rabbi Chanina ben Teradion, "that Heaven granted [the Romans] their power? How can you flaunt their decrees?"

"I really on the mercy of Heaven," Rabbi Yosi ben Kisma replied. "Tell me, will I have a share in the next world?"

"Have you ever done anything outstanding?" asked Rabbi Chanina ben Teradion.

"Yes, I have," said Rabbi Yosi ben Kisma responded. "I once had charity as well as my own money in the same pocket. They got mixed up, and I didn't know which was which. So I gave everything to charity."

"If so," said Rabbi Chanina ben Teradion, "may my own portion be as great as your portion, and may my destiny be as great as yours."

What can we make of this conversation? Rabbi Yosi ben Kisma is risking his life to teach Torah in public. He will probably die a horrible death at the hands of the Romans if he is apprehended. Yet this great act of heroism doesn't seem to guarantee him a share in the next world. What worthy act convinces Rabbi Chanina ben Teradion that Rabbi Yosi ben Kisma has earned a share in the next world? That he gave his own money to charity when it got mixed up with charity money! Amazing!

We see clearly from this Gemara how true greatness is measured. Headline-grabbing acts of heroism are not absolute proof of true greatness. On the other hand, giving away one's own money when it gets mixed up with charity money will never get a headline. In fact, no one will ever know about it. Such an act shows what a person is really made of. Such an act is a sure sign of true greatness.

Kindness and Truth

וַתִּפְתַּח וַתִּרְאֵהוּ אֶת הַיֶּלֶד וְהִנֵּה נַעַר בֹּכֶה וַתַּחְמֹל
עָלָיו וַתֹּאמֶר מִיַּלְדֵי הָעִבְרִים זֶה

And she opened [the box] and saw the boy,
and behold, he was crying, and she took pity
on him and said, "This is a Hebrew boy." (2:6)

PHARAOH'S DAUGHTER BASYA WENT DOWN TO THE RIVER to bathe, and she caught sight of a box floating among the bulrushes. She sent her attendants to fetch the box, opened it and saw a baby boy crying, and she said, "This is a Hebrew boy."

How did she know this? What made her conclude that the infant Moshe was a Hebrew child? It was not his appearance. It was not the sound of his crying. It was simply the conditions of his discovery. Why was a child adrift in a box on the river? It must be that his parents were trying to save him from Pharaoh's decree of death to all male Jewish infants.

Basya's logic was excellent, and she guessed right. But it seems to have taken her a while to figure it out. As soon as she saw that the box contained a boy, she should have realized that he was Jewish. But apparently, this is not what happened. According to the Torah, she noticed that "he was crying, and she took pity on him" and only afterward did she say, "This is a Hebrew boy." What took her so long?

Rav Nissan Alpert offered a beautiful solution to this question in the context of his eulogy for his *rebbi,* Rav Moshe Feinstein. Rav Moshe was universally recognized as by far the greatest Torah scholar of his time. His knowledge was vaster than vast, his insight razor sharp and his humility, sensitivity and kindness legendary. One might have thought it would be very difficult for a young scholar to receive a *haskamah*, a letter of approbation, for a new *sefer* from such a towering sage, but just the opposite was true. Rav Moshe gave *haskamos* readily and easily to just about anyone who asked for them. He also gave letters of recommendation and letters of endorsement for all sorts of projects with the same ease. It came to the point that people were no longer impressed by a letter from Rav Moshe, so easy were they to come by. Why did he do this? Why wasn't he more discriminating when it came to writing letters on behalf of people?

Rav Alpert explained that *chessed*, kindness, and *emes*, truth, are not really compatible concepts. Kindness flows from the heart. It is an instinctive emotional response. Truth is established by the brain. It is the product of scrutiny, investigation and logic. In a certain sense, truth is the antagonist of kindness. If we would do a thorough investigation of poor people that ask for charity we would probably reject most of them.

Indeed, when *chessed* and *emes* are mentioned together in the Torah (*Bereishis* 24:49; *Shemos* 34:6; *Yehoshua* 2:14), the word *chessed* always precedes the word *emes*. *Chessed* is quick and instinctive. *Emes* is deliberate and thorough. If *chessed* would wait for *emes*, it would never get off the ground.

A person's first reaction must be kindness. Only afterward should he set off in search for the truth. When a beggar asks for a handout, don't wait until you check out his credentials. Give him something right away. When an institution needs financial assistance, don't call for an audit to determine exactly what the problem is. When a young author comes for an approbation, give it to him! This was Rav Moshe's philosophy in life.

When Basya opened the box and saw the boy, concludes Rav Alpert, her first reaction wasn't to assess the situation, to consider who the child's parents were and why he was adrift on the river, to determine if it would be appropriate to rescue him. Her first reaction was kindness. "He was crying, and she took pity on him." Before she gave any thought to the situation, her kind heart went out to the crying child. Only afterward did she stop to consider the situation, and she came to the correct conclusion that "this is a Hebrew boy."

Parashas Va'eira
פרשת וארא

The Measure of Goodness

וָאֵרָא אֶל אַבְרָהָם אֶל יִצְחָק וְאֶל יַעֲקֹב

"And I appeared to Avraham,
to Yitzchak and to Yaakov." (6:3)

MOSHE'S FIRST VISIT TO PHARAOH DID NOT TURN OUT exactly as he had expected. As the messenger of Hashem, he had hoped to convince Pharaoh to release the Jewish people from bondage. But Pharaoh responded with disdain, "Moshe and Aharon, why are you making trouble? The people have work to do, and you're only getting in the way." Then Pharaoh had turned the screws of bondage even tighter. He decreed that the people had to go out and procure their own building materials, but the quota expected of them would not be lowered.

Moshe was upset, and he said to Hashem (5:22), "My Master, why have You treated these people badly? Why did You send me on this mission?"

Hashem took exception to Moshe's questions and rebuked him. "I am Hashem. I appeared to Avraham, to Yitzchak and to Yaakov, and they never questioned Me. I promised Avraham the entire land of Israel, yet he could not find a grave for his wife Sarah until he paid a high price for a burial ground. Did he complain? Did he question Me? I told Yitzchak to live in this land, that I would give it to him and his descendants, yet in order to find water he had to wrangle with the Philistine shepherds. Did he complain? Did he question Me? I promised Yaakov the entire land, yet he was unable to find a place to pitch his tent until he bought a place from Chamor ben Shechem for one hundred *kesitas*. Did he complain? Did he question Me? Only you had complaints, Moshe. Only you questioned Me. What a loss the patriarchs are to Me. What an irreplaceable loss!"

The patriarchs had also experienced adverse conditions. They had also had times when things did not go as well as they might have expected. But they never complained. They never questioned Hashem. Moshe did, and Hashem rebuked him for it.

If we think into it more deeply, however, it would seem that there is an important difference between Moshe and the patriarchs. They were private citizens, so to speak, individuals who were having a hard time. True, the promises they received from Hashem involved a future nation, but at the time they experienced their hardships, there was no nation as yet. Only they themselves were affected. Therefore, the patriarchs could, in all good conscience, suffer in silence and not complain.

Moshe, however, was the leader of an entire nation, responsible for the welfare of millions of people. It was his duty to advocate for them, to fight for their welfare, to complain when things did not go well for them. Why then did Hashem rebuke him? What did he do wrong?

When the Jewish people sinned with the Golden Calf, Moshe argued for their survival, otherwise, he said, "Erase me from Your book." And Hashem did not object. When Moshe came to their defense again and again in the desert, Hashem did not object. Why did He object now?

The answer lies in Moshe's choice of words. "My Master," he said, "why have You treated these people badly?" He characterized Hashem's actions as "bad." This was his mistake. True, it was his responsibility to advocate for the Jewish people. True, it was his responsibility to complain to Hashem when things did not go well for them. But at the same time, he had to recognize that everything Hashem did was good. All he could do was ask that it become better. In his position, Moshe should have had too profound understanding of the goodness of Hashem's actions to utter the words "treated them badly."

When Pharaoh asked Yaakov how old he was, he replied (*Bereishis* 47:9), "The years of my life have been few and bad." According to the Midrash, Hashem immediately said to Yaakov, "I saved you from Eisav and Lavan and I returned Dinah and Yosef to you, and now you are complaining that your years are few and bad? Your life will be shortened by the number of words in your complaint."

Yaakov never expressed his complaints to Hashem, but apparently deep inside he did not perceive the absolute good of everything Hashem had sent his way. Although his life may have been bitter, he should have realized that it was not bad. The confrontation with Eisav developed the Jewish people's ability to contend with Eisav's descendants in future generations. Yosef's removal to Egypt paved the way for the salvation of the nation. These were difficult, trying and even incomprehensible events, but ultimately, they were not bad. As the Chafetz Chaim points out, strong medicine may be bitter, but if it is effective, it cannot be considered bad.

This is where Moshe erred. In his great love and devotion for the Jewish people, he was distracted by their momentary affliction and lost sight of its ultimate good. For that brief moment when those fateful words slipped out, he failed to see that, in the broader scheme of things, Hashem was treating the Jewish people exceedingly well.

Stop and Think

הַיָּרֵא אֶת דְּבַר ד' מֵעַבְדֵי פַּרְעֹה הֵנִיס אֶת עֲבָדָיו

וְאֶת מִקְנֵהוּ אֶל הַבָּתִּים

The one among Pharaoh's servants
that feared the word of Hashem
whisked his servents and livestock indoors. (9:20)

MOSHE VERY GRACIOUSLY GAVE THE EGYPTIANS AMPLE warning that they were about to be stricken by *barad*, the seventh plague. Hailstones would rain down from the heavens and destroy everything in the field. If they wanted to save their livestock, they should bring them indoors quickly. What did the Egyptians do? The Torah tells us (9:20-21), "The one among Pharaoh's servants that feared the word of Hashem whisked his servants and livestock indoors. But the one that paid no heed to Hashem's word left his slaves and livestock in the field."

Statistic are usually quite reliable, especially when the percentages are very high. So far, Moshe was "six for six" in his predictions about the upcoming plagues. He had not yet made a single mistake. One would think the probability of his being right again regarding the seventh plague was pretty high. So why didn't all the Egyptians pull their slaves and livestock indoors until the danger passed, at least on the off chance that Moshe was right? Wasn't it stupid of them to leave everything outside where there was a good chance it would be destroyed?

The Midrash identifies "the one that feared the word of Hashem" as Iyov and "the one that paid no heed to Hashem's word" as Bilam, both of whom were advisers to Pharaoh.

Bilam was an interesting fellow. In some ways, he was intelligent, even brilliant, but in other he was quite obtuse, a person so focused on himself that that he "pays no heed" to what is going on around him.

Many years later, when Balak hired Bilam to curse the Jews, he mounted his trusted donkey and began the journey. Then his donkey saw a sword-wielding angel in the middle of the road and he came to a sudden stop, refusing to budge an inch no matter how much Bilam prodded and cursed him. Finally, miraculously, the donkey spoke to Bilam, "Is this my normal pattern of behavior? Have I not been your trusted donkey for all these years? Have I ever stalled on you once or given you a moment of trouble? So why are you beating up on me?" In other words, can't you see that something extraordinary is happening here? Why don't you pay attention to what's going on, Bilam? Wake up!

The Chafetz Chaim points out that the entire episode of Bilam in the Torah appears as one long uninterrupted narrative, no *stumos*, no *psuchos*, no breaks whatsoever. Why? Because Bilam never stopped to think about what he was doing. He never stopped to take stock and consider the wisdom of his actions.

This was Bilam. When Moshe issued his warning about the impending hailstorm, Bilam could not be bothered to "pay heed" to it. He was thinking about his own plans, his own agenda. His mind was made up.

We think this sort of behavior is bizarre. We laugh at Bilam's foolishness. But are we that much better ourselves? Consider just a small thing, the pace of life. It used to be that we had to spend inordinate amounts of time on tasks that are accomplished easily and quickly by modern appliances. We have automobiles, self-defrosting refrigerators, washing machines and dryers, fax machines. The list is practically limitless. So have we had a net gain in time? Have we managed to catch our breaths because of all these labor-saving devices? Do we have more time to learn, to spend with the family, to reflect, to rest?

In fact, just the opposite is true. We are more rushed than ever. The pace of life is so rapid that we can barely breathe. Something is wrong. But do we "pay heed"? Do we stop and think about what is going on around us? Do we stop to assess our lives to see if we may perhaps have gone a little off the track? It is not only Bilam that fails to stop and think.

Parashas Bo
פרשת בא

The Message of the Firstborn

קַדֶּשׁ לִי כָל בְּכוֹר פֶּטֶר כָּל רֶחֶם

*Sanctify for Me every firstborn,
those who open every womb. (13:2)*

THE LAST AND MOST SPECTACULAR OF THE PLAGUES was *makas bechoros*, during which Hashem skipped over every Jewish firstborn and slew every Egyptian firstborn. Because of this miracle, the firstborn of the Jewish people, human and animal, are forever sanctified. Originally, the firstborn were to be the priests who performed the holy service in the *Beis Hamikdash*, but they lost this privilege when they sinned with the Golden Calf. Nonetheless, despite their fall from grace, the firstborn still remained sanctified regarding *pidyon haben*, firstborn animals and other observances.

Rav Simchah Zissel, the Alter of Kelm, once wrote a letter to Baron Rothschild, praising him for his exertions on behalf of the Jewish people. In this letter, Rav Simchah Zissel raises an interesting question. What did the Jewish firstborn do in Egypt to earn this high level of sanctification? True, they were involved in a great *kiddush Hashem*, but did they do anything at all to make it happen? They contributed nothing to their rescue during the plague. They also had nothing to do with their being born first. Everything happened without their involvement and assistance. Their role was absolutely passive.

Clearly, even passive participation in a *kiddush Hashem* is a very great thing. A person gains tremendous merit if Hashem chooses him to play a role in a *kiddush Hashem*, even if it is only a passive role.

"If this is the reward for a person who has a passive role in a *kiddush Hashem*," wrote Rav Simchah Zissel, "how can we even begin to imagine the reward of a person that actively makes a *kiddush Hashem*? You, Baron Rothschild, considering who you are and what you have done, have actively and publicly sanctified the Name of Hashem, and there is no limit to the honor, respect and gratitude you have earned."

This is the lesson we must all draw from the *mitzvah* of *pidyon haben*. If a passive contribution to a *kiddush Hashem* sanctified the firstborn, we can be sure that an active contribution would certainly provide at least such a level of sanctification if not a greater one. And the opportunities are always there for us. We can make a *kiddush Hashem* in the way we conduct our daily lives, the way we walk, the way we talk, the way we negotiate, the way we do business, the way we treat other people, both Jewish and non-Jewish. It is within our power to cause people who observe us to remark (*Yoma* 86a), "Look at him! Look how beautifully a religious Jew behaves." This is such an easy way to make a *kiddush Hashem*, such an easy way to gain tremendous reward both in this world and the next.

One of the rules of *pidyon haben* is that only the natural firstborn of the mother is sanctified as a *bechor*, a holy firstborn. If the child is the first for the father but not for the mother, or if he is delivered by caesarean section, he is not a *bechor*.

Let us think for a moment. What is the reason for the *mitzvah* of *bechor*? It reminds us that Hashem skipped over the Jewish firstborn while He was slaying the Egyptian first-born. Now, the Talmud tells us specifically that Hashem slew all the firstborn of Egypt, both the firstborn for the mother and the firstborn for the father or any other way they can be construed as a firstborn. If so, shouldn't the *mitzvah* of *bechor* also extend to both the firstborn for the mother and the firstborn for the father?

The Avnei Shoham offers a solution based on an analogy to the *mitzvah* of *bikurim*, the offering of the first fruits. What is the purpose of bringing the first fruits? The Torah tells us (*Devarim* 8:17-18), "And you may say in your heart, 'My power and the strength of my hand created all this wealth.' Then you shall remember Hashem your Lord, for He is the One that gives you the power to create wealth."

A person can easily fall into the trap of thinking that everything comes to him naturally. He planted the seed. He nurtured it. The tree grew. It gave fruit. It was all natural, with no involvement from Hashem. But when we bring the first fruits to the *Beis Hamikdash* we are reminded that the most natural process still requires the miraculous intervention of Hashem, that we are always dependent on Divine providence no matter how naturally everything seems to be coming our way.

The *mitzvah* of *bechor* has a similar message. When we have a firstborn child, we may easily fall into the same trap. When people have all sorts of trouble having a child, they turn to Hashem and plead with him. And when the child is finally born, they know full well that it is a priceless gift from Hashem. But when things go normally, they may not realize that the child is just as great a gift from Hashem. People get married, they have a child, and they think: What could be more normal, more natural? They forget that they owe Hashem an enormous debt of gratitude. This is the role of the *mitzvah* of *bechor*. It reminds them that Hashem spread a protective wing over all the firstborn Jewish children in Egypt. Just as those firstborns were a Divine gift to their parents, so are all the firstborns and all other children for all generations.

The Torah, however, chooses to give us this reminder only when everything goes normally and naturally, because that is when we are most likely to forget that we have to thank Hashem. We are less likely to make this mistake when things do not go with the greatest smoothness, and therefore, the Torah does not deem a reminder necessary.

When a child is the firstborn to his mother by natural birth, everything has indeed gone as expected. But when he is the firstborn only to his father and not to his mother, something has obviously gone off the track. The mother may have had a child by a previous marriage that didn't work out. If the child was born by caesarean section, it is also a deviation from the normal and natural. In such cases, we are already painfully aware that our fate is in Hashem's hands, and we don't need the *mitzvah* of *bechor* to remind us of it.

Parashas Beshalach
פרשת בשלח

Financial Wisdom

וַיִּקַּח מֹשֶׁה אֶת עַצְמוֹת יוֹסֵף עִמּוֹ כִּי הַשְׁבֵּעַ
הִשְׁבִּיעַ אֶת בְּנֵי יִשְׂרָאֵל ַ

*And Moshe took Yosef's remains with him, for he
had made the people of Israel take an oath. (13:19)*

WHILE THE JEWISH PEOPLE WERE BUSY GATHERING the treasures of Egypt, in fulfillment of Hashem's promise to Avraham that his descendant would come forth from captivity "with great wealth," Moshe was doing some gathering of his own. He was preparing the remains of Yosef for transportation to Eretz Yisrael. The Talmud (*Sotah* 13a) praises Moshe for being a "wise heart gathering *mitzvos*" (*Mishlei 10:8*) while the rest of the people were gathering money.

After *Havdalah*, when we sing *Hamavdil*, we come across the phrase "*zareinu vechaspeinu yarbeh kachol*, may He increase our children and our money like the sand." The Vilna Gaon changed the text to read "*zareinu uzechuyoseinu*, our children and our merits." As it stands, commented the Gaon, "This is not a Jewish prayer. We ask for a decent livelihood. We do not ask for wealth."

A man once came to the Vilna Gaon with a plea. "*Rebbe*, I want to make sure that all my children, grandchildren and great-grandchildren will be learned and observant Jews. How can I accomplish this? Is there any special *mitzvah* I can do? Is there a *segulah*, a charm, for this purpose? Should I say a particular chapter of *Tehillim* every day? Or should I perhaps learn something in the Gemara? What should I do? What will do the trick?"

The Vilna Gaon looked at him intently. "There is something you can do," he said. "There is special prayer you can say in the *Shema Koleinu* blessing of *Shemoneh Esrei*."

The man was a little disappointed. "You mean I should pray they should be learned and observant during the *Shema Koleinu* blessing?"

"Not at all," said the Gaon. "This is what you should say: *Yehi ratzon*, may it be Your will, Hashem my Lord and the Lord of my fathers, that my children should not be rich. Do not pray that they should be poor, just that they should not be rich. That will be their best protection."

This, according to the Vilna Gaon, was the *segulah*, the charm, for having good Jewish children. He did not mean that rich Jews are somehow less Jewish than others are. It is certainly feasible for a rich Jew to be as learned and devout as any other Jew. It just takes more effort. Riches come along with tremendous temptation. All doors are open to the rich person, and it takes courage and determination not to step through some of the ones that are exceedingly enticing. In the long run, looking ahead to further generations, which rich person can feel confident that all his grandchildren will be equally strong and righteous? Experience has certainly shown us otherwise. Therefore, the best *segulah* for keeping all one's descendants securely within the Jewish fold is to shield them from the temptations of wealth.

On *Shabbos Mevarchim*, we ask Hashem for *chaim shel osher vechavod*, a life of wealth and honor. Why didn't the Vilna Gaon object to this wording as well as "not a Jewish prayer"? Why do we ask for wealth when it is such a dangerous commodity?

Many years ago, I met a Jew who had just come back from Jerusalem. While there, he had visited a family — consisting of two parents and eleven children in a tiny one-room apartment. He remarked to me that he could not imagine how a family could live like that. He also expressed his amazement at the exceptional respect with which the children treated their parents and each other. Finally, he commented to me that the apartment was neat and clean, a place of dignity. It was one of the most amazing things he had ever seen.

This family undoubtedly did not have a large bank account. They did not have holdings and investments. But their lifestyle was certainly one of "wealth and honor." It could not have been more so had they lived in a sprawling mansion.

A person can have millions of dollars without having a life of wealth and honor. Perhaps his wife complains constantly, his kids drive him crazy and everyone is fighting. Is that a life of wealth and honor? What difference does it make that he has a million dollars if everyone is constantly bickering and nothing is ever good enough? On the other hand, it is possible to have eleven children, live in a one-room apartment and enjoy "a life of wealth and honor."

You Can Take It With You

וַיִּקַּח מֹשֶׁה אֶת עַצְמוֹת יוֹסֵף עִמּוֹ כִּי הַשְׁבֵּעַ
הִשְׁבִּיעַ אֶת בְּנֵי יִשְׂרָאֵל

*And Moshe took Yosef's remains with him, for he
had made the children of Israel take an oath. (13:19)*

MOSHE HAD THE FORESIGHT TO OCCUPY HIMSELF
with *mitzvos* when everyone else was occupied
with material things. While the rest of the Jewish
people were collecting the treasures of Egypt, Moshe "took
Yosef's remains with him," arranging to have them transported and reburied in Eretz Yisrael.

There seem to be two redundant words in this phrase.
What does the Torah add by telling us that he took Yosef's
remains "with him"? Wouldn't it have been sufficient to say,
"And Moshe took Yosef's remains"?

Rav Mordechai Ilan explains that he actually took the
bones "with him." He took the *zchus* of this *mitzvah* with him
to *Olam Haba*. It became his forever. The Talmud (*Sotah*
13a) applies to Moshe the verse in *Mishlei* (10:8), "The wise
heart gathers *mitzvos*." Moshe was very wisely collecting an
everlasting treasure. We all know that "you can't take it with
you." But Moshe knew that there were some things he could
take with him. *Mitzvos*.

The Chafetz Chaim used to illustrate this idea with a
beautiful parable.

There was a man who was so poor that his earnings could
barely keep his family from the edge of starvation, let alone
feed them properly. One day, he heard about a faraway
island where jewels were scattered on the ground, free for the
taking. The thought of those jewels captured his imagination,

and for weeks, he could think about nothing else. If only he could spend five minutes on that island, he thought, his problems would be over. All he had to do was get there.

He told his wife and children about this dream, and they encouraged him to try it. After all, things couldn't get much worse than they were right now. The man hired himself out as a deckhand on a ship and set sail for the faraway island. He still couldn't believe that such a thing could be true, but he would soon find out.

A few months later, he stepped off the ship onto the island and looked around. He couldn't believe his eyes. It was true! Jewels — diamonds, rubies, sapphires, emeralds — were scattered on the ground like pebbles. Everywhere he turned he saw the glitter of exquisite jewels.

Quickly, he filled his pockets with jewels. He thought of getting a few bags to fill as well, but then he decided there would be plenty of time for that. The jewels didn't seem to be going anywhere.

After walking around for a while on a cloud of elation, he realized he was hungry. He walked into a grocery store and filled a basket with a loaf of bread and various other staples. When it came to pay, he reached into his pocket and pulled out a stunning four-carat diamond.

"My good man," he said as he handed the diamond to the grocer, "do you have change for one of these, or would you perhaps prefer something smaller?"

The grocer laughed. "Diamonds you give me? You must be one of those greenhorns that come here all the time. If I want diamonds, you think I need you? I can just go out and pick a few myself. Besides, why would someone want diamonds?"

"What do you mean?" said the man. "Look how beautiful they are. Don't you appreciate beauty?"

"Of course, they're beautiful. But they aren't worth anything. All I have to do is stand at the door and enjoy their beauty. The baker has to work hard to make a loaf of bread. He wants something of value for it, not a diamond."

"But what has more value than a diamond?" asked the man. "Schmaltz!"

"Schmaltz? Animal fat? Are you serious?"

"I certainly am. We don't have much schmaltz on this island. It is a rare commodity, and people will pay a fortune for it. A small drop of schmaltz will get you a whole loaf of bread."

The man was stunned, but what could he do? He needed a place to live, something to eat. It was time to get down to work.

He emptied his pockets of all those worthless stones and got a job. The man began to deal in schmaltz, and after a while, he became quite good at it. But he never considered the island his permanent home. He missed his family back home, and he couldn't wait to be reunited with them. But before he could return, he had to accumulate enough riches to provide for them for many years to come. At this point, however, he had slipped into the mentality and the lifestyle of the island, and his concept of wealth was a large accumulation of schmaltz.

After a year on the island, the man had filled several warehouses with schmaltz, and he decided it was time to go home. He had his schmaltz packed in special cartons and loaded onto the ship. The next day, he set sail for home.

When he reached home, his family awaited him on the dock. After the excited welcome, they couldn't wait to see the riches he had brought back from the island.

Beaming ear to ear, he called to the stevedores to unload a few of his cartons. They went down to the hold and emerged with grease-soaked cartons. The stench was unbearable.

"What is this?" his wife wanted to know. "Where are the jewels you were supposed to bring back?"

"Jewels?" he said. "What are jewels worth? This is schmaltz!"

"My dear husband, have you lost your senses?" said his wife. "Whatever schmaltz is worth, you cannot transport it home. It is spoiled now, totally worthless. But the main thing is, where are the jewels? Where are all those precious jewels you were supposed to bring back from there?"

Fortunately for this poor family, a few small jewels remained in the pockets of the suit he had worn the day he landed on the island. They sold the jewels and lived comfortably on the proceeds for the rest of their lives. But the man could never get over how he could have come home with his pockets full of diamonds—if only had not been swept up in the lifestyle and values of the islanders.

This world, says the Chafetz Chaim, is like that island. Hashem sends us here to gather *mitzvos* and they are scattered all over, ours for the taking. If we had the sense, we could return home to *Gan Eden* with our pockets full of *mitzvos*. But we are swept up in the values of this world. We disregard the *mitzvos* and pursue money. But when we eventually come back to the *Olam Ha'emes*, the World of Truth, all our money is worthless. The only benefit we have is from the few *mitzvos* we find in the linings of our pockets. Ah, but if we had been wise enough to fill our pockets with *mitzvos* when there were so many there for the taking! This is a regret that we can never overcome. It will be too late.

Moshe never had these regrets. He knew the value of *mitzvos*. "The wise heart gathers *mitzvos*."

Parashas Yisro
פרשת יתרו

The Truth Seekers

שֵׁם הָאֶחָד גֵּרְשֹׁם כִּי אָמַר גֵּר הָיִיתִי בְּאֶרֶץ נָכְרִיָּה

The name of the first was Gershom,
because he said, "I was
a stranger in a strange land." (18:3)

MOSHE AND HIS WIFE TZIPPORAH, THE DAUGHTER OF Yisro, had two sons. The names of the children tell the story of his wandering before he returned to Egypt as Hashem's messenger to redeem the Jewish people (18:3-4). "The name of the first was Gershom, because he said, 'I was a stranger in a strange land.' The name of the other was Eliezer, because 'the Lord of my father helped me and rescued me from Pharaoh's sword.'"

The origin of Eliezer's name is given directly, "because 'the Lord of my father helped me and rescued me from Pharaoh's sword.'" But the origin of Gershom's name—"because he said, 'I was a stranger in a strange land'"—features the seemingly extraneous words "he said." Why couldn't the Torah have simply stated "because 'I was a stranger in a strange land'"?

The Baal Haturim explains that these words allude to a Midrash in *Parashas Shemos*. The Midrash states that Yisro gave Moshe permission to marry Tzipporah only on the condition that he deliver his firstborn son to be trained for the priesthood of *avodah zarah*. Moshe had no choice but to comply and allow Yisro to have his firstborn son, who turned out to be Gershom. The words "because he said" allude to Yisro. Why did Moshe have to give Gershom to Yisro? Because Yisro had reminded him that he was a stranger in a strange land and was not in a position to reject his prospective father-in-law's conditions to the marriage.

The Baal Haturim further explains that Moshe believed this was the right thing to do. He wanted to bring Yisro close to Hashem and the Jewish people, and he felt he could accomplish this by marrying Tzipporah. Even though he had to agree to Yisro's terrible condition, Moshe believed his father-in-law would ultimately come around.

The truly puzzling question is: What was Yisro thinking?

According to the Midrash, Yisro was a real truth seeker. He came to the realization that the *avodah zarah* of Midian was nonsense. He then traveled all over the world to investigate the cults of different kinds of *avodah zarah*, and he rejected all of them. Then he returned to Midian, resigned his high office in the indigenous cult and renounced *avodah zarah* altogether.

Yet here is the mystery. He placed the condition on Moshe's marriage to Tzipporah after he renounced all *avodah zarah*. Why would he insist that his grandson be trained for the priesthood of the Midianite *avodah zarah* when he had already determined it was worthless? It makes no sense!

Rav Chaim Shmulevitz, *Rosh Yeshivah* of the Mirrer Yeshivah in Jerusalem, offers a penetrating insight into Yisro's mentality. Apparently, Yisro was the ancient counterpart of a 60's flower child. He believed that the best way to arrive at the truth was through a journey of discovery, just as he had done. Yisro believed that the Torah was definitely the truth. But he had learned this important information by experiencing what all other cultures had to offer and determining that the Torah was superior.

This was also how he wanted his grandson to discover the truth. He did not want him brought up in one narrow ideology, sheltered from all other cultures and ideologies. Better that he should use the inquiring mind he would inherit from his grandfather and then follow in his grandfather's footsteps, starting in the priesthood of Midian and then eliminating one false ideology after the other until he discovered the truth of the Torah. This would be intellectually fulfilling and satisfying. His grandson would know he had made his own decision, and he would be comfortable with it.

But this is not the way of the Torah. We do *mitzvos* because we are obligated to do them, because we are servants of Hashem obligated to obey Him, not because we choose to do these things because we have decided they represent the truth. If Gershom was the son of Moshe, he did not have the luxury of going on a journey of discovery, even it were somehow guaranteed that he would arrive at the appropriate destiny at the end of his journey. Jewish children cannot nibble at the smorgasbord of the ideologies of the world. They have a duty to serve Hashem. This was something Yisro simply did not understand.

Let us take this thought a little further. The Torah introduces (20:1) the Ten Commandments with the words, "And the Lord spoke all these things, saying." Rashi cites a Midrash that at first Hashem spoke "all these things" simultaneously, something that the human brain cannot absorb or comprehend. Only afterward did He articulate the Commandments individually.

What was Hashem's purpose in first speaking them all at once if no one could understand what He was saying anyway?

Rav Yosef Dov Soloveitchik points to the difference between the first five commandments and the second five. The first five relate to *bein adam laMakom*, the relationship between man and his Creator. Everyone understands that these decrees are of Divine origin. But the second five, the set that relates to *bein adam lachaveiro*, the relationship of man to his fellow man, may not seem to be Divine in origin. "You shall not murder. You shall not commit adultery. You shall not steal. You shall not lie. You shall not covet." We think we understand these Commandments on a different level. They appear to be the rational attempts of society to regulate and protect itself. Do we need a Divine decree to tell us these things? They seem self-explanatory and self-evident. After all, what kind of society would sanction murder and adultery?

Although they may seem logical to us, that logic is not the rationale for these Commandments. We do not refrain from murder and adultery only because it makes sense to us. We refrain because Hashem has forbidden these things. That is why Hashem first spoke all the Commandments at once. It was to impress upon us that they are all the same, that they are all unfathomable Divine decrees that we must obey without question because such is the will of Hashem.

In today's society we see clearly the difference between a secular prohibition of murder and a Divine one. If murder is forbidden because we consider it logical, then changing attitudes can permit abortion, euthanasia and even infanticide, which is not unheard of in certain societies. But when the prohibition is Divine, it is absolute. We do not obey because it makes sense to us. We obey because we bow to Hashem's will.

Yisro came to Judaism through rational investigation. Therefore, he made the serious error of directing his grandson toward the priesthood of the Midianite cult. He wanted him to investigate for himself, to find the system that appealed to his reason. That is not the way of the Torah. We only apply reason to recognizing Hashem. Afterwards, it is all obedience.

Reminders of Exile

שֵׁם הָאֶחָד גֵּרְשֹׁם כִּי אָמַר גֵּר הָיִיתִי בְּאֶרֶץ נָכְרִיָּה

The name of the first was Gershom,
because he said, "I was
a stranger in a strange land." (18:3)

OTH OF MOSHE'S SONS WERE NAMED AS REMINDERS of the trials and tribulations he had experienced during his lifetime (18-3-4). "The name of the first was Gershom, because he said, 'I was a stranger in a strange land.' The name of the other was Eliezer, because the Lord of my father helped me and rescued me from Pharaoh's sword."

Why did Moshe choose these names?

The Pardes Yosef explains that Moshe wanted to ensure that his children grew up with a sense of reality. Growing up in the placid environment of Midian, they could easily have developed a false sense of security. What were these children lacking? They lived with their parents in comfort and peace. They had grandparents. They were respected and honored. Their lives were as near to perfect as could be, but there are no guarantees in life. Jewish children have to be prepared. They have to be aware that they are always in exile, that persecution, hunger, chaos, terror can appear suddenly out of nowhere. Everything can change in one day.

By choosing these names for his children, Moshe was reinforcing this message in their hearts. Look at me, he was saying. I used to be a prince in Pharaoh's palace. I had everything imaginable. I was a child of privilege. Then everything turned over, and I had to flee for my life, and if the Lord of my father had not rescued me, Pharaoh's executioner would have killed me.

The Pardes Yosef brings the story of the Jews of Spain as an illustration. There was a time when the lives of the Jews in Spain were close to perfect, a true golden age. They were secure, respected and prosperous. They lived in a warm and beautiful land. Their leaders, such as Rav Shmuel Hanagid, were the honored advisers of kings and sultans. The Torah flourished in their midst. And then things changed. Forces hostile to the Jewish people gained supremacy. The Jews lost favor. Terrible pogroms broke out, and a century of turbulence ended with the expulsion of the Jews from Spain in 1492 on Tishah b'Av. Could anyone living during the golden age have imagined it would come to this?

Had the Pardes Yosef lived to see the Holocaust, he could have brought an even better illustration of the tables turning on the Jewish people. Things may have been very good for Jews in Germany in the 19th century, but they were still in exile, as time would so painfully tell.

Here in America, we also live under the illusion that we are no longer in exile. This is truly a wonderful country, a merciful country, a blessed country, and may Hashem protect and watch over this country forever. My father, Mr. David Frand, of blessed memory, a true and honest Jew, would buy United States Savings Bonds when they were paying 3.5 percent. "Can't you get a better return on your money?" I once asked him when I was still a youngster. My father told me that the United States took him in when he was running away from Frankfort in 1939, and he felt obligated to acknowledge the favor by buying government bonds even at rates as low as 3.5 percent. That is how we must feel about this country. And yet, there are no guarantees.

The Talmud relates (*Bava Basra* 73b) in the name of Rabbah bar bar Channah, "We were once traveling on a boat and saw what turned out to be a fish. It was so huge that sand collected on its back, and we thought it was an island. We got off the boat and stepped onto this supposed island. We baked and cooked. But when it got too hot for the fish, he rolled over, and we fell off. Had we not been close to the boat, we all would have drowned."

According to the Maharsha, this story is a parable. We are all adrift on the stormy sea of exile, and suddenly we see an island. We think we have found a safe haven. We cook and bake and buy houses and made weddings and bar mitzvahs. We have children and grandchildren and great-grandchildren, and everything is wonderful. And we say, "We are no longer in exile. We are in a land flowing with milk and honey." And then the island turns over and we realize we have been sitting on the back of a fish all along. And now we consider ourselves fortunate if only we do not drown in the sea of our exile.

Parashas Mishpatim
פרשת משפטים

The Problem Is in the Ear

וְרָצַע אֲדֹנָיו אֶת אָזְנוֹ בַּמַּרְצֵעַ וַעֲבָדוֹ לְעֹלָם

*And his master shall drill his ear with an awl,
and he shall serve him in perpetuity. (21:6)*

S IX YEARS IS MORE THAN ENOUGH FOR A JEW TO BE AN
eved Ivri, an indentured servant to another Jew. But
what if he likes the comfort and security of a life of
servitude? Can he stay? The Torah describes a process by
which this can be accomplished. The owner drills his ear near
the doorpost, and then he can remain with him in perpetuity
until the *Yoveil* year interrupts his servitude.

Why is his ear drilled? The Talmud explains (*Kiddushin*
22b) that this is the ear that heard Hashem say on Mount
Sinai, "*Avadai heim*. They are My servants." Therefore, if he
chooses to remain in servitude, his ear is pierced.

The Sfas Emes is puzzled. Why is the *ear* pierced? Why not
the brain? Why not the heart? After all, the brain and the heart
make all the decisions. The ear is but one of their tools, their
receptors of information. Why does the ear take on such dis-
proportionate importance here?

The problem, explains the Sfas Emes, really is in the ear,
because Hashem's message never reached the brain; it

remained in the ear. This man may have heard Hashem state on Mount Sinai, "They are My servants." But the import of the words never penetrated to his brain and heart. He never really gave them much consideration. He never viewed himself as Hashem's servant, and therefore, he saw no conflict n becoming the servant of another man.

Rabbi Michel Twerski of Milwaukee, a practicing rabbi and psychologist, pointed out to me that patients in therapy can often discuss a problem and see the solution but they just can not implement it. They hear what needs to be done, but it does not penetrate to their brain. They cannot translate it into a personal reality. Rabbi Twerski believes that we have become a spectator society. People are conditioned by movies and television to become spectators to the point that they view even their own lives as soap operas. They see the problems, they even see the solutions, but they have no real control. They cannot act to improve their lives and change what is going on in their lives any more than they can change what is happening on the screen. The problem is in the ear.

Widows and Orphans

אִם עַנֵּה תְעַנֶּה אֹתוֹ כִּי אִם צָעֹק יִצְעַק אֵלַי שָׁמֹעַ
אֶשְׁמַע צַעֲקָתוֹ

If you surely afflict him,
then if he surely cries out to Me,
I will surely hear his outcry. (22:22)

NO ONE EVER HEARD THE CHAFETZ CHAIM SAY, "THAT person is talking *lashon hara*. He is going to get it!" No one ever heard him say, "Look at that person desecrating the Sabbath. He is going to be punished." But when it came to widows and orphans, it was an altogether different story.

During the years when the Cantonist decrees were in force in Czarist Russia, Jewish children were conscripted into the Russian army for twenty-five-year terms. A good many of them did not survive the rigors at all, and among those who did manage to survive, only a handful remained loyal, observant Jews; it was next to impossible to remain observant in the Russian army for one year, let alone twenty-five.

Not every Jewish child was forced to go to the army. There was a quota of Jewish conscripts, and when it was filled the recruiters left, not to return until the following year. Parents would do anything to protect their children from the draft. Heavy bribes often exchanged hands before a child was exempt. A good proportion of the conscripted children were, therefore, orphans who had no one to fight or offer bribes on their behalf.

One time, a wealthy Jewish butcher bribed an army officer to take an orphan rather than his son. When the Chafetz Chaim heard this story, he said, "Wait and see. This man will be punished severely. He will pay a heavy price for what he has done." Thirty years later, the butcher's son came down with cholera and died. The *Chevrah Kaddisha* was afraid to touch the contaminated body for fear of the contagious disease. The butcher had to dig the grave and bury his son with his own hands.

Why was the Chafetz Chaim so emphatic about the retribution of the butcher who had tormented an orphan when he was never so emphatic regarding other serious sins?

The answer is explicit in the Torah (22:21-23). "Do not torment any widow or orphan. If you surely afflict him, then if he surely cries out to Me, I will surely hear his outcry. Then My anger will flare, and I will slay you by the sword, then your wives will be widows and your children orphans."

The Rambam writes (*Yad, Hilchos De'os* 6), "One must be heedful of orphans and widows . . . because punishment is spelled out in the Torah . . . Hashem made a special covenant with widows and orphans that He will respond to them whenever they are tormented and cry out."

The Kotzker observes that all the verbs in the verse appear in the emphatic double form. "If you surely afflict (*aneh se'aneh*) him, then if he surely cries out (*tza'ok yitz'ak*) to Me, I will surely hear (*shamoa eshma*) his outcry." This indicates that tormenting widows and orphans inflicts twice the normal pain. Every taunt, every jibe not only inflicts humiliation, it also reminds them of their earlier loss, that there is no one to come to their defense. The orphan can think, perhaps if I had a father I would not be treated like this. The widow can think, perhaps this would not be happening to me if I my husband were alive. Hashem hears both levels of the torment, and He responds with an appropriate punishment to the tormentor.

Rav Chaim Ozer Grodzinski was the Rav of Vilna and author of the classic *Achiezer*. He was also the active leader of Lithuanian Jewry the world over. "For years, I thought my entry to the World to Come would be my *Achiezer*," he used to say when he was an old man. "However, now I believe it is the money I raised for widows and orphans throughout Europe that will get me into the World to Come."

Rav Yechezkel Abramsky, the brilliant author of *Chazon Yechezkel* and head of the London rabbinical court, spoke about this topic when he eulogized Rav Chaim Soloveitchik, the Rav of Brisk. "Rav Chaim was a very humble man," said Rav Abramsky. "He always referred to himself as simply Chaim Soloveitchik when he introduced himself or when he signed letters, never as the Rav of Brisk. Except for one occasion. He once heard that a certain widow in Brisk was depressed, and he decided to pay her a visit to cheer her up. When he was still a block away from the widow's house, he sent his attendant ahead with instructions to tell the widow that 'Rav Chaim Soloveitchik, the Brisker Rav, the Chief Justice of Brisk is coming.' To make a widow feel important, Rav Chaim was willing to forgo his natural modesty and use his full title. Otherwise, never."

Rav Abramsky himself was also outstanding in his treatment of widows and orphans. In the last year of his life, when he was already in his frail 90's, he was at his table on Friday night when a widow came to visit his *rebbetzin*. Rav Abramsky rose from his chair, walked over to the widow and said, "Good Shabbos." He then got a coat from the closet and showed it to the widow, "They just bought me this coat. What do you think? Is it a nice coat?" Amazing! Did Rav Abramsky, a man in his 90's, one of the great men of the generation, care very much about his new coat? All he wanted was to find something kind to say to a widow, something that would make her feel recognized and important.

Parashas Terumah
פרשת תרומה

The Ark of the Oral Law

וְצִפִּיתָ אֹתוֹ זָהָב טָהוֹר מִבַּיִת וּמִחוּץ תְּצַפֶּנּוּ

And you shall cover [the ark] with pure gold,
from within and without shall you cover it. (25:11)

R AV SAADIAH GAON WAS LIVING IN EGYPT WHEN HE WAS
invited to become the head of the *yeshivah* in Sura in
what is now Iraq (and thereby assume the honorary
title of Gaon). His first immediate responsibility as the new
rosh yeshivah, one all too familiar to modern-day *roshei
yeshivah*, was to raise money for his *yeshivah*.

Rav Saadiah wasted no time. He approached one of the
wealthy Jewish merchants of the Egyptian Jewish community and secured an extremely large donation. The man had
one request. He wanted a plaque bearing his name affixed to
the *aron kodesh*, the holy ark of the great and famous
yeshivah of Sura. Rav Saadiah agreed, and the man turned
over the funds.

When he arrived in Sura, Rav Saadiah discovered that a
plaque bearing someone else's name was already affixed to
the *aron kodesh*. Someone else had already dedicated the
aron kodesh!

Rav Saadiah wrote a letter to the donor from Egypt in which he explained that the *Aron Kodesh* had a dual significance, symbolizing both the Written Torah and the Oral Torah. It was the receptacle of the *Luchos*, the Tablets of the Ten Commandments. And it also symbolized the Torah scholar. Our Sages tell us that a person who wants to progress in Torah study should incline his head toward the south when he prays, because the *Aron Kodesh* was in the southern part of the *Heichal*, the Sanctuary.

"The *aron kodesh* in the yeshivah is the place of the Written Torah," he wrote to the donor in Egypt. "It contains the Torah scrolls. But where is the Oral Torah in the *yeshivah*? It is certainly not in the *aron kodesh*. It is in the hearts and minds of the rabbis and the students. It is to be found wherever someone is sitting and studying the Torah. By giving a contribution that enables people to sit and learn, you are, in effect, dedicating the *aron kodesh* of the Oral Law!"

If the Ark symbolized the Torah scholar, what was the significance of the gold covering within and without? The Talmud tells us (*Yoma* 72b), "Any Torah scholar who is not *tocho kebaro*, identical inside and out, is no Torah scholar." Just as the Ark was gilded within and without, so must the Torah scholar be a person of genuine character and integrity.

Elsewhere (*Berachos* 27b), the Talmud relates the famous story about Rabban Gamaliel's dispute with Rabbi Yehoshua. While Rabbi Gamaliel was head of the yeshivah he had followed an exclusive admission policy, accepting only those students who were *tocham kebaram*, who were identical inside and out. As a result of his dispute with Rabbi Yehoshua, he was removed from office, and Rabbi Elazar ben Azariah took his place. Rabbi Elazar changed the admission policy. He opened the doors to all comers, and several hundred new chairs were added. When Rabban Gamaliel heard about this, he was crestfallen, fearing that he had unfairly withheld Torah from the Jewish people.

The Chiddushei Harim wonders why Rabban Gamaliel was upset. He had known perfectly well that all these prospective students wanted to join the *yeshivah*. He had seen their applications. He had tested them, interviewed them and rejected them. And for good reason. He was looking for students who were *tocham kebaram*, genuine rather than superficial people, the real thing. He could have invited them all in, but he had chosen not to do so. Why should he suddenly have regrets when Rabbi Elazar ben Azariah let them in?

The Chiddushei Harim explains that he did not have those regrets immediately. But after a while, he noticed an amazing thing. All those students who had appeared superficial when he first met them were changing. The Torah they were learning was transforming them, penetrating into their hearts and minds and making them the real thing, the genuine article, true Torah scholars, gilded within and without. This was the cause of his regrets. He had not given these young men the opportunity to be exposed to Torah. He had seen them as they were and rejected them, when he should have realized that Torah study itself would change them into the genuine Torah scholars they could have become from the beginning.

Buried In A Dining-Room Table

וְעָשִׂיתָ שֻׁלְחָן עֲצֵי שִׁטִּים

And you shall make a table
of acacia (shittim) wood. (25:23)

THE TABLE, AS WELL AS THE ARK AND THE ALTAR, WAS made of acacia wood. This was undoubtedly an extremely fine wood, fitting for such a high purpose as forming the holy furnishings of the *Mishkan*. Rabbeinu Bachya finds an additional homiletic significance to the use of this wood, which is called *shittim* in Hebrew. This forms an acronym for the words *shalom*, *tovah*, *yeshuah* and *mechilah*, which mean peace, goodness, salvation and forgiveness. In other words, all the gifts the Jewish people enjoyed, which these four blessings encompass, came to them through the conduit of the holy furnishings and vessels of the *Mishkan* and the *Beis Hamikdash*.

But what about our own times, when we no longer have these furnishings and vessels? How can we continues to receive these gifts?

Rabbeinu Bachya answers this question by citing a famous passage from the Talmud (*Chagigah* 27a), "Now that the *Beis Hamikdash* is no longer standing, a person receives atonement through his own table."

Which "table" atones for us and brings us blessing now that we don't have the *Beis Hamikdash*? Our dining-room table! If we feed the poor, welcome the traveler and host guests at our table, then the dining-room table — or the kitchen table for that matter — becomes our own personal altar of atonement.

Rabbeinu Bachya concludes on an awesome note, "There is a custom among the pious people in France to construct their coffins from wood taken from their dining-room tables."

Think of the imagery. The people who have known the deceased, who have sat at his dining-room table, come to his funeral and see him being buried in a coffin that looks exactly like his dining-room table!

The message is clear, says Rabbeinu Bachya. A person take nothing along with him to the World of Truth except for the Torah he learned, the *mitzvos* he performed, the charity he gave and the goodness that he shared with other people around his dining-room table.

Parashas Tetzaveh
פרשת תצוה

The Power of Tumim

וְנָתַתָּ אֶל חֹשֶׁן הַמִּשְׁפָּט אֶת הָאוּרִים וְאֶת הַתֻּמִּים

*You shall place the Urim and the Tumim
on the Breastplate of Judgment. (28:30)*

IT MUST HAVE BEEN VERY CONVENIENT FOR THE *KOHEIN
Gadol* to have the power of the *Urim* and *Tumim* at his
disposal. Whenever he needed to know something important, all he had to do was put on the *Choshen Mishpat*, the
Breastplate of Judgment into which were set precious jewels
representing all the Jewish tribes, and ask a question. Lights
would flash, and an answer would appear. This is what I
thought when I was a young child. The reality was not quite
so simple.

The Ramban explains that the Divine message was
received through a combination of the *Urim* and *Tumim* pow-
ers. The message used the letters of the names of the tribes
engraved on the stones of the *Choshen Mishpat*. When the
Kohein Gadol asked his question, a number of letters would
light up. This was the power of *Urim*. But those letters still
needed to be arranged and deciphered. A set of holy Names
also appeared. These provided the *Kohein Gadol* with a spe-

cial ability to decipher the message, called the power of *Tumim*, akin to *ruach hakodesh*, Divine inspiration.

Sometimes, the Kohein Gadol erred in his interpretation. For instance, we are told (*I Samuel* 1:13) that Eli Hakohein made a serious error regarding Chanah, the prophet Shmuel's mother. The Gaon of Vilna explains that the letters *shin, kaf, resh* and *heh* lit up. They spelled out the word *kesheirah*, worthy woman. But Eli thought they spelled out the word *shikorah*, drunken woman, and he treated her as such. At that precise moment, Eli did not have the power of *Tumim*.

The Beis Av explains the modern-day form of the *Urim* and *Tumim*. There are many people who are great in Torah. When they are presented with a question, they look into the Torah, and many words, verses and passages light up for them. They see the lights, and they feel confident they can interpret their message. But this is only the power of the *Urim*, the lights. Only a few people in each generation also have the power of *Tumim*, which gives then the ability to interpret the lights correctly. They are the ones that have true *daas Torah*. They can discover the Divine message by looking into the Torah.

A profound example of the *Urim* without the *Tumim* can be found in story of the prophet Shmuel and King Shaul (*Shmuel I* 15). Shmuel told Shaul in the Name of Hashem to destroy Amalek, to wipe them out, man, woman, child and all the animals, from camels to donkeys. But Shaul disobeyed. He allowed Agag, the Amalekite king, to live, and he did not kill the animals that could be used for sacrifices to Hashem. For these failures, he would lose his throne.

The next day, Shmuel came, and Shaul went out to greet him. What would we expect him to say to Shmuel? "I'm sorry. I made a terrible mistake. I know I should have followed your instructions, but I was overcome by misplaced mercy." That is what one might have expected, but incredibly he said, "I have fulfilled the word of Hashem."

What was Shaul thinking? Did he expect to fool Shmuel? How could he claim to have fulfilled the word of Hashem?

Clearly, Shaul believed he had indeed fulfilled Hashem's will. He was great in Torah, and somehow, he arrived at a different interpretation of the instructions he received from Shmuel. This is the classic example of having the power of *Urim* but not the power of *Tumim*. And so, he could in all honesty tell Shmuel he had fulfilled the word of Hashem, at least according to his understanding. And yet, he was completely wrong.

At the end of *Sefer Shoftim*, we read about one of the most sordid affairs in Jewish history, the story of "*pilegesh b'Givah*," the concubine of Givah. Without getting into the details, suffice it to say that one thing led to another, and soon all the tribes were filled with righteous anger and mobilized against the lonesome tribe of Binyamin. There was a war, and the tribe of Binyamin was just about wiped out. Afterwards, they realized they had gone too far and tried to make amends to revive the stricken tribe.

How could such a thing happen? How could the well-meaning tribes of the Jewish people make such a mistake that an entire tribe was nearly eradicated forever?

The answer lies in the last verse of *Sefer Shoftim*, "In those days, there was no king in Israel, and everyone did as he pleased." Here is the problem. People can have the best intentions, the most righteous motivations, they can see the lights in the Torah and read in those lights support for their own opinions, but all that is no more than the *Urim*. If they do not have to answer to a higher authority, if they are not compelled to seek the guidance of sages who also have the power of *Tumim*, they can make tragic errors. If there is no king in Israel, if there is no bona fide leader who possesses the power of *Tumim*, if each individual can do as he pleases, then even the best and the brightest can easily go astray.

Getting It Right

אֶת הַכֶּבֶשׂ הָאֶחָד תַּעֲשֶׂה בַבֹּקֶר וְאֵת הַכֶּבֶשׂ הַשֵּׁנִי
תַּעֲשֶׂה בֵּין הָעַרְבָּיִם

You shall prepare the one sheep in the morning,
and prepare the second sheep in the afternoon. (29:39)

EVERY SINGLE DAY THE *MISHKAN* AND THE *BEIS* Hamikdash stood, including Shabbos and Yom Kippur, the *korban tamid*, the daily sacrifice, was the same, one sheep in the morning and one in the afternoon. This exact *korban* was also brought as part of the *chanukas hamizbeiach*, the dedication of the Altar during the first week of the sacred service.

There is one difference, however, between the way this *korban* is presented in these two contexts. The description of the *korban tamid* in *Parashas Pinchas* refers to "one sheep in the morning and a second in the afternoon." Here, regarding the dedication, the Torah refers to "the one sheep in the morning and the second in the afternoon," using the definite article "the." What is the significance of this difference?

The Brisker Rav explains that the pair of sheep brought for the everyday *korban tamid* were independent of each other, just as the *tefillin shel yad* and the *tefillin shel rosh* are independent of each other. If someone only has a *shel rosh*, he puts it on, because it is a complete *mitzvah* in itself. Similarly, if for some reason the *korban tamid* had not been brought in the morning, a sheep could still be brought for the *korban tamid* in the afternoon. During the dedication, however, the two sheep were interdependent. One could not be brought without the other (*me'akvin zeh es zeh*).

The Shemen Tov sees in this law an important lesson for life. Our Sages say, "*Kol has'chalos kashos,* all beginnings are difficult." The beginning is always critical; the way something is established at the outset determines its character forever. Therefore, it would not have been acceptable during the dedication week to perform only one part of the *tamid* service without the other. Both sheep had to be there. In the future, however, one could be accepted without the other.

It is said of the Vilna Gaon that when a new *shul* was being built he insisted that even the axe handles should be crafted by pious Jews. If this is done, he said, all the prayers within this *shul* would be uttered with utmost concentration. The beginning would set the tone for the future.

When Yeshivah Ner Yisrael dedicated a new *beis midrash*, Rav Ruderman, my *Rosh Yeshivah*, forbade idle talk in it, at least for the first week. The future success of this *beis midrash* for generations and generations of students who would come through its doors depended on an auspicious beginning during its very first week.

In every aspect of life, beginnings are crucial: the beginning of a marriage, the beginning of a child's *chinuch*, the beginning of a position, job or any other endeavor. If the beginning is imbued with Torah values and ideals, if we get it right the first time, the chances are we will get it right just about every time afterward.

Parashas Ki Sisa
פרשת כי תשא

Instant Turnaround

וַיִּקַּח אֶת הָעֵגֶל אֲשֶׁר עָשׂוּ וַיִּשְׂרֹף בָּאֵשׁ וַיִּטְחַן עַד אֲשֶׁר דָּק

*And [Moshe] took the calf they had and burned it,
in the fire, and he ground it into tiny pieces. (32:20)*

BECAUSE OF A MISCALCULATION, THE DISASTER OF THE Golden Calf came to pass. The people thought Moshe was supposed to come down from the mountain one day earlier than he was really scheduled to come. When he didn't arrive, they got nervous. And then things started going downhill.

Satan managed to convince the Jewish people that Moshe was dead. They went wild, fearing that they had lost their only connection to Hashem. Ill-advisedly they sought to create a new conduit to the Divine by constructing the Golden Calf.

Events gathered speed like a runaway train. Moshe's nephew Chur tried to put on the brakes, but the people were in a frenzy. They killed Chur and proceeded with their plans.

Aharon wanted to stop them, but he was afraid he would meet a fate similar to Chur's. Instead, Aharon tried to join them and stall for time. But events were hurtling ahead, out of control. The people built the Golden Calf and started to dance around it.

Just then, Moshe came down from the mountain. He took one look at what was going on, raised his hands and said, "Stop!" And everything stopped. Just like that. One minute the Jewish encampment was in a fever pitch, and the next it was immobilized.

How could such a thing happen? How could all this activity be brought to such an instant, screeching, grinding halt?

The Beis Av explains that such is the power of *emes*, truth. The sin of the Golden Calf was based on *sheker*, falsehood, a miscalculation and Satan's artifice. Once Moshe appeared, once the truth became apparent, it was as if someone had switched on a light in a dark room. The darkness was instantly dispelled. Unadulterated truth stops falsehood in its tracks.

We may sometimes wonder about the Messianic times. The prophets tell us that "the earth will be filled with knowledge." In our prayers on Rosh Hashanah and Yom Kippur, we say that "every creature will know that You created him." How will such a thing come about? How will all those religions and cults and atheists suddenly turn around and acknowledge everything they have been denying for thousands of years? Will it be a miraculous phenomenon, something beyond human conception?

This *parashah* provides us with the answer. Moshe came down, and all the hullabaloo instantly ceased. Truth stops falsehood right away. Mashiach will bring truth to the world, and all falsehood will just crumble away.

I once heard in the name of Rav Avraham Pam that the collapse of the Communist world was a message from Hashem to prepare us for the times of Mashiach. Those of us who grew up under the shadow of the Iron Curtain, remember how ominous and pervasive was the Communist threat.

We could not believe that something like that would cease in our own lifetime. And then, within a few short months, the entire edifice collapsed. It did not need to be assaulted or even dismantled. It fell to the ground in a cloud of dust. And then it was gone—poof!—as if it had never been there.

Mashiach will arrive, speedily and in our time, with the truth, and all the edifices of falsehood will crumble into dust. And the light of the pure truth of the Torah will penetrate to the farthest dark corner of the earth.

Only The Landowners

וְלֹא יַחְמֹד אִישׁ אֶת אַרְצְךָ בַּעֲלֹתְךָ לֵרָאוֹת אֶת פְּנֵי
ד׳ אֱלֹקֶיךָ שָׁלֹשׁ פְּעָמִים בַּשָּׁנָה

No one shall covet your land when you go up to be seen before the God your Lord three times a year. (34:24)

THREE TIMES A YEAR, ALL JEWISH MALES ARE REQUIRED to fulfill the *mitzvah* of *aliyah laregel* by going to the *Beis Hamikdash* in Yerushalayim and celebrating the festivals "before the Master, God, the Lord of Israel." But who is going to keep an eye on the farm while everyone is away? No one. The Torah assures us (34:34) that it will not be necessary, because "no one shall covet your land when you go up to be seen before the God your Lord three times a year."

This is quite a strong promise, and it is obviously meant to allay the fear of the more hesitant souls. It does not seem to be central to the *mitzvah* of *aliyah laregel*. And yet, the Talmud derives (*Pesachim* 8b) from this verse that only landowners are required to make the pilgrimage to Yerushalayim. Landless people, to whom the promise of "no one shall covet your land" cannot be applied, are not required to go.

Why should someone be deprived of "being seen by God your Lord" just because he doesn't own any real estate? Is this fair? What is the connection between going up three times a year and owning land?

We also find here a Name of Hashem —Adon, the Master—that rarely appears in the Torah — only twice, here and in *Parashas Mishpatim* (23:17), both regarding to the *mitzvah* of *aliyah laregel*. What does this signify?

Sforno in *Parashas Mishpatim* points out that the title Adon, the Master, is used to indicate that Hashem is the Master of the Land. In this light, perhaps we can see the *mitzvah* of *aliyah laregel* from a new perspective. The essence of the *mitzvah* is not only to celebrate the festivals in Yerushalayim in the *Beis Hamikdash*, which is indeed a wonderful thing. On a deeper level, however, the *mitzvah* impresses on each of us that the whole world belongs to Hashem and not to me. I can leave my house and my farm and my property unattended, and I don't have to worry about it. Why? Because essentially it is not mine. Hashem promises that "no one shall covet the land" and I will be able to return and pick up the thread of my life. And I can be very calm about it, because it is not really my land after all is said and done. It all belongs to Hashem.

If so, we can well understand why a landless person is exempt from the *mitzvah*. He can certainly go to Yerushalayim and celebrate if he wishes, but the *mitzvah* of *aliyah laregel* does not include him since he has no land anyway, and the critical message of the *mitzvah* does not apply to him.

The Kotzker Rebbe offers a different answer to this question. Why is a landless person exempt from the *mitzvah* of *aliyah laregel*? Because he doesn't need it.

Only the landowner, whose vision is blurred by material-ism, needs to go up to Yerushalayim to see the *Shechinah*. The landless person, the poor man who lacks material things and whose vision materialism has not blurred, does not need to go to Yerushalayim to see the *Shechinah*. He sees It everywhere.

Parashas
Vayakhel-Pikudei
פרשת ויקהל-פקודי

Mirrors of Faith and Hope

וַיָּבֹאוּ כָל אִישׁ אֲשֶׁר נְשָׂאוֹ לִבּוֹ וְכֹל אֲשֶׁר נָדְבָה רוּחוֹ
אֹתוֹ הֵבִיאוּ אֶת תְּרוּמַת ד' לִמְלֶאכֶת אֹהֶל מוֹעֵד

And every man whose heart inspired him came,
and everyone of generous spirit
brought his offering to the Tent of Meeting. (35:21)

WHEN THE TIME CAME TO BUILD THE *MISHKAN*, THE people came forward to contribute to its construction, the men and the women alike. The *Daas Zekeinim Baalei Hatosefos* comments that the women contributed eagerly to the building fund, readily surrendering their gold jewelry for this holy purpose. The men thought that the women would be reluctant to part with their jewelry, but the women proved them wrong.

The *Daas Zekeinim*, based on the Midrash, goes on to draw a sharp delineation between the men and the women. During the incident of the Golden Calf, the women refused to relinquish their gold jewelry for the construction of the Calf, and the men had to take it from them by force. For the construction of the *Mishkan,* on the other hand, many men were reluctant to contribute, but the women did so enthusiastically.

For this gallant spirit, the women were rewarded with a special connection to the minor festival of Rosh Chodesh, on which women, but not men, customarily refrain from work (*Orach Chaim* 417:1).

What is the specific relationship between the contribution of the women and the reward of Rosh Chodesh?

The Shemen Tov offers a beautiful interpretation based on another Midrash. The Torah states (38:8), "And he made the washing basin of copper and its stand of copper from the mirrors of the multitudes who thronged the entrance to the Tent of Meeting."

What was the history of these mirrors? The *Midrash Shir Hashirim,* quoted by Rashi, explains that during the worst times of the Jewish bondage in Egypt the men gave in to despair. They lost hope, and they separated from their wives. What was the point of bringing children into this world if their lot would be endless suffering and misery as slaves of the Egyptians? But the women refused to give up. They had faith that the bondage would end someday, that the Jewish people would be redeemed, that a future of freedom and opportunity awaited any children they would bear even in the darkest hour of their enslavement. And so, the women beautified themselves in front of their mirrors and went out into the fields where their husbands were laboring. Thus beautified and made up, they drew their husbands back to them and convinced them that it would be good to have more children.

The mirrors these women used to make themselves up were the symbol of the survival of the Jewish people. Had it not been for those mirrors, there would not have been any more Jewish children. Therefore, Hashem said, "These mirrors are more precious to Me than anything else. Use them to make the washing stand of the *Mishkan.*"

The women were the strong ones among the Jewish people. When the men were ready to surrender to despair, the women were the steady anchor of the people, the ones that kept the faith strong, the ones that never gave up hope, the one that insisted, "We must go on."

When the *Mishkan* was constructed, the men once again were overcome by depression. Before the sin of the Golden Calf, there would have been no need for the *Mishkan*. The *Shechinah* would have dwelt among all the people. The entire Jewish encampment would have been its domicile. But the Jewish people fell from grace when they sinned. They were no longer worthy of having the *Shechinah* among them. From that point on, the encampment would be divided into the Camp of the *Shechinah*, the Camp of the Levites and the Camp of the Israelites. The *Shechinah* would dwell in seclusion behind the walls of the *Mishkan*.

As long as the construction of the *Mishkan* did not begin, the men held out hope that perhaps there would be a last-minute reprieve. Perhaps things would revert to the way they were, the way they should have been. Perhaps the *Shechinah* would yet dwell among all the people. But when the construction got under way, the writing on the wall was clear. The damage cause by the sin of the Golden Calf would be everlasting. There would be no reprieve. This was a very depressing thought, and many of the men fell into despair. They could not being themselves to contribute to the *Mishkan*, to put the nails in their own coffin, so to speak.

But the women, rocks of stability, once again came forward and saved the situation. "This is not a time to despair," they said. "What's done is done, and no matter how much we've lost, it cannot be undone by being depressed. Now is the time to look to the future, to embrace this holy *Mishkan* enthusiastically, to bring about a renaissance of the Jewish people."

In Egypt, the faith and hope of the women had saved the Jewish people physically. At the construction of the *Mishkan*, the faith and hope of the women saved them spiritually. It gave them hope to reach for a new closeness with the Master of the Universe. And for this, they were rewarded with a special status regarding Rosh Chodesh.

According to our Sages, Rosh Chodesh, the festival of the new moon, celebrates the concepts of rebirth and renewal. The moon is always waning and waxing. Even in its darkest phase, we know it will once again recover its full illumination. It is the symbol of faith and hope for the Jewish people who also go through cycles of darkness and light. Therefore, it is the Jewish women, who have shown themselves most sensitive to the ideas of faith and renewal, that are most closely connected to the festival of Rosh Chodesh.

Rejoice on the Final Day

וַיָּבִיאוּ אֶת הַמִּשְׁכָּן אֶל מֹשֶׁה אֶת הָאֹהֶל וְאֶת כָּל כֵּלָיו

And they brought the Mishkan to Moshe,
the Tent and all its vessels. (39:33)

ACCORDING TO THE MIDRASH, THE BOARDS OF THE *Mishkan* were so heavy that the people could not hold them up erect next to each other long enough for them to assemble the *Mishkan*. They kept toppling over. In frustration, the people brought all the boards and poles to Moshe, and he assembled it with miraculous strength that Hashem granted him especially for this purpose.

The Torah, however, states that the Jewish people "brought the *Mishkan* to Moshe." This would seem to imply that they brought him a completely assembled *Mishkan*. How can the Midrash be reconciled with these words?

Regarding this same verse, the Midrash quotes from *Mishlei* (31:25), "Might and splendor are her garments, and she will rejoice on the final day." The Midrash goes on to illustrate this idea with a story concerning Rabbi Abahu's departure from this world. On the threshold, he was shown all the reward that awaited him in the World to Come, and he remarked with astonishment, "All of this is for Abahu? I thought I had been toiling in vain, and now I see I have a great portion in the World to Come!"

What point is the Midrash making by bringing this story in connection to the erection of the *Mishkan*? And how do we understand Rabbi Abahu's surprise? Did he really expect that having spent his life learning Torah and doing *mitzvos* he would not be rewarded in the World to Come? Did he really think he was laboring in vain?

Rav Shlomo Breuer explains that Judaism is a deed-oriented religion. It is not enough to say, "I am a Jew at heart." Deeds are what count, learning Torah, performing *mitzvos*, doing *chessed*. Being a Jew is about doing, from the moment we arise until the moment we go to bed. Our religion is not one of sentiment, it is one of deed.

At the same time, however, intent also plays a great role in Judaism. If someone is prevented by circumstances beyond his control from doing a *mitzvah*, the Torah considers it as if he had done the *mitzvah* (*maaleh alav hakasuv k'ilu asahu*). Judaism demands deeds but not necessarily results. As long as a Jew puts in the honest and sincere effort, he is rewarded even if he is not successful. Hashem considers his intentions as deeds.

This is what Rabbi Abahu was saying, "There were so many times in my life when I tried, I made the effort, but I was not successful. I had assumed that on these occasions my efforts had been in vain. Now I see that I have been rewarded even for my intentions, for my efforts, even when they were unsuccessful." Therefore, Rabbi Abahu "rejoiced on the final day."

When the time came to assemble the *Mishkan*, the Jewish people made every effort to do it by themselves. Sweat pouring from their brows, veins bulging on their foreheads, they strained and they pushed those heavy boards with all their might, but they could not erect the *Mishkan*. It was simply beyond them, and they had no choice but to turn to Moshe for help.

Nonetheless, the Torah reports that they "brought the *Mishkan* to Moshe," because that is what they intended to do and what they tried to do with all their hearts. Hashem considered it as if they had erected the *Mishkan* themselves, and He rewarded them. Therefore, they "rejoiced on the final day."

A Long Waiting Period

בְּיוֹם הַחֹדֶשׁ הָרִאשׁוֹן בְּאֶחָד לַחֹדֶשׁ תָּקִים
אֶת מִשְׁכַּן

On the first day of the first month,
you shall erect the Mishkan. (40:2)

CONSTRUCTION ON THE *MISHKAN* BEGAN RIGHT AFTER
Moshe came down from the mountain for the second
time. Six months later, on Rosh Chodesh Nissan, it
was finally erected. According to the Midrash, the entire
labor of construction was completed miraculously within
three months, but Hashem did not want it erected until Rosh
Chodesh Nissan, the month when Yitzchak was born.

The obvious question presents itself. If Hashem didn't
want the *Mishkan* erected until Nissan, why did He work a
miracle to have the work completed within three months?
Why didn't He just allow the work to proceed normally so that
it would be finished by Nissan? If that, too, would have
required a miracle, then so be it. But why make a miracle that
leads to the completion of the project three months early?

The *Be'er Yosef* explains that the waiting period was necessary for the *Mishkan* to fulfill its purpose. Our Sages tell us
that the *Mishkan* was an atonement for the sin of the Golden
Calf. Let us then consider what were some of the human fail-
ings that led to that fiasco.

Impatience was certainly at the heart of it. As soon as
they perceived, mistakenly, that Moshe was late returning
from the mountain, they pushed the panic button. Did they
ask Aharon what to do? Did they consult with the elders? Did
they step back and try to deal with the situation in a calm
manner? Did they try to determine what Hashem wanted

them to do? They did none of these things. They plunged right ahead impatiently and impulsively and caused tremendous damage for the Jewish people for all future generations.

This was the sin for which the *Mishkan* was an atonement. Therefore, Hashem wanted to teach the Jewish people the virtue of patience. Don't be in such a rush. The construction of the *Mishkan* is complete by Teves, but you have to wait until Nissan. There is a time to do everything, and Hashem is the One Who determines that time. The servant does not call the shots, the Master does. This was the lesson they had to learn right away in order for the *Mishkan* to be an effective atonement for the sin of the Golden Calf.

Vayikra

Parashas Vayikra
פרשת ויקרא

Hearing the Voice

וַיִּקְרָא אֶל מֹשֶׁה וַיְדַבֵּר ד׳ אֵלָיו מֵאֹהֶל מוֹעֵד לֵאמֹר

*And He called out to Moshe,
and God spoke to him from
the Tent of Meeting, saying. (1:1)*

ASHEM "SPOKE TO MOSHE FROM THE TENT OF Meeting." Rashi explains that the voice of Hashem reached Moshe's ears, but the Jewish people did not hear it. The voice stopped at the walls of the Tent. One might think that it stopped because it was soft and faint, but Rashi assures us that this is not the case. It was a powerful voice, a voice that "breaks cedar trees." And yet, this powerful voice came to a sudden stop and was not heard outside the Tent of Meeting. Had someone placed his ear right up against the wall of the Tent, he would also not have heard Hashem's voice.

How could such a thing be? Was it a miracle?

Not necessarily, writes Rav Yaakov Neiman in his *Darchei Mussar*. It is possible that only Moshe heard the voice of Hashem because only he was attuned to it. As for the others, it passed right by them without their being aware of it.

We all know that different ears are set for different audio frequencies and that sounds heard by one species may not always be heard by another. In order to hear the voice of Hashem, a person's ears would have to be set to a high spiritual frequency. Otherwise, he would hear nothing. Moshe was attuned to that frequency, and he heard Hashem's voice. The rest of the Jewish people were not attuned.

The Mishneh tells us (*Avos* 6:2) in the name of Rabbi Yehoshua ben Levi, "Every day a heavenly voice (*bas kol*) goes forth from Mount Chorev and proclaims, 'Woe to humanity because of the Torah's humiliation.'" Has any of us ever heard this heavenly voice? I don't think so. But that does not contradict Rabbi Yehoshua ben Levi's statement. He certainly heard that voice, as did other people of his stature in his times, people attuned to the spiritual frequency on which heavenly voices travel. We, however, who are not attuned to that frequency, cannot hear the heavenly voice.

Having the faculty of hearing does not guarantee that we will really hear. Having the faculty of sight does not guarantee that we will really see. The sounds and the images may reach us, but that does not mean they will make an impression on our brains and hearts. They may just be left to languish on the surface.

By way of illustration, I would like to discuss an event that most of us remember vividly and all too painfully—the Persian Gulf War of 1990. We all recall our terror and anxiety as we waited for Iraq to carry out its threat to rain Scud missiles on Israel. And then it happened. Thirty-nine Scuds landed in Israel, but miraculously, only three people were killed.

I say miraculously not as a figure of speech but as an internationally acknowledged description of what had happened. It was beyond incredible that thirty-nine Scuds should cause such minimal casualties. And if we had any doubt about it, a Scud missile struck an American barracks in Saudi Arabia and killed scores of American servicemen.

These were no firecrackers. But they did virtually nothing to Israel.

We all knew we were witnesses to a great miracle, but did it penetrate deep into our hearts and minds? Was our appreciation just superficial or did it cause profound changes in our lives, in the way we thought and felt, in the essence of who we are? Did we really "see" the miracle, or did it go right by us at the edge of our superficial awareness?

Rav Eliahu Lopian once said that *emunah*, faith, is not manifest in the intensity of the prayers we say during a crisis but by the intensity of the praises we offer up to Hashem when the crisis has passed. To pray when in danger is a natural reaction; as the common saying goes, there are no atheists in a foxhole. But faith reaches much deeper. It reflects a profound relationship with Hashem sometimes forged in the fire of experience. But when the fire passes, is the relationship still as intense? That is the test of true faith. We may have seen miracles in our time, but did they penetrate beyond the surface and effect changes in who we are? That is the question we must ask ourselves. Did we really "see" the miracles?

The Mystical Power of Torah

וְהֵבִיא אֹתָם אֶל הַכֹּהֵן

*And he shall bring them
to the Kohein. (5:8)*

THE ROLE OF THE *KOHEIN* BROUGHT HIM INTO CONTACT with numerous Jewish people and gave him the opportunity to have a positive effect on them. The Midrash, describing how Aharon, the *Kohein Gadol*, dealt with other people, quotes from the prophet *Malachi* (2:6), "The Torah of truth was in his mouth . . . and he turned many away from sin."

We think of Jewish outreach as a new phenomenon, but apparently, Aharon was already an outreach activist back then. He embraced people and drew them toward the Torah. How did he do this? By telling the truth.

"He did not forbid that which is permitted," the Midrash states, "nor did he permit that which is forbidden." He did not compromise. He did not waffle. He was straightforward and consistent, telling things exactly as they were, and people responded to him. People are not necessarily seeking *heterim*, leniencies, or *chumros*, stringencies. They want the truth. They can handle it. Furthermore, Aharon drew them close by learning Torah with them, and this was perhaps his most effective tool.

Let me tell you a story about a man who is very active in Jewish outreach. When he was just married, he was learning in a *yeshivah* in Eretz Yisrael, and he couldn't afford to spend much on rent. As it turned out, he found an apartment within his range, but it was in a nonreligious area. In fact, he was the only observant Jew in his building.

It seems that his natural talents and tendencies were already budding then, because as soon as he moved into his apartment he set out to draw his neighbors to Torah. Some Israelis are harder to reach than unaffiliated American Jews. Sometimes, they can be very antagonistic to observant Jews. But he was undaunted. He invited his neighbors to come and learn Torah in his apartment once a week. And he was successful! A number of his neighbors agreed, and he organized the session.

As the night of the session drew near, he gave a lot of thought to the subject matter of his presentation. Should he learn Jewish philosophy with them? Perhaps the Rambam's *Guide to the Perplexed*? Or maybe *Chumash* would be best? Or how about some of the great works of *Mussar*? He couldn't make up his mind.

Then, providentially, on the morning before his presentation, he met Uri Zohar in *shul*. Uri Zohar had been an icon of Israeli secular society—entertainer, comedian, television and radio host, social satirist, movie star, film producer. Everyone knew Uri Zohar. Then, at the height of his fame, he went and did a shocking thing. He became fully observant. Afterward, he wrote the very popular *Waking Up Jewish* and became active in the *teshuvah* movement.

"What should I do?" the young man asked Uri Zohar. "What should I learn with these people?"

"Well, what are you learning in yeshivah?" Uri Zohar asked.

"I'm learning *Bava Kama*."

"Then learn *Bava Kama* with them."

"*Bava Kama*? Are you serious?" asked the young man. "Do you think they'll be interested in an ox that gores a cow? In pits and fires? This will bring them to Judaism?"

"My dear friend," said Uri Zohar with a wry smile, "you don't believe in Torah! If you doubt that learning *Bava Kama* with them is going to bring them back, then you don't fully believe and appreciate the power of Torah."

To this day, the young man, who is a lot older now, learns *Bava Kama* with his adult beginners. And it works just fine. Better than fine.

Torah, regardless of the subject matter, has tremendous spiritual power. It has a mystical, almost magical effect on the soul. It is the nourishment the Jewish soul craves. Aharon fed Torah to the people who came to him, and by doing so, "he turned them away from sin."

Parashas Tzav
פרשת צו

Clean-Up Work

וְהֵרִים אֶת הַדֶּשֶׁן

*And the Kohein shall
take the ashes. (6:3)*

EVERY MORNING, THE *KOHEIN* COMES INTO THE *BEIS
Hamikdash*, puts on the splendid priestly garb and
prepares for a day of sacred service. What is the first
task he is assigned? The removal of the ashes accumulated
on the top of the Altar from all the sacrifices consumed by
the fires on the Altar throughout the long night.

The *Chovos Halevavos* explains that this is deliberate.
The Torah did not want the *Kohein's* high station to go to his
head. Walking into the *Beis Hamikdash* as a member of the
select priestly caste, the *Kohein* could easily turn to arro-
gance. He could begin to think that he is somehow better
than other people are. Therefore, the first duty he is assigned
humbles him. Don't think you're so great and so haughty.
Take out the ashes!

Just as the Torah is concerned that the *Kohein's* ego
should not become too inflated, it is also concerned that the
poor man's ego should not become too deflated. The Talmud

tells us (*Bava Kama* 92a) that when the people brought the *bikurim,* the first fruits, to the *Beis Hamikdash,* the rich would bring them in baskets of gold and silver, while the poor would bring them in baskets of woven reeds. When the rich stepped forward, the *Kohein* would take the fruits from their baskets and return the baskets to them. When the poor stepped forward, the *Kohein* would take the fruits along with the baskets. "The poor get poorer," the Talmud observes ruefully.

Granted that circumstances somehow construe that the poor get poorer, but why indeed did the *Kohein* differentiate between the rich and the poor donors?

Rav Aharon Bakst explains that it was done for the protection of the poor. The rich had fine orchards that produced bounteous fruits, and their *bikurim* offerings were lavish. When the *Kohein* took their succulent and luscious fruits, their skins bursting with juice, out of the baskets and laid them in front of him, they were a sight to behold. But the poor had perhaps a few scraggly trees that produced, just barely, a few meager fruits. Had the *Kohein* taken the poor man's fruits out of the basket, he would have caused him embarrassment. Therefore, he kept the basket along with the fruits, and the poor man retained his dignity.

Some time ago, there was a *hachnasas kallah* campaign in Baltimore. A well-known and respected family was marrying off a child, and they had no money to cover their expenses. A committee was formed to raise the money.

A question arose. Should the identity of the family be revealed to potential donors? This would probably generate much more money, since the people in the community really liked and respected this family. On the other hand, should their identity perhaps be kept secret to avoid embarrassment?

The question reached my *Rosh Yeshivah,* Rav Ruderman, and he immediately said, "The identity of the family should not be revealed. A family's honor is worth a great deal."

Inside a Thank You

אִם עַל תּוֹדָה יַקְרִיבֶנּוּ

*And if he brings it as
a thanksgiving offering. (7:12)*

JUST ABOUT EVERY JEWISH CHILD KNOWS HOW TO SAY thank you in Hebrew: *todah*. There is also a sacrifice called the *korban todah*, the thanksgiving offering. The Midrash states that in the future all the sacrifices will be discontinued, except for the thanksgiving offering. There will always be a need to say thank you to Hashem.

Rav Yitzchak Hutner observes that the Hebrew word for thanksgiving is *hodaah*, and the exact same word also means an admission. This is no coincidence, explains Rav Hutner. In order to give proper thanks, a person has to admit that he needed help, that he is not all powerful and that the one you are thanking did something important for you. Admission is an integral part of thanksgiving, and therefore, the same word is used for both.

How can we tell, concludes Rav Hutner, if the word *hodaah* is being used to indicate thanksgiving or a different kind of admission, such as an admission of guilt? By looking at the part of speech that follows it. If the preposition *al*, for, follows, it means "thanksgiving for." If the particle *she*, that, follows, it means an "admission that."

In the seventeenth blessing of the *Shemoneh Esrei*, we say, "*Modim anachnu lach she . . .*" *Modim* is the present plural form of the word *hodaah*. It is generally understood to be the thanksgiving blessing of the *Shemoneh Esrei*, which indeed it is. And yet, it is followed by the particle *she*. Clearly, the thanksgiving blessing is incomplete unless it begins with an admission, acknowledging all the wondrous things Hashem does for us day in and day out.

When the *shaliach tzibbur*, the representative of the congregation who repeats the *Shemoneh Esrei* aloud, gets to the *Modim* blessing, the congregation says its own version called the *Modim d'Rabbanan*. Why is this necessary? Why can't the *shaliach tzibbur* represent the congregation in this blessing as he does in all the others?

The Avudraham explains that you can appoint a *shaliach*, a surrogate, for everything: to pray for healing, for a livelihood and so forth. But you cannot appoint a *shaliach* to say thank you. You have to say it yourself.

Parashas Shemini
פרשת שמיני

The Sins at the Beginning

קְחוּ שְׂעִיר עִזִּים לְחַטָּאת וְעֵגֶל וָכֶבֶשׂ

Take a young goat as a sin offering,
and a calf and a sheep. (9:3)

URING THE DEDICATION OF THE *MISHKAN*, THE JEWISH
people were required to bring many *korbanos*, sacrifices — a goat for a sin offering, a calf and lamb for
a burnt offering and a bull and a ram for peace offerings.

Why so many? The *Toras Kohanim* explains that the Jewish
people had an account with Hashem, with "sins at the beginning
and sins at the end." The "sins at the beginning" refer to the sale
of Yosef, when the brothers dipped his coat in goat's blood. The
goat comes as atonement for that sin. The "sins at the end" refer
to the Golden Calf, for which the calf is brought as atonement.

We can readily understand why the Jewish people had to
make amends for the sin of the Golden Calf during the dedication ceremony of the *Mishkan*. The erection of the Golden
Calf as an intermediary to Hashem was tantamount to *avodah
zarah*, a direct affront to Him. Therefore, when the *Mishkan*
was being dedicated and the *Shechinah* was about to dwell
within it, amends were very much in order.

But what was the connection between the sale of Yosef and the dedication of the *Mishkan*? It was not a recent occurrence. Why then should it be brought up again in this context?

The *Yalkut Yehudah* points out that an underlying element of jealousy led to the sale of Yosef. The brothers could not bear that Yaakov singled Yosef out for a special role, that he gave him special treatment, that he provided him with special garments. If Yosef was so special, that meant they were less special. Unable to bear the thought, they plotted against him and eventually sold him into slavery.

What was happening when the *Mishkan* was being built? One family was being singled out to be the priestly caste, to perform the sacred service, to wear special priestly garb, to be given the priestly gifts, to be treated as special in every way. The *Kohanim* were an easy target for jealousy, as indeed came to pass during Korach's rebellion, when they declared (*Bamidbar* 16:3), "The entire congregation is holy and God is among them; why should you lord it over the assembly of God?"

The dedication of the *Mishkan* was, therefore, a time to remember that in Judaism there are roles. There are roles for *Kohanim*; there are roles for Levites; there are roles for men; there are roles for women. Not everyone is alike. Not everyone has the same strengths. Not everyone is going to have the same duties and responsibilities. Not everyone is going to get the same benefits and privileges. Everyone must be content with the role Hashem has assigned to him.

This then was an exceedingly appropriate time to bring sacrifices to atone for the sin of selling Yosef. This would impress upon the people the extreme danger of giving in to jealousy. It had led to disaster in the past, and it could lead to disaster in the future, unless it was nipped in the bud.

Special Qualifications

וַיֹּאמֶר מֹשֶׁה אֶל אַהֲרֹן קְרַב אֶל הַמִּזְבֵּחַ

And Moshe said to Aharon,
"Draw near to the Altar." (9:7)

AFTER MOSHE GAVE AHARON ALL THE DETAILED instructions regarding his duties in the dedication of the *Mishkan*, he said to him, "Draw near to the Altar." What happened? Why did he need special encouragement? Why did Moshe have to coax him forward?

The *Toras Kohanim* explains that Aharon suddenly saw the Altar in the shape of an ox, and he shrunk back. As the Ramban explains, the shape of the ox reminded Aharon of the sin of the Golden Calf, in which he had played an unwilling role.

In his great righteousness, Aharon did not consider himself worthy of approaching the Altar. "How can I come near to the Altar?" he said. "I, too, participated in the Sin of the Golden Calf."

"My brother, you're afraid of that?" Moshe told him. "You of all people don't have to fear what the ox represents."

That is why, the *Toras Kohanim* concludes, Moshe said to Aharon, "Draw near to the Altar."

The *Toras Kohanim* leaves us somewhat in the dark. Why indeed did Aharon have nothing to fear from the image of the ox? What was wrong with his reasoning? Even if he was not fully guilty, it was certainly a matter of concern. What did Moshe mean when he told him that "you of all people don't have to fear" the memory of the Golden Calf?

The *Yalkut Yehudah* offers an explanation based on the Midrash. Why indeed did Aharon participate in the construction of the Golden Calf? Even after he saw Chur murdered, why didn't he put his foot down and take a stand? Why didn't he say, "I will not allow this. Over my dead body will you make an idol"?

According to the Midrash, Aharon had the best interests of the Jewish people in mind. "If I let them build the Calf," Aharon reasoned, "the sin will be forever on their heads. Better that I should build it. Better that I should be blamed than the Jewish people. Better that I should bear the sin."

Hashem told Aharon, "Your love for the Jewish people was such that you were willing to sacrifice your righteousness to save them. Therefore, you will be anointed High Priest."

Because of his self-sacrifice, because he was willing to give up his *Olam Haba* for the Jewish people, because he placed the welfare of the people above his own, precisely for these reasons was he deemed worthy of being the *Kohein Gadol*.

"My brother, you are afraid of that?" Moshe told Aharon. "That's precisely why you were chosen. Draw near to the Altar!"

Perfect Faith

וַיִּדֹּם אַהֲרֹן

And Aharon was silent. (10:3)

AHARON'S TWO OLDER SONS, NADAV AND AVIHU, WERE men of extraordinary stature, righteous leaders who were worthy of someday stepping in the shoes of Moshe and Aharon. And then, during the joyous dedication of the *Mishkan*, they made a small error, and a fire reached out from the Holy of Holies and snuffed out their lives.

We cannot even begin to imagine the shock to Aharon, a father who witnessed his two glorious sons perish right before his eyes. What went through his mind in that split second? His own loss, the loss suffered by the entire Jewish people, the loss suffered by the two deceased sons themselves. So much loss. Such a gaping void.

What was Aharon's reaction? The Torah tells us that "Aharon was silent." Silence. Complete acceptance. Unshakable faith. One of the most eloquent and powerful exhibitions of faith recorded in the Torah.

The Torah forbids excessive mourning over a deceased relative (*Devarim* 14:1). "Do not mutilate yourselves, and do not tear out your hair between your eyes over the dead." The Ramban writes that self-destructive mourning shows a lack of faith in Hashem. If we believe in the immortality of the soul and that all Hashem does is ultimately for the good, we do not mourn too much, even in the face of tragic youthful death.

A few years ago, the Baltimore community suffered a tragic loss on Erev Pesach. Mr. and Mrs. Israel Weinstein's son and his wife were killed in an automobile accident while coming from Lakewood to Baltimore for Pesach.

I was not there to witness it personally, but I heard from others that Mr. Weinstein's faith and acceptance were incredible. It is hard to conceive how a man who has just been told that his two beloved children had been torn away from him can walk into the Pesach *Seder* and make the *Shehechianu* blessing, thanking Hashem for sustaining life and bringing us to this joyous occasion. It is hard to conceive how such a man can walk into *shul* the next day and say "*Gut Yom Tov*" to everyone without a trace of his grief on his face so as not to disturb the festival spirit. It is hard to conceive how such a man, sitting in *shul*, can reach out and affectionately pat the cheek of a little child that happens to walk by. It could only be accomplished by a man whose heart is full of a rare and unshakable faith.

During the *Shivah*, the father of the boy whose cheek Mr. Weinstein had patted asked him, "How, in the moment of your most profound grief, could you still bend down to a child and pat him on the cheek?"

"At that exact moment," Mr. Weinstein responded, "when your little boy walked past me, with everything I was feeling in my heart, I realized how special each and every one of our children is. Sometimes we take our children for granted. Times like these clear our vision."

A person can only have such strength if he has a clear vision of the eternal light that shines at the end of every dark tunnel, if he has a strong and abiding faith in the Master of the Universe. Such a person, like Aharon before him, can be silent.

Parashas Tazria
פרשת תזריע

The Holiness of Childbirth

אִשָּׁה כִּי תַזְרִיעַ וְיָלְדָה זָכָר וְטָמְאָה שִׁבְעַת יָמִים

*A woman who conceives and gives birth to a son
shall be unclean for seven days. (12:2)*

BIRTH IS ONE OF THE TRANSCENDENT MOMENTS IN LIFE. After a long period of anticipation, the mother releases a new and glorious life into the world. It is a miraculous moment, an occasion of sheer magic. One would think that at such a time the mother would be elevated and exalted, but in fact, she becomes *tamei*, ritually impure. Why is this so? Ordinarily, we associate *tumah* with defilement, death, *tzaraas* and other negative experiences. How does childbirth fit into this list?

Furthermore, we find a distinction between the birth of a son and the birth of a daughter. A woman that gives birth to a son is *tamei* for seven days, while a woman that gives birth to a daughter is *tamei* for fourteen days. Twice as much! Why should this be so? What is wrong with a girl? Why should her birth cause more *tumah* than the birth of a boy?

The first child ever born was Kayin, the son of Adam and Chavah. Why was his name Kayin? Because Chavah said

(*Bereishis* 4:1), "*Kanisi ish es Hashem*. I have gained a man with Hashem." Chavah felt that by bearing a child and giving birth to him she had literally become a partner "with Hashem."

The Talmud identifies (*Nidah* 31a) three partners in the creation of a person: his father, his mother and Hashem. Chavah felt this very keenly. Until then, she had been a creature, and now, she had become a creator. She had brought a life into this world, and she memorialized this exalted feeling in the name she gave her son. She had come as close to being like the Creator as a human being can possibly come. She had created a new life, and in doing so, she gained a touch of the Divine and became sanctified.

But this state of heightened sanctity does not last long. It builds and grows as the months of pregnancy progress. It reaches its climax at the moment of childbirth. And then it is gone. The mother, that exalted creator of human life, returns to an ordinary existence. She is just another human being, another creature on this earth. She is no longer a creator. That is all past. Her sanctified state is all history, a thing of the past.

What is *tumah*? How do we define this state of spiritual impurity? The *Kuzari* defines *tumah* as the void left by the absence of *kedushah*, holiness. Whenever *kedushah* is withdrawn from the world, the void it leaves behind is filled with *tumah*.

In this light, we can understand how a blessed event such as childbirth brings *tumah*. During her pregnancy and through the moment of delivery, the mother achieves a spark of the Divine. She is a creator of human life, a facsimile of the Creator, and this gives her a great *kedushah*. But right after childbirth, this additional *kedushah* leaves her, and the void it leaves behind was filled with *tumah*.

Following this line of reasoning, it seems that the greater the *kedushah*, the greater the void its withdrawal leaves behind, the more *tumah* rushes in to fill it. The higher the level of *kedushah* the mother achieves during pregnancy and childbirth, the more *tumah* she will experience afterwards when the *kedushah* departs.

Perhaps we can suggest that when a woman is pregnant with a girl she rises to a much higher level of *kedushah*. Not only has the mother herself become a creator, the child she is carrying is also a potential creator. Therefore, when she gives birth to the girl she was carrying she loses more *kedushah* than she does after the birth of a boy, and consequently, her *tumah* is proportionately greater.

Changing the Eye

וְהִנֵּה לֹא הָפַךְ הַנֶּגַע אֶת עֵינוֹ

*And behold, the lesion
has not changed appearance. (13:55)*

WHEN A *TZARAAS* LESION REMAINS ON A GARMENT after all the instructions of the *Kohein* have been followed, he examines it one last time. If it "has not changed appearance," the garment is burned. The exact Hebrew language is *"lo hafach hanega es eino,"* which translates literally as "the lesion has not changed its eye." Although the meaning is clear, we cannot help but wonder why the Torah chose such an unusual form of expression.

The affliction of *tzaraas* is spiritual rather than medical in nature. The Talmud discerns (*Arachin* 16a) seven different causes for *tzaraas*, the most famous of which is *lashon hara*, improper speech. The other six are not as well known. One of them is *tzarus ayin*, which translates literally as "narrowness of the eye." It refers to mean-spiritedness, a tendency to see the negative and overlook the positive in everything. It is a singular lack of generosity in all things, a constricted view of the world and everything in it.

If this affliction of the spirit caused the lesion on the garment, then the therapy is to transform the trait of *tzar ayin* into *tov ayin*, literally "a person with a good eye." Instead of being a sour-faced, mean-spirited curmudgeon, he must become a smiling, generous, expansive, optimistic, warm and friendly person. Then the lesion will fade away. If he does not change, the lesion remains on the garment, and it must be incinerated.

This is what the Torah means, explains the Chiddushei Harim, by the words "*lo hafach hanega es eino*, the lesion has not changed its eye." The owner of the garment has not changed his narrowness of the eye into goodness of the eye; he has not transformed himself from a mean-spirited person into a kind and generous man. Therefore, the garment is burned.

The Chiddushei Harim concludes with a classic *chassidishe vort*, an interpretation in the Chassidic style. The Hebrew word for lesion or affliction is *nega*. The opposite of affliction is pleasure, which is *oneg* in Hebrew. Both words are constructed of the same three letters. *Nega* is spelled *nun, gimmel, ayin*. *Oneg* is spelled *ayin, nun, gimmel*. The only difference is in the placement of the *ayin*. Move it from the back to the front, and affliction is transformed into pleasure. The Torah is telling us that "the lesion has not changed its eye (*ayin*)." He is the same narrowed-eyed person he was before. Therefore, the *nega* was not transformed into *oneg*.

Parashas Metzora
פרשת מצורע

The Measure of Distinction

זֹאת תִּהְיֶה תּוֹרַת הַמְצֹרָע . . . וְהוּבָא אֶל הַכֹּהֵן

This is the law of the metzora...
he shall be brought to the Kohein. (14:2)

HE AFFLICTION OF *TZARAAS* IS NOT CAUSED BY A microbe or by impurities in the water supply. The Talmud tells us (*Arachin* 16a) that it is caused by any of seven sins. The most famous of these is *lashon hara*, improper speech, he was afflicted with *tzaraas* as a not very subtle message from Heaven that he had better shape up and watch his mouth. Such a person would have to seek the assistance of a *Kohein* who would hopefully help him mend his erroneous ways.

Rav Nissan Alpert observed that the word the Torah uses here for a person is *adam*, which generally denotes a person of greater stature and distinction than does the word *ish*. It seems peculiar that when discussing a person who speaks *lashon hara*, the Torah would use language that denotes a person of distinction.

Clearly, the measure of a person that determines whether or not he has stature or distinction is not if he speaks *lashon hara*. Unfortunately, most people fall into the trap of doing so. The opportunities and the snares are so many that it is almost impossible to avoid it altogether without a tremendous focused effort. The measure is rather how a person deals with it. A person of distinction is mortified that he has spoken *lashon hara*. He wants to improve himself, to fortify himself against any recurrence of such a thing. A smaller person rationalizes or shuts it out of his mind altogether.

A distinguished person can stumble and inadvertently speak *lashon hara*, but as long as he demonstrates a desire to change and improve he can still be considered distinguished. He has to make the effort. The Torah says that "he shall be brought to the *Kohein*." The language implies a measure of coercion. He has to force himself to go. He has to be ready to take his medicine. That is the measure of distinction.

One Chol Hamoed morning, Rav Isser Zalman Meltzer was sitting in his study with Rav David Finkel, one of his students. They were discussing various subjects when Rav Isser Zalman suddenly touched his forehead as if he had forgotten something.

"Could you please bring me a pencil and a piece of paper?" he asked.

Rav David was perplexed, since it is only permitted to write on Chol Hamoed in case of emergency. Perhaps it had momentarily slipped Rav Isser Zalman's mind that it was Chol Hamoed. "Ahem," he said, "isn't it forbidden to write on Chol Hamoed?"

"This is different," said Rav Isser Zalman. "It's practically a matter of life and death."

"Is something wrong, *Rebbi*?" Rav David cried out. "Is something going on? What can I do to help?"

Rav Isser Zalman shook his head. "You can bring a pencil and paper."

Rav David hurried off and returned momentarily with a paper and pencil. He gave them to Rav Isser Zalman and stood back, trembling with apprehension.

To his amazement, Rav Isser Zalman wrote out a quotation from *Mishlei* (4:25), "Let your eyes look straight ahead, and your eyelids will straighten your path." Then he put down the pencil.

"That's it, *Rebbi*?" asked Rav David. "That's practically a matter of life and death? To write down a few words from *Mishlei* that you already know by heart?"

"In a certain way," said Rav Isser Zalman, "this is very much a matter of life and death. For me, that is."

"I don't understand," said Rav David.

"I will explain it to you. On Chol Hamoed, hundreds of people here in Yerushalayim come to pay me a visit. Among them are many fine and respectable people, Torah scholars, pious Jews, friends and relatives. But there are also plenty of the less-distinguished residents of Yerushalayim. For some reason, it has become like a 'thing to do' on Chol Hamoed. Go visit the Meltzer house."

He paused for a sip of water.

"If you stay here for a while, you will see the type of people that come visit me on Chol Hamoed, braggarts, nasty people, lunatics, derelicts, fools, and I have to welcome all these people with patience and kindness. I have to sit here patiently and listen to all of them and smile. Sometimes, I feel my patience being tried sorely. I am tempted to lash out at them with a few well-chosen sharp words. I have to hold myself back. I have to control myself, but I am afraid I will make a mistake and say something I shouldn't say. So I've worked out a system for myself. I write down this verse from *Mishlei*. Here, take a look at it."

Rav David read it and returned it.

"I once heard a homiletic interpretation," continued Rav Isser Zalman, "that reads it as saying, 'When your eyes look at someone else, turn them inward.' When you see someone else's flaws and shortcomings, don't focus on him. Focus on yourself. Look at your own shortcomings. You are also far from perfect. This is what I think about at those moments when I am close to losing control. If I wouldn't have the paper there on my desk, staring me in the face, I am afraid I would just lash out. But then I see the paper, and it stops me. I always write this paper out before Yom Tov, so that it should already be prepared for Chol Hamoed. This year, I forgot. That is why I have to write it now. Otherwise, I would be in trouble."

Rav Isser Zalman was a very great man, and he knew that keeping away from all forms of *lashon hara* is a struggle. He worked hard to avoid criticizing others and looking at their faults. He felt it was practically a matter of life and death.

There are only two types of people in the world, those who view the glass as half empty and those who view the glass as half full. Those who speak *lashon hara* always view the glass as half empty; they only see the faults of others, not their virtues. Those who look away from the faults of others take a more positive view of the world; they see the glass as half full. In the long run, these people are the happiest. They see the positive in their spouses, their children and their surroundings. But one who speaks *lashon hara* is miserable in the end, because it makes him into a negative and destructive person. As destructive as he is to others, he is most destructive to himself.

Parashas Acharei Mos
פרשת אחרי מות

The Stuff of Life

וּשְׁמַרְתֶּם אֶת חֻקֹּתַי וְאֶת מִשְׁפָּטַי אֲשֶׁר יַעֲשֶׂה אֹתָם
הָאָדָם וָחַי בָּהֶם אֲנִי ד׳

*And you shall keep My decrees
and My laws, that a person shall do them,
and he shall live by them, I am God. (18:5)*

MARTYRDOM IS DEMANDED OF A PERSON ONLY RARELY. He must allow himself to be killed rather than cause a *chillul Hashem*, a desecration of the holy Name. He must also be prepared to die rather than commit one of the three cardinal sins — idolatry, illicit relations and bloodshed. Otherwise, he is allowed to violate any prohibition in the Torah in order to save his life.

The Talmud (*Sanhedrin* 74a) derives these guidelines from the verse, "And you shall keep My decrees and My laws, that a person shall do them, and he shall live by them, I am God." The Torah wants the Jew to "*vechai bahem*, live by them," not to die by them. If you have to eat *chametz* on Pesach in order to survive, do so. If you have to desecrate the Sabbath to save your life, do so. If you have to eat nonkosher food to avoid starvation, do so. Your first priority is to "live by them," not to die.

There is a general misconception about this passage in the Talmud. At a cursory glance, the Talmud seems to be saying that life is a higher value than the fulfillment of the *mitzvos*. But what does this mean? How does one define the life that is so precious even though it is devoid of *mitzvos*? What makes it so precious? Watching the sunrise on the beach? Reading a good book? Sipping a cup of heavenly coffee?

This is not what the Talmud is saying. Onkelos translates the words *vechai bahem* as "he will live forever [in the World to Come]." Rashi also follows that translation, pointing out that "it cannot mean in this world, because he will eventually die."

Accordingly, Rav Moshe Feinstein in *Igros Moshe* sees the Talmud as telling us something totally different. On the contrary, the most precious thing in life is *mitzvos* because we "live by them"; they bring us to the World to Come, to eternal life. Therefore, in case of danger it is better to violate a prohibition of the Torah if by doing so one will survive to fulfill many more *mitzvos* for years to come. The Talmud tells us (*Yoma* 85b), "Desecrate Shabbos for him once in order that he should observe Shabbos many times." For the Jewish people, *mitzvos* are the stuff of life.

The Gerrer Rebbe offers a *chassidishe* interpretation of this phrase, "*vechai bahem,* that you shall live by them." What do we call "living by them"?

In the *yeshivah* world, one often hears the question, "Where do you get your *chius*?" Literally, this means, "Where do you get your life?" The question touches on a profound issue. Where do you find the spark of life? What brightens up your day when you get out of bed in the morning? What excites you? What gives you the zest for life? For some people, it is the prospect of learning Torah. For others, it is the opportunity to do some good work in Jewish outreach. And for yet others, it is the prospect of a good steak or a good game of baseball.

This, says the Gerrer Rebbe, is what the Torah is telling us. A person should "live by the *mitzvos*." His *chius*, his zest for life, should derive from the prospect of doing *mitzvos*. These should be the entire *raison d'être* for his existence in this fleeting material world.

Before you turn around, your life in this world is over, even if you were blessed with a ripe old age. It is all a dream, an illusion. You cannot look for the meaning of life in this world, only in the eternal World of Truth, and only *mitzvos* will bring you there. Only *mitzvos* will give you an everlasting, meaningful life.

You should never seek to accumulate money for its own sake. What will it get you? A little extra pleasure in this world? Is that life? Is that where you are expecting to find your *chius*? You should work as much as you have to in order to provide a livelihood for your family, but you should seek your *chius* from doing *mitzvos* and chessed with your wife and children, your family, your community, all the Jewish people. You should seek your *chius* in the Torah. You should seek your *chius* in building a close relationship with the Master of the Universe. That is the key to eternal life.

Parashas Kedoshim
פרשת קדושים

Effective Rebuke

הוֹכֵחַ תּוֹכִיחַ אֶת עֲמִיתֶךָ וְלֹא תִשָּׂא עָלָיו חֵטְא

*You shall surely rebuke your fellow man,
and you shall not bear a sin over him. (19:17)*

ALL JEWS ARE RESPONSIBLE FOR EACH OTHER.
Therefore, if a Jew sees another committing a sin,
he must rebuke him and set him straight. But how
does one rebuke another Jew? This is a very difficult thing to
do. In fact, it is one of the most difficult *mitzvos* to perform
properly.

The final words of the commandment are "*velo sisa alav
cheit*, and you shall not bear a sin over him." What exactly
does this mean? Rashi explains that if you embarrass the
person you are rebuking, you are committing a sin. This is
an important guideline for the *mitzvah* of giving rebuke. It
must be done carefully, discreetly and oh so gently.
Otherwise, you will embarrass him. Then you will not only
have failed in your rebuke, but you will also have committed
a very grave sin.

Rav Gedaliah Schorr suggests a further interpretation
based on a variant translation of the words *velo sisa alav*

cheit. They can be read as "do not raise up the sin over him." Do not magnify the sin and minimize the person.

If you see someone doing a sin, do not place the emphasis on the magnitude of the sin. Do not say, "How could you do such a terrible thing?" You are raising up the sin over him, dwarfing him by the magnitude of what he has done. You are making the person feel about two inches tall. This is not the way to offer rebuke. It is offensive, and it is also almost guaranteed to be ineffective. Better to place the emphasis on the person and say, "How could a person such as you do such a thing?" Better to raise him up over the sin, to show him that to do such a thing is beneath him, that he is too great to do such a thing. This is the way to rebuke with genuine kindness and lasting effect.

A rabbi was once asked to be guest speaker in a neighboring town, and he chose rebuke as his topic. After speaking about the importance of giving rebuke properly, he told a story.

"I do not know this story firsthand," he began. "But I've heard many times, and I believe its is true. The Chafetz Chaim had a *yeshivah* in the Polish town of Radin. In those days, during the early part of the 20th century, there were many pressures on *yeshivah* boys. Some of their peers were leaving their faith and seeking greener pastures in socialism, secular Zionism or just plain secularism. I suppose it was inevitable that some of the boys in the *yeshivos* would also be affected, that a tiny number of them would do things no *yeshivah* boy would do today.

"One of the boys in the Chafetz Chaim's *yeshivah* was caught smoking on Shabbos. The Chafetz Chaim was told about it, and he summoned the boy to his room. The boy stayed in the Chafetz Chaim's room for about two minutes, and afterward, he kept Shabbos scrupulously.

"Can you imagine what the Chafetz Chaim's rebuke must have been like? Ah, if only we could have an inkling of what went on in that room for those two minutes! What did the Chafetz Chaim say to this boy? It would be like a beacon of light for us. I'm sure all of us would love to know what he said. But we don't. And so we just have to try and do the best we can."

After the rabbi finished speaking, a man came over to him. His face was tear stained. "Rabbi, I can tell you what the Chafetz Chaim said to that boy," he declared. "You see, I was that boy."

The rabbi was stunned. "Please tell me," he whispered.

"When I was called to the Chafetz Chaim's room," he said, "I was terrified. What could I say to the great *tzaddik*? How could I justify smoking on Shabbos? And right in his *yeshivah*! I couldn't even justify it to myself. It was one of those rash and foolish things young people often do without thinking. I walked into his room, and there, he was, his holy face distorted in a grimace of pain. He walked over to me, his head barely reaching to my chest, and he took my hand in his. 'Shabbos,' he said softly, and he began to weep. After a minute, he looked up at me and said it again, 'Shabbos.' His hot tears dripped onto my hands, and the sound of his weeping penetrated my heart. That was all it took. Two minutes of the Chafetz Chaim's pain."

The Chafetz Chaim did not put this boy down. He did not berate him or belittle him. He gently but powerfully impressed on him the sacred nature of Shabbos. That was the most effective rebuke he could have given him.

Rabbi Akiva's Principle

וְאָהַבְתָּ לְרֵעֲךָ כָּמוֹךְ

*Love your neighbor
as you do yourself. (19:18)*

ONE OF RABBI AKIVA'S MOST FAMOUS SAYINGS IS, "*Ve'ahavta lereiacha kamocha.* Love your neighbor as you do yourself. This is a fundamental principle of the Torah." This *mitzvah* is one of the pillars of the entire Torah. We find a similar thought expressed by Hillel. The Talmud relates (*Shabbos* 31a) that a prospective gentile convert to Judaism asked Hillel to teach him the entire Torah "while standing on one foot." Hillel replied, "Do not do to others that which is hateful to you. This is the essence of Torah. All the rest is explanation."

It seems to me that Rabbi Akiva was most suited to speak about the importance and centrality of this *mitzvah*. Rabbi Akiva was a great *rosh yeshivah* with many thousands of students, and he experienced a shattering tragedy. All of his twenty-four thousand students died during the Omer period between Pesach and Shavuos. It is an incredible number, a number that fails to penetrate the consciousness even in our day of huge *yeshivos*.

How would one of us have dealt with such a blow? What would we have done if all twenty-four thousand—twenty-four thousand!—of our students had died in one fell swoop due to some character flaw, a catastrophe that inevitably must have reflected somewhat negatively on their *rosh yeshivah*? First, we would, of course, have to deal with a serious bout of depression and despondency. And if we managed to get over that, we would probably retire with a broken heart.

What did Rabbi Akiva do? The Talmud tells us (*Yevamos* 62b), "When Rabbi Akiva's students died and the world was desolate, he went to the south of Eretz Yisrael and started over again!"

Rabbi Akiva clearly had unbelievable resilience. No matter how great a disaster he suffered, he would find a silver lining in the darkest cloud. He would discover something positive, something to give him new hope, and this would give him the strength and the confidence to start all over again. "All is not lost!" he would exult when he had lost just about everything.

Rabbi Akiva lived through the destruction of the *Beis Hamikdash*. The Talmud relates (*Makkos* 24a) that several Sages were walking past the ruined *Beis Hamikdash* and saw a fox emerging from the site of the Holy of Holies. They all burst into tears, except for Rabbi Akiva, who began to laugh. "Why do you laugh?" they asked him. He replied, "Because if the prophecy of destruction has come true so literally, then the prophecy of redemption will also come true literally."

This ability to find the glimmer of light in the deepest darkness, to find the positive, the spark of hope, in the worst of times, made Rabbi Akiva singularly attuned to the *mitzvah* of loving others. He — more than anyone else — was able to see the worth in all people and love them for it.

The Baal Shem Tov give us an additional insight into the concept of loving your neighbor "as you do yourself." When a person gets up in the morning and takes stock of himself, he thinks, "I am basically a good person. I have my faults and foibles; I am not perfect. But I am more good than bad." This, the Baal Shem Tov says, is how we must evaluate our neighbor. He is basically good. I can overlook his faults.

Parashas Emor
פרשת אמור

Inconsistent Defense

אֱמֹר אֶל הַכֹּהֲנִים בְּנֵי אַהֲרֹן

*Speak to the Kohanim,
the sons of Aharon. (21:1)*

THE MIDRASH TELLS US THAT HASHEM SHOWED MOSHE each generation and its judges, each generation and its kings, each generation and its sages, each generation and its robbers. Hashem also showed Moshe the image of King Shaul and his son Yonasan dying by the sword during a battle with the Philistines.

Moshe asked, "Why should the very first king of the Jewish people die by the sword?"

Hashem replied, "Why complain to me? Shaul massacred Nov, the city of *Kohanim*. Speak to the *Kohanim*!"

This, concludes the Midrash, is the implication of the verse "Speak to the *Kohanim*."

The commentators are exceedingly puzzled by this Midrash, which seems to run counter to the reasons the Torah gives for Shaul's premature death. We read in *Sefer Shmuel* that Shaul disobeyed the prophet Shmuel's command to exterminate the Amalekites, men, women and children. Shaul took mercy on Agag, the Amalekite king, and spared him. The result of this misguided kindness was the career of Agag's descendant Haman, the implacable enemy of the Jews, centuries later. When Shmuel arrived and saw what Shaul had done, he specifically told him that Hashem would rip his kingdom from him. How then can the Midrash connect Shaul's death to his massacre of the *Kohanim* of Nov?

The Reisher Rav, in his *Hadrash Veha'iyun*, explains that Shaul's primary sin was indeed his failure to wipe out Amalek, but he might have been given a less painful form of death. For Shaul really could have argued convincingly in his defense. He could have said, "I didn't mean to be disobedient. But I guess I have a soft heart. I'm just too compassionate. I couldn't bring myself to kill Agag." Such a defense would not have excused him, but it might have mitigated his guilt somewhat.

But the massacre of the *Kohanim* of Nov slammed the door in the face of any such defense. Where was his soft heart when he attacked Nov? Where was his compassion when he exterminated all the *Kohanim*? No, the failure to kill Agag did not stem from uncontrollable compassion. Shaul's guilt was not mitigated. Why did Shaul die such a violent death? "Speak to the Kohanim."

Many commentators write that exactly this should be our greatest concern when we are brought to judgment before the Heavenly Court after one hundred twenty years. We may have all kinds of arguments in our defense, but who knows if our own actions won't refute them.

Hashem may listen to our arguments and say, "Oh, is that the reason why? You didn't have any money. But for that thing you did have money? You say you didn't have any time. But for that other thing you did have time? You say you were not smart enough. But for that thing you were smart enough?" And that is when all the defenses of the inconsistent people will crumble and fall.

Teach the Children

אֱמֹר אֶל הַכֹּהֲנִים בְּנֵי אַהֲרֹן וְאָמַרְתָּ אֲלֵהֶם

*Speak to the Kohanim, the sons
of Aharon, and say to them. (21:1)*

ASHEM TOLD MOSHE TO "SPEAK TO THE *KOHANIM*"
and "say to them" to avoid contact with the dead.
These two phrases seem redundant. "Speaking to
the *Kohanim*" obviously includes "saying to them" whatever
needs to be said. What is the purpose of these additional
words?

The Talmud infers (*Yevamos* 114a) that it comes
"*lehazhir hagedolim al haketanim*, to caution the adults
regarding the children." There is a special obligation on adult
Kohanim to train the young *Kohanim* to maintain the purity
of their persons. Accordingly, the verse is stating, "Speak to
the *Kohanim*," meaning the adults, that they should "say to
them," the minors, that a *Kohein* must avoid contact with the
dead.

The only problem with this interpretation is that it does-
n't seem to fit into the words. There is no hint in the verse
that the *Kohanim* are meant to repeat what they hear to others. The plain meaning of the words is that the objective pro-
noun "them" refers back to the object "*Kohanim*."

The Beis Av suggests that the Torah is indeed talking only
to the adults, once for themselves and the second time for
the benefit of the children.

We all know how to teach children to do *mitzvos*. When a
boy is young, we buy him a pair of *tzitzis*. When he gets a little older, we learn Torah with him. We teach our daughters to

make blessings, to pray, to appreciate Shabbos. This is all relatively simple. We can condition our children to do the acts, but how can we inspire them? How can we instill in them a true *yiras shamayim*, a true awe of living in the presence of the Almighty so that they should love to do *mitzvos* and find sins abhorrent?

The only way this can be accomplished is if the children see *yiras shamayim* in the parents. Teach them by example. Children must see their parents recoil from food whose kosher status is questionable. They must see their parents suffused with the joy of a *mitzvah*. They must see their parents trembling in awe of the Almighty. Only then will *yiras shamayim* become real to them. They too will be caught up in the mood and the atmosphere of the home, and they too will become accustomed to living in the presence of the Almighty.

Here is just one example of what I consider true *yiras shamayim*. When the Steipler Gaon was a young man, he once went to meet with a young lady who was a prospective match. While they were sitting at the table and talking, he nodded off and fell asleep.

The young lady let him sleep and just sat there waiting patiently. Presently, he awoke and realized where he was and what had happened.

"You must excuse me," he said.

"Oh, it is nothing," said the young lady. "Don't worry about it."

"No, it is something. I must explain. You see, I was very tired."

The young lady smiled. "Well, that was obvious."

He cleared his throat. "Look, you know I had to travel twelve hours by train today to get here."

"Yes, I know. Twelve hours on a train can make anyone tired."

"No, it is not so simple. I knew that I could not learn that much traveling on a train, so I stayed up and learned all last night. I expected I would be able to catch a few hours' sleep on the train and come here reasonably rested. But when I saw the upholstered seats on the train, it seemed to me that the material might have *shaatnez*. I couldn't very well take a chance, could I? So I remained standing for the whole journey. And of course, I didn't get any sleep at all. So you must forgive me for falling asleep in your company. Please don't take offense."

Incidentally, the young lady married him.

To remain standing for twelve hours on a train — after having stayed up the entire night — because of a suspicion that there might be *shaatnez* in the train's seats, this is *yiras shamayim*.

Now we can understand the seemingly redundant words of the Torah. First, Hashem told Moshe to "speak to the *Kohanim*" and inform them of the *mitzvah*. Then He told Moshe to "say it to them" again, to impress on them that it would not be enough simply to obey and fulfill. A higher level of performance was required of them, a type of performance that would carry forward to the next generation when the children see the diligence, inspiration and awe with which the adults embrace the *mitzvah*.

Parashas Behar
פרשת בהר

Peer Pressure

תַּעֲבִירוּ שׁוֹפָר בְּכָל אַרְצְכֶם

*You shall sound the shofar
throughout the land. (25:9)*

O N YOM KIPPUR OF EACH FIFTIETH YEAR, THE *YOVEIL*
year, the *shofar* was sounded "throughout the
land." We know the purpose of the sounding of the
shofar on Rosh Hashanah. It is to remind us of the *Akeidah*
of Yitzchak and to inspire us to repent. But what was the
purpose of sounding the *shofar* in the *Yoveil* year?

The *Chinuch* explains that it was for the benefit of all
those who owned Jewish indentured servants. According to
the law, all Jewish servants had to be set free in the *Yoveil*
year, regardless of when they were bought or their particular
type of servitude. This was a very difficult thing to demand
of the owners. It meant a great financial loss.

It must have been very convenient owning slaves and
indentured servants. It really kept the overhead low. There
were no salaries, no benefits, no Social Security, no pension,
no four weeks' vacation. All the owner had to do was provide
bed and board and treat his slaves humanely. A few years of

this, and it could become quite hard to give it up. The *Yoveil* year really presented a dilemma.

Therefore, the Torah decreed that the *shofar* be sounded throughout the land as a signal to all slaveowners to set them free. The knowledge that he was not alone, that thousands of other slaveowners throughout the land were experiencing the same wrenching ordeal, this gave each individual slaveowner the strength and courage to do what he knew was right. True, he knew perfectly well even without the *shofar* that thousands of others were in the same boat. But he didn't feel it. He did not see them struggling with the same ordeal. When he heard the *shofar*, however, the idea that he was not alone came to life in his mind, and he was able to do what he had to do. He found the strength to set his slaves free.

The *Sefer Hachinuch* emphasizes that this is a powerful means of reinforcing the human spirit. The knowledge that "everyone is doing it" goes a long way toward removing the obstacles to a difficult course of action.

Peer pressure is an incredible thing. The desire to conform to peers is an overriding motivation for just about anyone. We see all around us how peer pressure is a powerful negative force. In today's society, drugs are wreaking enormous havoc. There is not a kid in all of America that does not know that drugs are bad for him or her. So why are so many fooling around with drugs? Don't they know that drugs kill, that they destroy lives? Are these kids all idiots? The answer is, "Everybody is doing it." Peer pressure can induce a person to do something that he does not want to do.

The same peer pressure can also be a power for the good. When a person's peers are exerting themselves to do *mitzvos* even when it doesn't come easy, he is also drawn to behave in the same way, even though he may be reluctant to do so deep down. When everyone around him is setting his slaves free, even though this means suffering a great financial loss, he is also strengthened in his own resolve.

The lesson to be learned from this is the importance of community. We do not outgrow our susceptibility to peer pressure. When we were teenagers, we had to deal with peer pressure, and as adults we also have to deal with peer pressure, but perhaps in a somewhat different form. All we can do is try to arrange our lives so that the peer pressure we face is positive rather than negative. That keeping up with the Cohens pushes us to do more *mitzvos*, not to build larger homes and drive fancier cars. Therefore, it is imperative to find a community that wants the right things out of life.

The *Beis Av* raises a question with the interpretation of the *Chinuch*. If the purpose of sounding the *shofar* was to provide positive peer pressure for slaveowners, it should have been enough to sound one long blast. The Talmud states (*Rosh Hashanah* 34b), however, that the sounding of the *shofar* on Yom Kippur of the *Yoveil* year followed the exact same pattern as the sounding of the *shofar* on Rosh Hashanah, with long, short and *staccato* blasts. Why was all this necessary?

The answer is that the recollection of the *Akeidah* was also of great importance on this occasion. When we sound the *shofar* on Rosh Hashanah, we are reminded of the self-sacrifice of the patriarchs. Avraham was prepared to sacrifice his beloved son Yitzchak if that was the will of the Creator, and Yitzchak was equally ready to give up his life for the same purpose. That is a very important message to the slaveowners who must set their slaves free. Granted, it is not an easy thing the Torah is asking of them. Granted, it requires sacrifice, great sacrifice. But sacrifice when it comes to obeying Hashem is in our heritage. Our patriarchs instilled it in our blood.

The Talmud tells us that there are two types of self-sacrifice. One is "*bechol levavcha uvechol nafshecha,* with all your heart and soul." This refers to readiness to give up one's life. The other is "*bechol me'odecha,* with all your wealth." On

Rosh Hashanah, we concentrate on the first. During *Yoveil*, we concentrate on the second.

In actuality, the second is not necessarily easier than the first. Let's not kid ourselves. People love their money. The Talmud tells us (*Sanhedrin* 74a) there are certain people for whom parting with their money is a greater sacrifice than parting with their lives. We ask ourselves incredulously, "Do such people really exist?" The answer is absolutely yes. That is why people work fourteen, sixteen, eighteen hours a day. That is why do people have coronaries as a result of their businesses. During the race riots in Baltimore in 1968, a man in my neighborhood went down to his liquor store in West Baltimore with his shotgun to fend off the rioters. Crazy? He is just a little crazier than many of us who give their sweat, tears and energy and the best years of their lives to the pursuit of financial gain.

Rav Avraham Pam once said that the previous generation, the one that lived through the Holocaust, was put to the trial of "with all your hearts and with all your souls." Our generation, the Jews in America at the turn of the millennium, is being put to the trial of "with all your wealth." How do we relate to money? What do we do with it? Do we give enough to *yeshivos*, to the poor, to the community *mikveh*, to Jewish outreach? These are the questions posed to us. It is the trial of our generation.

The Perfect Antidote

וְכִי תִמְכְּרוּ מִמְכָּר לַעֲמִיתֶךָ אוֹ קָנֹה מִיַּד עֲמִיתֶךָ

אַל תּוֹנוּ אִישׁ אֶת אָחִיו

When you sell to your friend
or buy from your friend,
do not cheat each other. (25:14)

SMACK IN THE MIDDLE OF ITS INSTRUCTIONS REGARDING *Shemitah*, the Torah inserts the singular prohibition of *onaah*. "Do not cheat each other." Why does it belong here? Furthermore, the laws of *Shemitah* apply to the usage of the land, requiring that it lay fallow for the entire seventh year. It is essentially real-estate law. But the law of *onaah* does not apply to real estate, since the dynamics of land prices are different. Why then does this law, which applies to movable property, appear in the midst of the *Shemitah* laws that apply to the land?

The *Beis Av* explains that the underlying concept of the *Shemitah* year is to impress on people that, in the final analysis, everything we have comes from Hashem. Do not think that the more you toil the more you earn. Here you will see that you can leave your land fallow for an entire year, and your livelihood will not suffer.

This concept very much negates the rationale for cheating. A person may think he can beat the game. He may think that his underhanded methods will bring him additional money that he would not have had otherwise. But if he honestly believes that everything comes from Hashem, he certainly cannot expect to outsmart Him. He may gain a few dollars by cheating, but then his air conditioner will break or his car will need a new transmission, costing him the same amount of money he thought he had gained. In the end, the bottom line will be what Hashem wants it to be.

If a person keeps the *mitzvah* of *Shemitah*, if he absorbs its message, he will understand that cheating is not only wrong. It is futile.

Let us follow this reasoning one step further. We have identified the connection between *Shemitah* and cheating. But *onaah* also includes *onaas devarim*, which forbids snide and scathing remarks to other people. What is the connection between *Shemitah* and this type of *onaah*? What do such remarks have to do with business dealings and livelihoods?

I once heard from my *Rosh Yeshivah*, Rav Yaakov Weinberg that the root cause of all putdowns is an underlying attitude of rejection. It is as if we were saying, "He does not belong. He should not be getting so much honor. I am smarter and better than he is." And then we cut him down to size.

Looking more closely, we notice that the motivation behind the snide remark is really a lack of satisfaction with one's own portion in life. It reflects an insufficient trust and faith in Hashem. Verbal abuse, therefore, stems from a lack of belief that the Master of the Universe is fully in charge. Therefore, the *mitzvah* of *Shemitah* is the perfect antidote.

Parashas Bechukosai
פרשת בחקתי

A Vessel Called Peace

וְנָתַתִּי שָׁלוֹם בָּאָרֶץ וּשְׁכַבְתֶּם וְאֵין מַחֲרִיד

And I will make peace in the land,
and you will recline without fear. (26:6)

HASHEM PROMISES THINGS WILL GO WELL AS LONG AS the Jewish people follow His decrees. The land will be fertile, and the crops will be plentiful. Then He adds, "And I will make peace in the land." Rashi quotes from the *Toras Kohanim*, "You might say, 'We have what to eat, and we have what to drink. But if there is no peace, there is nothing.' Therefore, the Torah adds, 'And I will make peace in the land.' From here we see that peace is worth as much as everything else combined."

Peace is the greatest blessing for a family, a community or a nation. Any other blessings we may enjoy turn to ashes in our mouths if we are embroiled in conflict. This is the message of the concluding *mishneh* in the Talmud (*Uktzin* 3:12), "The Holy One, Blessed is He, found no vessel to contain the blessings for the Jewish people other than peace."

The Ksav Sofer explains that jealousy is the most common destroyer of peace. People who are dissatisfied with their own lot cannot bear to see others enjoying privileges they feel should have been theirs. And they will most likely not take this perceived injustice lying down. They will fight and struggle with those whom they envy and undercut them at every step of the way as long as there is an imbalance. And there goes peace. The person who breaks the peace is consumed with jealousy and is never happy. He cannot enjoy those blessings he already has. Clearly, all blessings are worthless unless they are contained in this vessel called peace.

In 1980, Rav Yaakov Kamenetsky traveled to the Knessiah Gedolah of Agudath Israel in Jerusalem. At that particular time, he was feeling extremely weak and incapable of making the trip; in fact, he was so weak that he left word that if he were to pass away in Eretz Yisrael he wanted to be buried there. Nonetheless, he succumbed to pressure and went.

Because of his physical condition, Rav Yaakov did not travel or give *shiurim* while in Eretz Yisrael. But he did insist on visiting Yeshivas Kol Yaakov. Rav Yaakov was taken to this *yeshivah*, and when he got up to speak, he began to cry. "All my life I wanted to greet Mashiach. I now feel that I won't have this merit. I don't feel I'll live much longer. But if I can't greet Mashiach myself, at least I want to be among a group of people that will undoubtedly be among those who greet Mashiach. I know that this *yeshivah* will be among those that greet him."

What was so special about this *yeshivah*? This *yeshivah* made peace between Ashkenazim and Sephardim, with both communities more or less equally represented in the student body. It was a *yeshivah* that produced that precious commodity called peace.

The Blessing of Desolation

וַהֲשִׁמֹּתִי אֲנִי אֶת הָאָרֶץ וְשָׁמְמוּ עָלֶיהָ אֹיְבֵיכֶם
הַיֹּשְׁבִים בָּה

And I will lay waste the land,
and your enemies who dwell in it
will be wretched. (26:32)

THE *TOCHACHAH* IS PROPHECY IN ITS MOST FRIGHTENING
form. Each verse, each phrase, each word is a har-
binger of future calamity in different times in Jewish
history. For instance, the Ramban writes that "Hashem will
send you back to Egypt in boats" refers to the enslavement
of the Jews under the Roman emperor Titus. He also writes
that "the king you appoint for yourself" refers to Agrippa who
was a cruel and incompetent monarch.

In the midst of this litany of misery, we find the statement,
"And I will lay waste the land, and your enemies who dwell
in it will be wretched." What does this mean? The Ramban
sees it as a blessing slipped in among the curses, a word of
consolation in middle of the *Tochachah*. It is an assurance to
the Jewish people that even when they are in exile the Holy
Land will not be hospitable to other peoples who seek to settle there. This, concludes the Ramban, is a great proof of
Divine providence, since "no other land throughout the world
is as good and fertile" as the Holy Land once was, and now
it has lain desolate for many centuries.

Think about what the Ramban is saying. For the last two
thousand years, Eretz Yisrael, that land flowing with milk and
honey, has been under foreign dominion—Romans, Persians,
Arabs, Turks, British—and what became of it? A dusty, arid
wasteland sparsely populated by hardscrabble tillers of the

soil. As the Torah assured us, no vibrant communities arose on the land during our absence, no deep-rooted prosperous cities.

Imagine if the Indians tried to reclaim Manhattan Island. "We want to renegotiate," they say. "We sold this island to you for $24 worth of wampum. We will reimburse your purchase price and give you a 100 percent return — $48. And all in cash. You don't have to take any wampum . . . Not enough? We understand. Inflation really eats up the dollars over three hundred and fifty years. And then there is what you could have earned in mutual funds all these years. All right, fair enough. How about 48,000? Forty-eight million? Forty-eight billion? Still no sale? Ugh!"

Manhattan Island is just about priceless.

Well, imagine if the gentile settlers had been able to develop Eretz Yisrael over the last two millennia. Imagine if in the 20th century it was like one long Manhattan Island. Would it have been possible for the Jewish people to recover this real estate for a national homeland? It was only the blessing of "your enemies who dwell in it will be wretched" that has made it possible for us to recover the land.

I have always been mystified by the placement of oil reserves in the Middle East. Saudi Arabia has oil, as do Iraq, Kuwait, Quatar, Bahrein, Aden, Yemen and even Egypt to a certain extent. But from Eretz Yisrael, we cannot squeeze a drop of oil—petroleum, that is. But look at the other side. If Eretz Yisrael had been oil rich, would we have been able to recover it from the gentiles? Not a chance. Once again, the blessing of desolation preserved the land for our people.

If we open our eyes, we see clearly the Divine providence by which Hashem has guided and continues to guide all the Jewish people.

Bamidbar

Parashas Bamidbar
פרשת במדבר

Under Pressure

אִישׁ עַל דִּגְלוֹ בְאֹתֹת לְבֵית אֲבֹתָם יַחֲנוּ בְּנֵי יִשְׂרָאֵל

The Jewish people should encamp,
each man according to his flag,
by the signs of his clan. (2:2)

CCORDING TO THE MIDRASH, MOSHE WAS CONCERNED about the flag system Hashem had told him to institute. He was afraid it would bring trouble and lead to "divisions and disputes among the tribes." He was afraid that if he told this tribe to travel on the west, they would insist on traveling on the east, that those he sent to the north would clamor for the southern flank. Whatever he did would not be good enough. The tribes would bicker and fight with each other as they jockeyed for position, and strife would reign in the Jewish encampment.

But Hashem reassured him that all would go well. Yaakov had already established the pattern of the travel formations by assigning specific positions to his sons when he gave instructions for his funeral procession from Egypt to Canaan. The positions around Yaakov's coffin were the same as those around the *Mishkan*. Therefore, the people were already accustomed to their assigned positions.

But questions still remain. Why would the people be willing to accept formations based on funeral formations hundreds of years in the past? How would the pattern of Yaakov's funeral procession prevent dissension and strife in the travel formation in the desert?

Rav Mordechai Rogov explains that human nature is very sensitive to the environment. When things are going well in society, when peace and prosperity reign in the land, people are more inclined to be civil, even genteel to each other. But when the going gets tough, the veneer of politeness thins very quickly. Nerves fray. Tempers grow short. Before you know it, all civility is gone, and people are at each other's throats.

Moshe was concerned that the Jewish people would not react well to the rigors of traveling through the desert, a place rife with feral animals and ringed by hostile nations. Despite the protection of the Cloud Pillars, they would feel apprehensive. This would lead them to discard their civil manners and jockey for better positions. It's one thing to be civil in ordinary times and quite another in times of war and famine.

You don't need to worry, Hashem assured Moshe. The death of Yaakov was also a crisis for the fledgling Jewish nations. It could easily have led to bickering and dissension among the brothers. Under pressure of the situation, they could have jostled for positions around the coffin. But Yaakov gave them specific instructions about their positions around his coffin, and by following those instructions, they learned to get along in times of crisis. This lesson sank deep into their consciousness and became part of the national character. Therefore, Moshe, you don't have to worry that the Jewish people will break down and fight among themselves. They have been conditioned to keep to a higher standard. Not only now but also throughout history, throughout the worst pogroms and inquisitions and massacres, the Jewish spirit will retain its refinement and nobility. You don't have to worry, Moshe.

We have all heard many stories about the conduct of Jews during the Holocaust, the quiet heroism, the indomitable spirit. There is one simple story I heard not long ago. It is not especially dramatic, but it illustrates the point of the Midrash very sharply.

Many Holocaust memoirs devote an inordinate amount of attention to bread, because at the time, bread consumed all their thinking hours. To a concentration-camp inmate, a piece of bread was life itself. Each inmate was given a piece of bread once a day, and he had to decide what to do with it. What should he do? Should he eat the bread right away or should he perhaps nibble at it all day? Should he save it until he is very tired and hungry at the end of the day so that he would not have to go to sleep on an empty stomach? Difficult questions. Weighty questions.

A Jew in a concentration camp was summoned to the commandant's office. This could mean only one thing. His time was up.

Every Jew was aware that the moment of death could come at any time, and this Jew was no different. He sighed and said *Vidui*, making peace with his Maker. Then he exchanged his clothes with the other inmates. He gave his shoes to a man whose feet were swaddled in rags. He gave his coat to one friend. And the precious piece of bread in his pocket, the piece of life he was saving all day, what was the point in wasting a good piece of bread when he had maybe minutes to live? He gave the bread to another friend and set out for the commandant's office.

Wonder of wonders, the commandant needed something trivial and had no intention of killing him, at least at that particular time. As the man walked back to his barracks, he felt certain he would get his clothing back, but what about the bread? The friend to whom he had given it could easily say he had already eaten it.

In the barracks, the first person to greet him was that friend. "You're alive!" he shouted ecstatically. "They didn't kill you. Here, take back your piece of bread. You must eat it; it is yours. Oh, thank Heaven, you are still among the living, not among the dead."

Where does a Jew get the strength to behave like an angel when he is being treated like an animal? It dates back to Yaakov's funeral procession from Egypt to Canaan, when his sons learned to conduct themselves on the highest levels of humanity in the midst of terrible tragedy.

Not Enough Respect

וַיָּמָת נָדָב וַאֲבִיהוּא . . . וּבָנִים לֹא הָיוּ

Nadav and Avihu died . . .
and they had no children. (3:4)

NADAV AND AVIHU, AHARON'S SONS, DIED SUPERNATURAL and mysterious deaths. The Torah tells us (*Vayikra* 10:1-2) that they brought a "strange fire" into the *Mishkan*, and that a fire snaked out from the Holy of Holies and snuffed out their lives.

Why did they die? There are different opinions among the Sages. Some say they were in a state of mild intoxication at the time they entered the *Mishkan*. Others say they issued a legal ruling in front of their teacher Moshe, presumptuously acting on their own without seeking guidance. Be that as it may, the common denominator seems to be a certain lack of respect where respect is due, a slight shortcoming in people of such an exceedingly august stature.

In *Bamidbar*, however, we encounter a completely new approach. "Nadav and Avihu died, and they had no children." The Talmud infers (*Yevamos* 64a) from here that whoever does not make the effort to have children deserves to die. This would seem to indicate that Nadav and Avihu died because they did not try to have children; it contradicts the opinions that they died because of intoxication or insubordination.

The Chasam Sofer suggests that there is no conflict whatsoever. The problem with Nadav and Avihu was indeed a deficiency in their demonstrating respect, a minuscule lack of *midos*. Every person really has to grapple with the same issues. Every person has to learn to acknowledge the authority and full worth of others. Every person has to sensitize himself to the sanctity of the holy places. Unfortunately, however, most people tend to see themselves as sufficiently respectful. It does not occur to them that they are deficient. And if they do not think they are lacking in respect, they certainly will not work on developing their respectfulness. So how can a person measure the level of his own respectfulness? By his children. If his children are disrespectful to them, he can be sure that he is not sufficiently respectful to others.

Rav Wolbe, in his *Alei Shur*, applies this concept to all areas of *midos*. "There is no greater factor in improving one's *midos*," he writes, "than having children." People have a tendency not to see their own flaws, but they see the flaws of their children all too well. And if they are intelligent, thinking people, they will realize they do not have to seek too far for the source of their children's flaws, and they will make every effort to correct the situation.

This is what the Sages may have meant when they said that Nadav and Avihu died because they did not have children. Had they had children, they would have noticed any lack of respect in their behavior. They would have realized that they only had themselves to blame. They would have worked on their own characters to improve their respectfulness. Then they never would have considered entering the *Mishkan* in a state of intoxication or in ruling on legal matters in front of Moshe, and they would not have died.

Following the same line of reasoning, we gain new insight into the words of the *Mechilta*, which states that the Commandments on the right Tablet corresponded to the respective Commandments on the left.

The *Mechilta* goes on to describe the relationships of each corresponding pair. The fifth and final pair is "honor your father and mother" and "you shall not covet" that which belongs to your neighbor. What is the connection? "Any person who is jealous," explains the *Mechilta*, "will have a child who will curse his own father and give respect to someone other than his father."

When we covet what others have, whether it is their wealth or their possessions or their prestige or their standing in the community, what message are we sending our children? We are telling them loud and clear that the grass is always greener on the other side, that whatever other people have is better than what we have. His house is better than mine. His car is better than mine. And so forth. The children absorb this message and apply it to their own lives. What does a child really have in his own life? Does he have a house? A car? A job? No, he has a father. So when he thinks about fathers, he concludes that the neighbor's father is better than his own. Then he diverts the respect that should be going to his own father and directs it toward someone else's father.

Parashas Naso
פרשת נשא

That's an Orthodox Jew

אִישׁ אוֹ אִשָּׁה כִּי יַעֲשׂוּ מִכָּל חַטֹּאת הָאָדָם לִמְעֹל
מַעַל בַּיהוָה וְאָשְׁמָה הַנֶּפֶשׁ הַהִוא

*A man or woman that commits one of the sins
people commit to be very faithless
to God, that person shall bear guilt. (5:6)*

STEALING FROM ANYONE IS FORBIDDEN, BUT STEALING from a *ger*, a righteous convert, is an especially despicable sin. Our Sages tell us (*Sifrei* 5:13) that the Torah considers such people "very faithless to God." Why is this so? Sforno explains that stealing from a *ger* is also a *chillul Hashem*, a desecration of the Name.

One can just imagine the scene. A gentile has seen the light. He has come to the realization that the Torah is the truth and that the Jewish people are the chosen people. His heart is burning with a desire to join this exalted elite. He works hard. He envelops himself in the holiness of the Jewish people. He studies. He learns. And finally, he is accepted as a convert and comes under the wings of the *Shechinah*, so to speak. He walks into the *shul* for Minchah, puts down his briefcase and joins the congregation. He feels wonderful. He finishes his prayers and goes to retrieve his briefcase, but it is gone, obviously stolen by another Jew! What a humiliation for the Jewish people, for the Torah, for the holy *Shechinah!* This thief, whoever he was, did not only commit a crime of theft against the owner of the briefcase. He made an awful *chillul Hashem.*

People tend to think of *chillul Hashem* as a transgression of major proportions, but it is not. The Talmud tells us (*Yoma* 86a), "What is considered a *chillul Hashem?* Rav said, 'If I were to buy meat from a butcher and fail to pay my bill right away.'" The greater the Jew, the greater the potential for *chillul Hashem* in his deeds. For someone of Rav's stature, all it takes to make a *chillul Hashem* is a small thing like not paying the butcher on time. People look up to our great rabbis. They measure all the Jewish people and all of Judaism by the behavior of the great. Therefore, people of stature have an additional responsibility to act with great care and fore-thought. Hashem's honor depends on what they do.

The Rambam writes (*Yad, Hilchos Yesodei HaTorah* 5:11) that not only a *tanna* such as Rav but "any great person renowned for his piety" who transgresses even slightly is guilty of *chillul Hashem.* If the people of his generation look up to him, he bears the same responsibility as Rav in his generation.

Taking this reasoning a step further, Rav Yaakov Weinberg, my *Rosh Yeshivah,* suggested that in our times every Orthodox Jew is considered a "great person renowned for his piety." Whether we like it or not, whether we agree with it or not, millions of nonobservant Jews see all of us as holy rabbis serving Hashem all day every day, and they measure our actions accordingly. A nonobservant Jew would be shocked and scandalized if he would be cut off in traffic by a car whose driver has a beard and is wearing a black hat, and perhaps a bumper sticker promoting Shabbos or protesting *lashon hara.* This is as bad or worse than not pay-ing the butcher on time. It is a bona fide *chillul Hashem.*

This obligation also includes treating all people with appropriate courtesy. If you work in a place together with gentiles, you most certainly should not socialize with them, but you have to say, "Good morning."

It doesn't matter if you are not among the *gedolei hador*. It doesn't matter if you are not a *talmid chacham*. It doesn't matter if you are big on *chumros*. These people don't know the difference. They see you and say, "That's an Orthodox Jew." It automatically makes you a "great person renowned for his piety" as far as *chillul Hashem* is concerned.

Melodies and Songs

בְּכָתֵף יִשָּׂאוּ

*They shall carry [the Holy Ark]
on their shoulders. (7:9)*

ALTHOUGH THE TORAH EXPLICITLY INSTRUCTS THE House of Kehas to carry the Holy Ark on their shoulders and not to place it on a wagon as were the other planks and the curtains, King David apparently forgot this law. After the Holy Ark had been recaptured from the Philistines, King David ordered that it be brought to Yerushalayim on a wagon. This decision resulted in tragedy.

Why did David deserve such a punishment? The Talmud explains (*Sotah* 35a) that it was because he referred to the Torah as a *zimrah*, a song, as it is written (*Tehillim* 119:54), "Your statutes were like songs to me." Hashem was displeased and said, "If you refer to My Torah as a song, I will cause you to forget a law that even young schoolchildren know."

The Vilna Gaon asks what the problem is here since the Torah elsewhere refers to itself as a song (*Devarim* 31:19), "And write for yourselves this *shirah* (song)."

There is a major difference, explains the Gaon, between *zimrah* and *shirah*. The word *zimrah* refers to a melody, a piece of song that has a finite structure, a beginning and an end, like the *zemiros* of Shabbos. The word *shirah*, however, represents the infinite. It is the articulation and expression of a person's feelings without beginning and without end. It is his essence bursting forth with irrepressible song in no particular structure or form, just a joyous expression of the sentiments in the heart in the language of music. It may stop after a while, but it has no real end, no ultimate boundary.

Therefore, Torah can be called *shirah*, but it cannot be called *zimrah*. Torah has no beginning and no end. It is infinite.

Nesanel's Dilemma

בַּיּוֹם הַשֵּׁנִי הִקְרִיב נְתַנְאֵל בֶּן צוּעָר נְשִׂיא
יִשָּׂשכָר: הִקְרִב אֶת קָרְבָּנוֹ . . .

On the second day, Nesanel ben Tzuar
of the tribe of Yissachar brought.
He brought his offering ... (7:18-19)

EVERY *BAR-MITZVAH* BOY'S NIGHTMARE IS TO HAVE TO read *Parashas Naso*, which has one hundred seventy-six verses, more than any other *parashah* in the Torah. At least, that is what I used to think when I was a boy. But in fact, *Naso* is not such a hard *parashah* after all. The end of the *parashah* describes the dedication offerings brought by all twelve princes of the tribes, and they are all identical. The *bar-mitzvah* boy would find himself reading a fairly sizable group of verses twelve times. That shouldn't be too hard, should it?

But why is it so?

The Midrash relates that the prince of Yehudah, Nachshon ben Aminadav, brought his offering, and then it was Nesanel ben Tzuar's turn. He was faced with a dilemma. What should he bring? What would be the ramifications of his decision?

Let us use a *bar-mitzvah* as an analogy. It is not unusual for one shul to have a *bar-mitzvah* every Shabbos for twelve consecutive weeks. Now let us say that the food served at the first *bar-mitzvah* was a fruit cup, a quarter of chicken, a piece of potato *kugel*, glazed carrots and chocolate ice cream for dessert. Everything goes beautifully. Terrific.

Now comes week two. The mother of the next *bar-mitzvah* boy has a problem. What should she serve? Fruit cup is out, as is a quarter of chicken and *kugel* as well. Two weeks in a row? She would be a laughingstock in the community. So she opts for the chicken cutlet and the broccoli quiche. Everything goes well. Disaster has been avoided.

Now comes week three. The mother of this boy considers the gravity of the situation. Chicken is certainly out, as are chicken cutlet, *kugel* and quiche. Forget about the fruit cup and the chocolate ice cream. This situation obviously calls for roast beef and grilled asparagus stalks. And lemon meringue pie for desert.

You can imagine the anxiety by week twelve. What can they serve at that *bar-mitzvah* already? They would have to find the most exotic foods, and they would have to pay the most exotic prices.

All this went through Nesanel ben Tzuar's mind. Not *bar-mitzvahs*, of course, but escalation. Nachshon ben Aminadav had already brought his offering. If Nesanel were to go one up on Nachshon, there would be no end to it. The pressure would mount, as would the anger, the resentment, the jealousy and no doubt the *lashon hara* as well.

So Nesanel ben Tzuar did a wonderful thing. He brought exactly the same offering as Nachshon. This enabled all those behind him to do the same thing, and thus all their offerings were identical. Nesanel set the tone—all Jews are the same.

The Midrash concludes that Hashem showed His pleasure in an unusual way. A *korban yachid*, a private offering, is never brought on Shabbos, only a *korban tzibbur*, a communal offering. The offerings of the tribal princes, however, were brought on twelve consecutive days, including Shabbos, even though they were *korbanos yachid*.

Since these offerings were deliberately identical in order to avoid hatred and jealousy, since they promoted a sense of community and harmony, Hashem considered them as *korbanos tzibbur* and allowed them to be brought even on Shabbos.

Parashas Behaalos'cha
פרשת בהעלותך

The Mark of a Leader

דַּבֵּר אֶל אַהֲרֹן וְאָמַרְתָּ אֵלָיו בְּהַעֲלֹתְךָ אֶת הַנֵּרֹת

Speak to Aharon and say to him,
"When you light the lamps . . ." (8:2)

IMMEDIATELY AFTER THE PRINCES OF THE TRIBES BRING THEIR offerings to the dedication of the *Mishkan*, Aharon is com-manded to light the *Menorah*. What is the connection? The *Midrash Tanchuma*, quoted by Rashi, explains that when Aharon observed all the princes bringing their offerings, he was upset that "that neither he nor his tribe [of Levi] partici-pated by bringing offerings." Hashem, therefore, told him, "Your share is greater than theirs. You will light the *Menorah*."

Rav Yaakov Weinberg, my *Rosh Yeshivah*, takes note of the language of the Midrash in which Aharon bemoaned that "neither he nor his tribe" participated. Why should Aharon be advocating for his tribe? He was not the titular head of the tribe of Levi. If anything, it would have been Moshe. Why then was Aharon concerned about the omission of Levi? It was not his responsibility.

Clearly, Moshe was not the head of the tribe of Levi, and therefore, it was proper for Aharon to advocate for his brethren in the tribe of Levi. There are no dual offices in the leadership role of a Jewish leader. If Moshe was the *rabban shel Yisrael*, the teacher of all the Jewish people, then he could not at the same time be the specific leader of a particular group within the Jewish people. He wore one hat. He was the leader of all the people.

This is an important qualification for a Jewish leader of the broader community. Once he steps into that role, he must embrace all Jews. He is no longer the leader of his narrow group.

Further along in the *parashah*, we find another important leadership qualification. After Moshe complains that he cannot handle the entire burden of leadership by himself, Hashem tells him (11:16), "Gather for Me seventy men (*ish*)."

The Midrash wonders why the Torah uses the word *ish*, which denotes the singular rather than the plural. The Midrash replies that it is meant to bring to mind two other verses, both of which should define a Jewish leader. He must be similar to Hashem who is described (*Shemos* 15:3) as a "Man (*ish*) of war." He must also be similar to Moshe of whom the Torah states (*Bamidbar* 12:3), "The man (*ish*) Moses was the most modest of men."

Rav Shlomo Breuer explains that we see here the duality in the role of a Jewish leader. On the one hand, he must be "the most modest of men." Regardless of how much power has been entrusted in his hands, he must never abuse his office. He always must be humble and circumspect in the exercise of his office. He must treat each individual Jew with the honor and respect due the descendants of Avraham, Yitzchak and Yaakov.

At the same time, there must be a hand of iron inside the velvet glove. He cannot take humility too far, to the point that he becomes a doormat. He cannot be meek. He must be a "man of war," ready to breathe fire if the people step out of line. There are times when he has to stand up courageously and rebuke the people. He must put them in their place.

Moshe himself, that most modest of all men, did not hesitate to do this when the situation called for it. He declared (*Devarim* 9:24), "You were rebellious against God from the day I first met you."

This is what the word *ish* signifies. The Jewish leader must be a perfect blend of Moshe's modest attributes and Hashem's commanding presence.

At the very end of the Torah (*Devarim* 31:7), we read that "Moshe said to Yehoshua in front of all Israel, 'Be strong (*chazak ve'ematz*).'" This is the way the verse is normally read. But a close look at the cantillation marks (*trop*) reveals a different reading. "Moshe said to Yehoshua, 'In front of all Israel be strong (*chazak ve'ematz*).'"

Moshe was telling Yehoshua that he could be as modest as he liked most of the time, but when he found himself facing off against all the Jewish people, he should be strong (*chazak ve'ematz*). Don't back off. Don't let them intimidate you. Don't be frightened. Be strong. Be forceful. Stand by your principles. Those are not the times to be modest.

We find yet one more qualification for Jewish leadership in the *parashah*. Moshe tells Hashem (11:12) he cannot continue to carry the nation "as a nursing mother carries her suckling child." The Talmud derives (*Sanhedrin* 8a) from here that a Jewish leader must have patience with the people. He will have to deal with unrealistic expectations and bizarre demands, and he must do so with patience and forbearance.

Any person who has ever raised an infant is familiar with the following scenario. A little baby is dressed in his beautiful outfit, sitting on the lap of his beaming mother, who is herself wearing a gorgeous dress. She is entertaining company. All of a sudden, the disposable diaper does not perform as advertised.

What does the mother do? Yes, she is upset. But does she berate the child and punish him? Does she say, "How could you do this to me?"

Of course not. The mother understands that the baby is only a baby and that he did not mean to do harm. So what does the mother do? She takes the baby out of the room, washes him well and dresses him in fresh clothes. Then she changes her own dress and returns to her company. With a smile on her face.

This is the image of "a nursing mother carrying her suckling child." This is the standard set by which our Sages measure Jewish leaders. He has to have a bottomless reserve of patience to endure everything his people do. And he has to see everything in a positive light so that when the people step out of line he will try to excuse them. "They are too tired. Too hungry. They weren't thinking."

Comfort Levels

וְיֵשׁ אֲשֶׁר יִהְיֶה הֶעָנָן מֵעֶרֶב עַד בֹּקֶר וְנַעֲלָה הֶעָנָן
בַּבֹּקֶר וְנָסָעוּ אוֹ יוֹמָם וָלַיְלָה וְנַעֲלָה הֶעָנָן וְנָסָעוּ

And sometimes the cloud would be there from evening until the morning, it would rise in the morning and they would travel; or for a day and a night, and the cloud would rise and they would travel (9:21)

IF YOU EVER PACKED A FAMILY INTO A STATION WAGON FOR A trip, you know how difficult it is. By the time you reach your destination and unpack, you are exhausted. You cannot even begin to think about the return trip when you're going to have to do the whole thing all over again. Sometimes, you wish you could stay for a month. If you find this type of trip hard, you would have had your hands full with the travels in the desert.

The Torah tells us that the position of the Cloud Pillars signaled to the Jewish people if they should stay put or break camp. If the Cloud Pillars rested on the *Mishkan*, the people could leave the suitcases under the beds, but if the Cloud Pillars rose, it was time to pull out those suitcases and start packing.

According to the Ramban, the travel schedule was very erratic. Sometimes, they would arrive at a particularly uninviting, barren stretch of desert. They wanted to leave immediately, but the Cloud Pillars would settle in for a while. On other occasions, they came to a lovely spot and wanted very much to stay there. They would unpack their belongings and look forward to an enjoyable layover. But the next morning, the cloud rose, and they had to break camp. These travels were not easy. They were a real test.

One cannot help but wonder what was the purpose of all of this? Why make the sojourn in the desert so arbitrary and burdensome?

Rav Eliahu Dessler, in *Michtav m'Eliahu*, explains that Hashem may have been teaching the Jewish people that learning Torah and performing *mitzvos* should not be dependent on external conditions.

People often say, "If only we had a little more free time, we would learn more." Or else, "If only we didn't have to worry so much about making a living, if only we didn't have to worry about our children, oh boy, would we sit and learn Torah and pray slowly and with great concentration!"

In the *Yeshivah*, from time to time I have to make a remark to a *bachur* when he is not performing up to par. I hear all the excuses. "I am busy with schoolwork." Or else, "I'm having trouble with *shidduchim*. If only I had my *shidduch*, oh boy, would I sit and learn!" And many, many more.

But life is never perfect. It's always full of disturbances. We are not living in the Garden of Eden. There are financial problems. There are problems with parents, problems with children. There are always problems!

That is what Hashem was teaching us with the erratic travels in the desert. Life in the desert was no picnic. But Jewish life did not depend on conditions improving. A Jew must learn Torah and perform *mitzvos* under any and all conditions. Don't wait until you get comfortable.

Parashas Shelach
פרשת שלח

The Danger of Humility

וַיִּקְרָא מֹשֶׁה לְהוֹשֵׁעַ בִּן נוּן יְהוֹשֻׁעַ

Moshe changed Hoshea bin Nun's
name to Yehoshua. (13:16)

OSHE KNEW THAT THE MISSION OF THE SPIES WOULD come to no good. He was especially concerned for the safety and welfare of his beloved disciple Yehoshua who would be traveling as part of the infamous group. At this time, Yehoshua's name was still Hoshea. Moshe "changed [his] name to Yehoshua," adding the letter *yud* to his name as a spiritual protection.

Targum Yonasan includes an editorial comment in his translation of this verse, "When Moshe saw Hoshea's humility, he changed his name to Yehoshua." Apparently, in the opinion of *Targum Yonasan*, Yehoshua's humility put him at risk. How was this so? Isn't humility a desirable trait?

The *Avnei Shoham* offers an explanation based on a *Tosefta* (*Shabbos* 17:4). There was disagreement between the schools of Shammai and Hillel as to whether the bones left over after a meal may be handled on Shabbos. According to the school of Hillel, it is permitted to remove the bones and discard them normally. According to the school of Shammai, the bones are *muktzeh,* and the only way to remove the bones is by removing the entire table or tablecloth and shaking it clean. Rabbi Zechariah ben Avkilos chose a middle way. He would pick up the bones and toss them behind the couch. The *Tosefta* comments that this compromising attitude of Rabbi Zechariah ben Avkilos destroyed the *Beis Hamikdash.*

What does this mean?

The *Tosefta* is referring to a famous incident recorded in the Talmud (*Gittin* 56a) in which a renegade Jew denounced the Jews as rebels to a skeptical Roman emperor. "I'll prove it to you," said the renegade. "Send an offering to the Holy Temple in Jerusalem and have them sacrifice it on their Altar. If they refuse, you will know they are rebels." The emperor sent the renegade back along with a letter requesting the sacrifice and a fine animal for the purpose. The renegade secretly blemished the animal, rendering it invalid as a sacrifice. The Sages rejected it, the Romans attacked, and the *Beis Hamikdash* was destroyed.

The Talmud relates that the Sages did not reject it out of hand. When they noticed the slight blemish on the emperor's animal, they were in a quandary. Perhaps they should offer it up even though it was blemished in order to avoid offending the emperor. But Rabbi Zechariah ben Avkilos objected. "You can't do that," he said. "People may come to think that blemished animals are fit for the Altar." The Sages considered killing the renegade to prevent the emperor from learning what had happened. But Rabbi Zechariah ben Avkilos objected again. "You can't do that," he said. "People might think that bringing a blemished sacrifice is punishable by death." As a result, the Sages did nothing, the tragic chain of events was set in motion, and the *Beis Hamikdash* was destroyed. Commenting on this incident, Rabbi Yochanan said, "The humility of Rabbi Zechariah ben Avkilos destroyed our *Beis Hamikdash* and exiled us from our Land."

Modesty, humility, compromise and peacemaking are all wonderful attributes, but in certain situations, other qualities are more appropriate. Sometimes, one has to stand up and say, "Let the chips fall where they may, this is the way it has to be!" Sometimes, one must exchange peacemaking and compromise for a strong, unequivocal stance. This was Rabbi Zechariah's failing. He took his humility a little too far.

According to *Targum Yonasan*, Moshe feared that Yehoshua had a similar failing. He was too good, too accommodating, too great a lover of peace and compromise solutions. But in the company of the Spies and their nefarious plans, situations might arise where compromise would be impossible. Did Yehoshua have the tough backbone to be strong and resolute when that was required? Moshe wasn't sure. Therefore, he added the *yud* to Yehoshua's name to reinforce his courage and fortitude, to give him the ability to stand alone against the plot of the Spies.

Subjective Proof

הָאָרֶץ אֲשֶׁר עָבַרְנוּ בָהּ לָתוּר אֹתָהּ אֶרֶץ אֹכֶלֶת יוֹשְׁבֶיהָ הִוא

The land we crossed to scout it out is a land that devours its inhabitants. (13:32)

Hashem was very kind to the *Meraglim*, the Spies. He arranged that a number of Canaanites should die just as the *Meraglim* were passing through the land.

Instead of casting suspicious glances at the Jewish scouting party, the inhabitants would be busy attending funerals. Wherever, they went, the *Meraglim* saw huge crowds attending funerals and hardly any traffic on the roads. Ideal conditions for a scouting party, one would think.

But the *Meraglim* put an entirely different spin on the situation. Funeral processions everywhere! Canaan was clearly "a land that devours its inhabitants." They perpetrated a malicious slander and created a wave of public reaction against entering the Holy Land. As atonement, the Jewish people had to spend forty years in the desert. This was a seminal event in Jewish history.

But what was really wrong with what they did? They only reported the facts as they saw them. After all, it was not their fault that wherever they went, they saw large funeral processions.

The Steipler Gaon explains that the *Meraglim* saw what they wanted to see. They looked at the Holy Land with a jaundiced eye, and they saw the worst. According to the Baal *Haturim*, they were subconsciously concerned that they would lose their positions of prominence once the Land was conquered. Had they been more positive in their outlook, they would have understood that their interpretation of events was wrong.

Logically, if Canaan was indeed "a land that devours its inhabitants," if death was always rampant in Canaan, people would not be attending funerals in large numbers. How would society function if everyone spent a good part of his day marching in funeral processions? Nothing would ever get done. If people were really dying in droves, people would go to very few funerals. In fact, no one but the immediate family and closest friends would attend funerals. There would not be many large funeral processions.

Had the *Meraglim* made an honest assessment of the situation, they would have realized that such large funeral processions proved the exact opposite of what they had concluded; they showed that death was a rarity in Canaan. They proved that having so many funerals at once was a rare phenomenon that brought out the shocked crowds in great numbers. And if they had seen beyond their bias, they would have perceived the hand of Hashem clearing the land before them so they could scout undisturbed.

The Talmud relates (*Gittin* 45a) the story of Rabbi Ilish who was arrested and imprisoned. While sitting in his cell, a bird came to him and chirped something to him. It seemed to Rabbi Ilish that the bird had said, "Ilish, escape! Ilish, escape!" Rabbi Ilish, however, was not convinced. He asked his cellmate, "Did you hear what that bird said to me?" The cellmate replied, "The bird said, 'Ilish, escape! Ilish, escape!'" Convinced of the authenticity of the message, Rabbi Ilish made his escape from prison.

Rav Akiva Eiger, in the *Gilion Hashas*, wonders why Rabbi Ilish needed confirmation from his cellmate. According to the *Seder Olam*, Rabbi Ilish understood the conversation of birds. He certainly did not need the help of some jailbird to decode the message.

Rav Chaim Shmulevitz explains that Rav Ilish did indeed understand the conversation of birds, and it seemed to him that the bird was telling him to escape. But since that was what he wanted to hear, he could not trust himself. He needed the confirmation of an objective person.

A person hears what he wants to hear and sees what he wants to see. The *Meraglim* came into the Land subconsciously seeking something to criticize because of their own personal interests; they feared they would lose their political status in the Land. Therefore, they saw in the large funerals a sign that the "land devours its inhabitants" when, in fact, it proved the exact opposite.

A related theme emerges from a similarity of language between the episode of the *Meraglim* and the *parashah* of *tzitzis* at the very end of *Shelach*. When Moshe sent off the

Meraglim, he told them (13:18), "And you shall see (*ure'isem*) the land." When he gave the *mitzvah* of *tzitzis*, he said (15:39), "And you shall see (*ure'isem*) it and recall all God's commandments." What is the significance of this similarity?

The Talmud explains (*Menachos* 43b) how "seeing" the *tzitzis* leads us to recall the commandments. The key is the blue *techeiles* thread, which is reminiscent of the sea. The blue sea recalls the blue sky. The sky recalls the Throne of Glory, and the thought of the Throne of Glory reminds us to perform the *mitzvos*.

The *tzitzis* show us that a person can "see" far beyond the surface if he makes the proper effort. Moshe sent the *Meraglim* to "see" the land, and indeed, there was much to see. But they could not get beyond the surface. They saw giants and funerals, but they never really penetrated to its holiness. They never did "see" the land.

Parashas Korach
פרשת קרח

Do It for the Children

וַיִּקָּהֲלוּ עַל מֹשֶׁה וְעַל אַהֲרֹן וַיֹּאמְרוּ אֲלֵהֶם רַב לָכֶם

*And they beleaguered Moshe and Aharon,
and they said to them, "You have enough!" (16:3)*

ORACH WAS CONSIDERED ONE OF THE *GEDOLEI HADOR*,
the greatest people of his generation, but when he
chose to quarrel with Moshe, he met his ignominious
downfall. Furthermore, he brought down his entire family,
even the little children.

The Chafetz Chaim, in his *Shaar Hazechirah*, a work that
identifies the most pernicious sins, spends several chapters
discussing the sin of *machlokes*, dissension. This sin, writes
the Chafetz Chaim, is one of the most destructive, both in the
havoc it wreaks in people's lives and in the spiritual damage it
causes to the soul.

Furthermore, points out the Chafetz Chaim, *machlokes* is
particularly harmful to children. As the Midrash notes, the
courts punish a person when he or she reaches legal adult-
hood. The Heavenly Court punishes when a person is past
his adolescence, at least 20 years old. But in the Korach
rebellion, even infants were swallowed up by the earth.

A number of sins are associated with *machlokes* — slander, jealousy, hatred, causing public humiliation— but the

core evil of *machlokes* is the obsessive need to be victorious. The quarrel may begin over some genuine issue, but before long, it flares out of control and takes on a life of its own. The original issue is no longer so important. Winning is important.

Brothers may get into an argument over a few thousand dollars of inheritance. The quarrel begins with the money, which is moderately significant. But once it gets started it leads into all sorts of other directions. The brothers stop going to each other's *simchos*. They stop talking to each other. They burn with hatred and resentment. And all over what? Five thousand dollars? No, it is much more than that. It is a personality conflict. It is an ego thing. "I will not let him win out over me. I will show him who is right. It's not the money, it's the principle of the matter." Oho! Once you hear about "the principle of the matter" you know things have gone from bad to horrendous.

Look how insane is this thing called *machlokes*, comments the Chafetz Chaim. Ask any parent if he would allow someone else to harm his child. Of course not. Ask any parent if he himself would harm his child. Preposterous! But it is proven that *machlokes* harms the children. So how can people play this dangerous game? And yet they do. Their need for vindication, for validation, for victory is so great that they are blinded to the dangers. It is incredible.

Two people in the Chafetz Chaim's town became embroiled in a *machlokes*. As one would expect, the situation deteriorated as time went on, becoming uglier and messier. Then the children of the two antagonists mysteriously began to die.

The Chafetz Chaim decided that enough was enough. He went to one of the parties and said, " Don't you think it's time to stop? This is killing your children! Think about the children!"

An evil gleam appeared in the man's eyes. He leaned forward and said, "*Rebbe*, I will bury all of them, but I am going to win."

As a famous American sports figure once said, "Winning isn't everything. It's the only thing." This is not the Torah way. It is pagan.

The story of Korach teaches us how far we can descend once we embark on the road to *machlokes*. We must avoid taking even the first step.

The Mishneh states (*Avos* 5:17) that any argument *lesheim Shamayim*, for the sake of Heaven, will have lasting results, and any argument not for the sake of Heaven but for self-interests will not have lasting results. The Mishneh goes on to give examples for the two types of dispute. An argument for the sake of Heaven is like that of "the schools of Hillel and Shammai," who were always disagreeing with each other. An argument not for the sake of Heaven is like that of "Korach and his followers."

Many commentators are puzzled by the phrase "Korach and his followers." The Mishneh mentions only one side of the dispute. Shouldn't the Mishneh have said "the argument of Korach and Moshe," just as the Mishneh mentions "the schools of Hillel and Shammai," who represent both sides of the dispute?

Rav Shimon Schwab explains that in an argument for the sake of Heaven both parties are interested in hearing the opinion of the other. Their goal is to arrive at the truth, and in order to do so, they have to hear both sides of the argument. Afterward, they will decide what they believe, and if it differs from the other school, there will be a dispute.

But in an argument that is not for the sake of Heaven, such as that of Korach and his followers, there was no interest in discovering the truth. There was only a grab for prestige and power. Why would they want to hear what the other side had to say? They turned a deaf ear to all the arguments against their position. Therefore, their dispute did not really have two sides. There was only one—Korach and his followers.

The Talmud tells us (*Berachos* 58a), "Just as people's faces are not exactly alike, so are their opinions not exactly alike." Rav Shlomo Eiger discerns an important lesson in this comment. No one is bothered by the differences in appearance among people. No one needs that all people should be identical to him. By the same token, no one should feel that everyone must share his opinions exactly.

If we would be more tolerant, if we would accept that others have different views and opinions, and that this is as it should be, we would go a long way toward avoiding *machlokes*.

Parashas Chukas
פרשת חקת

The Limits of the Mind

זֹאת חֻקַּת הַתּוֹרָה . . . וְיִקְחוּ אֵלֶיךָ פָרָה אֲדֻמָּה

This is the decree of the Torah . . .
let them take for you a red heifer. (19:2)

WHEN THE TORAH DOES NOT PROVIDE THE RATIONALE for a *mitzvah*, it is considered a *chok*, a decree. This does not mean that it is impossible to discover the rationale; sages who reach the highest levels of wisdom can fathom the *chok* as well. It means that the performance is completely independent of an appreciation for its rationale.

The ultimate *chok* is the *mitzvah* of *parah adumah*, the red heifer. It is a true paradox. The ashes of the *parah adumah* were used to purify those who had become *tamei* through contact with the dead. However, anyone involved with the preparation of the *parah adumah* became *tamei*. In essence, therefore, the *parah adumah* purified the impure and contaminated the pure. A paradox!

The Midrash relates that King Solomon, the wisest of all men, was able to penetrate to the heart of every *chok*, but he could not solve the paradox of the *parah adumah*.

Chastened, he wrote (*Koheles* 7:23), "All this I tried to understand with my wisdom; I said I will comprehend it, but it is still distant from me." The Midrash goes on to say that Hashem explained the paradox of *parah adumah* to Moshe, but it would remain a mystery to all other human beings until the Messianic Era.

Why did Hashem want the paradox of the *parah adumah* to remain a mystery to everyone but Moshe, even from King Solomon to whom He revealed all wisdoms?

The *Be'er Yosef* offers a powerful insight. Hashem withheld the understanding of *parah adumah* in order to teach us that some things in life are inexplicable. We cannot go through life expecting to understand everything we encounter. Our minds are too small, too limited. People, especially intelligent people, have a tendency to rely too heavily on their intellect. They begin to think that if they cannot explain something it must be wrong, and that is where the trouble begins.

There are many things in life that we will not understand in this lifetime. For instance, the old question of why the good suffer and the evil prosper is one of the most baffling paradoxes. Logic would dictate just the reverse: A person is righteous, he is a noble Jew. Why should he suffer? Another person is wicked, he does everything that is forbidden, and he is wealthy and prospers and has honor. Does this make sense?

But this is the way Hashem made His world, and we have to accept it. In order to help us accept this and the other paradoxes and enigmas of life, Hashem gave us the *mitzvah* of *parah adumah*, which even King Solomon couldn't understand. Clearly, not everything can be understood.

You may wonder: How can an obscure *mitzvah* such as *parah adumah* bear a message that is so central to life? During the times of the *Beis Hamikdash*, however, the *mitzvah* of *parah adumah* was not at all obscure. In fact, it was as familiar and commonplace as the laws of *aveilus*, mourning, are to us today. In the normal course of events, most people will go through periods of mourning at least once or twice during their lifetimes. The older die before the younger.

Even the Jews who do not go to *shul* on Yom Kippur are familiar with the Jewish laws and customs of *aveilus*. The same was true of becoming *tamei* during the times of the *Beis Hamikdash*. If someone came into contact with a dead person, he became *tamei*. From that point on, his movements in the *Beis Hamikdash* were restricted. He could not eat from the *korbanos*. He could not eat *maaser*, or *terumah* if he was a *Kohein*. The only way to return to normal was through the ritual of *parah adumah*. Therefore, everyone was aware of it. It was a part of life, and its implicit lessons could be applied to other aspects of life.

The Talmud quotes (*Pesachim* 50a) the words of the prophet (*Zechariah* 14:9), "On that day, God will be One and His Name will be One." In this world, God's Name is not One? wonders the Talmud. The Talmud answers that in this world we say the blessing *Dayan Ha'emes*, the Judge of Truth, when we hear bad news and the blessing Hatov Vehameitiv, the Good and Beneficent, when we hear good news. But in messianic times, "on that day," we will say *Hatov Vehameitiv* for everything, because we will perceive that everything is good. All paradoxes will be resolved.

Then we will also be able to understand the reason for the laws of *parah adumah*. We will no longer need the lesson of the mysterious *parah adumah*, because we will no longer be faced with insoluble paradoxes.

The *Shibbolei Haleket*, quoted by the *Magen Avraham* (*Orach Chaim* 580), mentions that the public burning of twenty-four wagonloads of *Sifrei Torah, Neviim, Midrashim* and *Gemaras* in Paris in the year 5004 (1244 c.e.) took place on Erev Shabbos of *Parashas Chukas*. Consequently, some people follow the custom of fasting every Erev Shabbos of *Parashas Chukas* as a memorial to that terrible tragedy.

What, asks the *Shibbolei Haleket*, is the reason for this unusual custom? All other fasts are pegged to the calendar date. This fast should be observed on the day of the month of Tammuz on which this tragedy took place. Why is it observed on a particular day of the week?

The answer, writes the *Shibbolei Haleket*, is that they were told in a dream to do it this way so that the fast would always be connected to *Parashas Chukas*.

The infamous Paris burning was another of the insoluble paradoxes. How could such a thing be allowed to happen? But when the memory is connected to *Parashas Chukas*, to the lesson of the *parah adumah*, we gain some perspective. We are reminded that much is beyond our understanding.

News of Aharon's Death

וַיִּשְׁמַע הַכְּנַעֲנִי מֶלֶךְ עֲרָד . . . וַיִּלָּחֶם בְּיִשְׂרָאֵל

And the Canaanite king heard . . .
and he waged war with Israel. (21:1)

WHEN THE CANAANITE KING HEARD THE NEWS, HE decided that the time was auspicious for an attack on the Jewish people. What news did he hear? The Talmud tells us (*Rosh Hashanah* 3a) that he heard about the death of Aharon and the subsequent departure of the Clouds of Glory.

Why did Aharon's death cause the Clouds of Glory to depart? Why did his death leave the Jewish people vulnerable to attack?

The *Ateres Mordechai* explains that Aharon was the glue that held the Jewish people together. The Mishneh states (*Avos* 1:12) that Aharon "loved peace and pursued it, loved people and brought them near to the Torah." He reached out to people with a boundless, embracing love, and they could not help but respond.

Whenever Aharon saw a Jew doing something wrong, he did not respond with anger. He did not throw stones. He did not berate and criticize the transgressor. He greeted him with a smile, with an expansive "Good morning." He asked how he was and beamed with genuine pleasure when the news was good. When they parted, the transgressor felt warmed by Aharon's love. He felt good. And the next time he had the opportunity to sin, he held back. "How can I do such a thing?" he asked himself. "Aharon, who was so warm and loving to me, would be upset if I did such a thing. Perhaps I shouldn't do it." In this way, Aharon drew people to the Torah and inspired them to do *teshuvah*.

Mr. Harry Wolpert, a long-time supporter of Torah causes in Baltimore, had once been a student of Rabbi Baruch Ber Leibovitz, the *Rosh Yeshivah* of Kaminetz. When Mr. Wolpert came to Baltimore in the early 1900's he faced the test of Sabbath observance time and again. Today, we don't have such problems, *baruch Hashem*. Rare is the job or profession that presents an impediment to Sabbath observance today. But in those days, it was different. It was very common for an employer to say, "If you don't come in to work on Saturday, don't bother coming in Monday either." What kept Mr. Wolpert from succumbing was the memory of Reb Baruch Ber's tremendous love for each and every one of his students. Not his Torah. Not his *Mussar*. Just his love.

The *Avos d'Rabbi Nassan* observes that when Aharon died, "the entire House of Israel mourned" — both men and women. But when Moshe died, "the sons of Israel" — the men only — mourned.

Moshe loved the Jewish people with all his heart, but his

role was teacher and judge. He had to show the people the way, to correct their errors, to issue uncompromising judgments. The people respected, admired, revered and loved him, but there was a certain inevitable distance in the relationship. But Aharon was all love, and the people responded with unreserved love of their own.

Aharon pursued peace. He was the epitome of peace and acceptance. When Moshe came to Egypt as the messenger of Hashem, Aharon did not have the slightest fleeting touch of jealousy. His joy was genuine. He was at peace with the situation, with his brother, with everyone else in the world.

He also did everything in his power to spread peace among other people. When he knew of two people that were quarreling, he would approach one and say, "I know that the other fellow wants to make up with you, but he's just too embarrassed to come to you. If you are willing to make up with him, I'll be happy to serve as the go-between." The person undoubtedly accepted the offer of the illustrious Aharon. Then he went and told the same thing to the other fellow, and that was it. Peace!

The *Yalkut Shimoni* states that Hashem was reluctant, so to speak, to tell Aharon directly that it was time for him to die. Rav Meir Bergman, in *Shaarei Orah*, points out that nowhere do we find that Hashem was reluctant to tell Moshe that his time had come. Rav Bergman suggests that it was Aharon's merit of spreading throughout among the Jewish nation that gave him this special status.

But now, concludes the *Ateres Mordechai*, this great pursuer and paragon of peace passed away. The harmony among the Jewish people began to fray. Spats and disputes erupted here and there. People began to fight. There was suddenly *machlokes* again among the people. The Clouds of Glory departed, and the Jewish people became vulnerable to attack.

The *Ateres Mordechai* further connects this idea with the verse in *Sefer Bereishis* (12:6), "There was a quarrel between Avram's shepherds and Lot's shepherds, and the Canaanites were in the land at the time."

For what purpose does the Torah tell us that the "Canaanites were in the land at the time"? As long as there was peace between the shepherds of Avram and Lot, their unity protected them against the Canaanite foe. But as soon as the quarrels broke out, the Canaanites appeared in the land, just as they later would arrive as soon as Aharon died.

Parashas Balak
פרשת בלק

Threatening Moves

וַיָּגָר מוֹאָב מִפְּנֵי הָעָם מְאֹד כִּי רַב הוּא

*And Moav was very frightened of
the people, for they were numerous. (22:3)*

MOAV AND AMMON WERE PROTECTED NATIONS. Because of the two great women who would descend from them, Rus and Naamah respectively, the Torah forbade attacking them. But there was a difference between the two nations.

In their relations with Ammon, the Jewish people were not to strike a hostile posture or do anything that could be construed as a belligerent act. In their relations with Moav, however, they were allowed to make any threatening and belligerent moves, as long as they stopped short of outright hostilities. They could mass troops in full armor and battle-field gear at the Moabite border. They could whoop and yell and make bloodcurdling cries and brandish their swords in the air. But they could not shoot in anger. This explains why Moav was "frightened of the people."

Why does the Torah differentiate between Moav and Ammon in this regard? The Talmud explains (*Bava Kama*

38b) that the difference dates back to the circumstances of the birth of their founders. After Sodom was destroyed, Lot's daughters thought that they and their father were the only human beings left on the face of the earth. If the human race was to survive, they believed, they would have to conceive by their own father—which is what they did.

Each daughter gave birth to a son. The older one named her child Moav, "from my father," advertising the incestuous relationship. It is therefore permitted to threaten or harass the nation that emerged from this birth. The younger daughter named her child Ammon, "my nation," making no mention of the incestuous relationship with her father. She did not advertise to the world the illegitimacy of her son's birth. It is therefore forbidden to disturb the nation of Ammon with even the pretense of belligerency.

What is the connection between the birth of Moav and Ammon and their treatment at the hands of the Jewish people? The *Zohar* states that "*chutzpah* begets *chutzpah*." The older daughter was immodest and bold; she took an aggressive posture. Therefore, we are allowed to take an aggressive posture toward her descendants. The younger daughter was modest and discreet, the opposite of aggressive. Therefore, we are forbidden to be aggressive toward her descendants.

Consider these two women. Each had an incestuous relationship with her father. Each gave birth to an illegitimate son. The difference is that one felt shame, while the other did not. And this difference had ramifications for entire nations hundreds of years later.

One of the most profound changes on the contemporary cultural scene in America in the last forty years is the end of shame. People have always had failures and shortcomings, but they were not proud of them. They did not advertise them. They did whatever they did, and they concealed it and lied about it. Today, it is popular to be up front, to be open and honest about one's foibles, to come out of the closet and do your own thing. Shame is a thing of the past.

Which is better? Modest and dishonest or honest and immodest?

The Torah gave us the answer by rewarding the modesty and dishonesty of Lot's younger daughter.

The Stunning Miracle

וַיִּפְתַּח ד' אֶת פִּי הָאָתוֹן וַתֹּאמֶר לְבִלְעָם מֶה
עָשִׂיתִי לָךְ

And God opened the donkey's mouth, and she said to Bilam, "What have I done to you?" (22:28)

BILAM WAS NOT AN ORDINARY PERSON. HE WAS A famous wizard, a man who wielded extraordinary power with his tongue. Those he blessed were blessed, and those he cursed were cursed. He did not command armies and navies, but he was more powerful than generals and admirals. His one word could lay waste an entire country.

Balak, king of Moav, summons this famous and powerful wizard to employ his power against the Jewish people. Bilam is fully aware that Hashem does not approve, but he goes nonetheless. Along the way, his donkey stops and refuses to take another step. Bilam strikes the donkey, and suddenly, miraculously, the donkey opens its mouth and speaks.

Never in the history of the world has such a thing happened. A talking donkey? A donkey holding a conversation with a man? Impossible. And yet, there it was, happening right in front of him. Did this stunning miracle give pause to Bilam? Did it make him rethink his travel plans?

Imagine yourself driving on the highway, and suddenly, your car stops. You pump the gas pedal again and again, and the car says to you, "Enough already! Can't you see that I don't want to go there?" What would you do? Would you keep trying to get the car started? Or would you sit back and reconsider your trip? There is little doubt that all of us would be shaken to our very roots in such a situation. But Bilam, the wise and extraordinary Bilam, the famous wizard Bilam, was nonchalant about it.

Sforno compares the amazing miracle of Hashem's allowing the donkey to speak to the verse (*Tehillim* 51:17), "O God, open my lips and let my mouth speak Your praises." In other words, human speech is also a miracle. The ability to communicate, to express, to articulate is no less a miracle than a donkey speaking. This should have been clear to Bilam.

Bilam should have said to himself, "My strength is my speech. Who gave me that power? Hashem. And the same God Who can give me the power of speech just gave the power of speech to a donkey! Just as a talking donkey is a miracle, a human being talking is also a miracle. This must be a Divine message to me, a sign that I should not use my power of speech in a manner that Hashem does not approve. I should turn back and abandon this evil journey."

Yet for some reason, all of this went right by Bilam. He never stopped to consider the significance of what he had just seen and the ramifications of what he intended to do. For all his skill and wisdom, he missed the clearest of all messages. He was stricken with a strange myopia.

What lesson does this hold for us? It is that if it can happen to Bilam it can happen to every one of us! If Bilam can be blinded, we can also be blinded. When a person is driven by some personal motive, whether it is money or power or whatever else, he becomes blinded to reality. He only sees what he wants to see. He sees those things that will advance his purpose and is impervious to all else.

There are none so blind as those who will not see.

Parashas Pinchas
פרשת פנחס

The Covenant of Peace

פִּינְחָס בֶּן אֶלְעָזָר בֶּן אַהֲרֹן הַכֹּהֵן הֵשִׁיב אֶת חֲמָתִי מֵעַל
בְּנֵי יִשְׂרָאֵל ... לָכֵן אֱמֹר הִנְנִי נֹתֵן לוֹ אֶת בְּרִיתִי שָׁלוֹם

Pinchas the son of Elazar the son of Aharon the Kohein deflected My wrath from the people of Israel . . . therefore say, "I am giving him My covenant of peace." (25:11-12)

PINCHAS STEPPED INTO THE BREACH WHEN NO ONE ELSE knew what to do. A prince of one of the tribes had brazenly had relations with a Midianite woman in full view of the public, and a plague broke out among the Jewish people. It was an act so utterly sordid and so utterly stunning that no one knew how to react. No one remembered what the Torah demanded in such a situation.

According to the Talmud (*Sanhedrin* 82a), when Pinchas saw what was happening he was reminded of the ruling that "the zealous can take the law into their own hands and strike down a man who has relations with a gentile woman." With Moshe's blessing, he killed both the man and the woman with one blow, and the plague came to an end. For his valiant deed, Hashem rewarded Pinchas with His "covenant of peace" and the eternal priesthood.

Why does the Torah mention that Pinchas was descended from Aharon in this context?

The Midrash, quoted by Rashi, tells us that the public reaction to Pinchas' act was not so positive. People remembered that Pinchas was descended from Aharon on one side but from Yisro on another, and they saw in his violent deed signs of his bloodline from Yisro. "Look at this child of idolaters," they said. "Where does he get the audacity to cut down a Jewish prince?" Therefore, the Torah traces his genealogy to Aharon to show the correctness of his deed.

The question remains, however. No one had denied or forgotten that Pinchas was a grandson of Aharon. They had accused Pinchas of acting as his idolatrous maternal grandfather Yisro would have acted, not as his paternal grandfather Aharon, that consummate lover of peace, would have acted. They claimed to have discerned in Pinchas the dominance of his pagan bloodlines. How did Hashem's declaration that Pinchas was Aharon's descendant exonerate and vindicate him?

Rav Meir Bergman, in his *Shaarei Orah*, explains that when Hashem declared in this situation that Pinchas was Aharon's descendant, He was saying clearly that this is the bloodline that led him to perform his act of zealotry. Aharon himself would have come roaring into the camp with his spear extended and impaled the two miscreants with one thrust.

But how can such a thing be? How could a lover of peace such as Aharon commit such a violent act?

The Chasam Sofer takes note of the language of the Mishneh (*Avos* 1:12) that describes Aharon as "a lover of peace and a pursuer of peace." What is the significance of this dual description? It reflects two aspects of Aharon's personality. On the one hand, he was a lover of peace, a man who spread harmony and peace among people.

But sometimes he had to be a pursuer of peace, a man who drove peace away when that was the right thing to do. True peace (*shalom*) is the manifestation of a state of perfection (*shalem*). Compromise with the imperfect does not lead to true peace. In that case, when faced with the vile, the despicable, the quest for true peace demanded that Aharon shun a seemingly peaceful accommodation with the forces of evil. It demanded that he drive away such a peace, that he pursue it out of the Jewish camp. Only then would it be possible to arrive at a state of true peace, a state of peace between the Jewish people and their Father in Heaven.

The Brisker Rav, in the name of his father Rav Chaim Soloveitchik, makes a similar point from a slightly different perspective. Why did Hashem reward Pinchas with "My covenant of peace"? Pinchas had just committed a violent, albeit very commendable, act of zealous defense of the Divine honor. Therefore, he should have been rewarded with Hashem's "covenant of zealotry." Why His "covenant of peace"?

Imagine a brave soldier returning from the battlefield after heroically turning the tide of battle against the enemy. Would we award him the Congressional Medal of Honor or the Nobel Peace Prize? Was Pinchas, *lehavdil*, a candidate for the Peace Prize?

The answer is that Pinchas restored true peace between the Jewish people and Hashem. If that required a violent act, then so be it. The lover of peace would have to commit a violent act in order to achieve the higher goal of true peace. Sometimes, the road to true peace is not very peaceful.

We often hear criticism of great rabbis who take doctrinaire stands on various issues. "Why do they have to make *machlokes*?" people complain. "Why do they have to start up? Why can't they leave well enough alone? Is this peace? It's *machlokes*! It's divisiveness!"

We're familiar with these complaints. We've heard them since the people mocked Pinchas in the desert. Hashem answered these complaints by telling us that Pinchas' way was the way of peace. His actions were worthy of the covenant of peace. Today as well, those rabbis who stand up for the truth, for the integrity of the Torah, are the ones who spread true peace among the Jewish people.

Just Like at Mount Sinai

עֹלַת תָּמִיד הָעֲשֻׂיָה בְּהַר סִינַי לְרֵיחַ נִיחֹחַ אִשֶּׁה לַד'

*A regular olah offering such as was made at Mount Sinai,
for a pleasant aroma, a fire offering before God. (28:6)*

EVERY DAY OF THE YEAR, EVEN ON SHABBOS AND YOM
Kippur, there is a *mitzvah* to bring the *korban tamid*,
the regular daily sacrifice, one in the morning and
the second in the afternoon. The Torah describes the laws
that apply to the *korban tamid* and then adds the curious
remark that it should be like the one "made at Mount Sinai."

What additional information about the *korban tamid* are we
meant to glean by examining the *korban tamid* brought during
the dedication of the *Mishkan* at Mount Sinai? The *Sifrei* and the
Talmud (*Chagigah* 6b) discuss this question, and the Sages offer
various opinions regarding the derivation of specific particulars.

Rav Yosef Salant points out that the Sages are addressing
only the *halachic* derivations. There is also a very important
philosophical point that we derive ourselves.

Think back to the first time you put on *tefillin*. It took you
a long time. You pulled the *tefillin* from the velvet bag and
unwrapped the straps. You made the blessings slowly and
carefully, savoring each word. Then you wound them slowly
around your arm, lingering lovingly over every turn. But for
most people, things change with time. Eventually, they can
come running into the *shul* late, put their *tefillin* on in a flash,
and before you know it, they're almost caught up to the people who came on time.

When something is done day in day out, as wonderful as it
may be, it eventually becomes done by rote. It becomes stale.
It becomes automatic, without thought. The thrill is gone.

This is the pitfall of the *korban tamid,* the sacrifice brought every day, day in and day out, morning and evening, as long as the *Mishkan* and the *Beis Hamikdash* were standing. After a while, there is a risk that the novelty will wear off, that the enthusiasm will disappear, that the excitement will fade, that it will be brought mechanically, without feeling or inspiration.

Therefore, the Torah reminds us, "Bring the daily sacrifice as you made the one at Mount Sinai, when everything was still new, when your heart beat faster and you caught your breath with excitement. This is what you should do every day. Reach for that inspiration. It can be done."

Parashas Mattos-Masei
פרשת מטות-מסעי

Listen to the Mussar

וַיֹּאמֶר מֹשֶׁה לִבְנֵי גָד וְלִבְנֵי רְאוּבֵן הַאַחֵיכֶם יָבֹאוּ
לַמִּלְחָמָה וְאַתֶּם תֵּשְׁבוּ פֹה

*And Moshe said to the people of Gad
and Reuven, "Your brothers will go to war
and you will remain here?" (32:6)*

HE FIRST GERRER REBBE WAS THE CHIDDUSHEI HARIM. The second Gerrer Rebbe, the Sfas Emes, was not his son but his grandson. The Sfas Emes' father passed away when he was a child, and his grandfather raised him. He was an *illui*, a prodigy, the apple of his grandfather's eye.

One night, when he was still a young boy, the Sfas Emes learned with his *chavrusa* straight through the night. He nodded off right before Shacharis, resting his head on the Gemara. After a few minutes, he awoke with a start. He washed his hands and hurried to the *shul*, but he was already a little late.

After Shacharis, the Chiddushei Harim called him over.

"What's this with coming late to Shacharis?" he said in a sharp tone. "It's bad enough for yourself, but think how it will affect others. If the grandson of the *rebbe* can come late, what kind of example is that for other boys? Or even men! It's a *chillul Hashem*, no less!"

The Chiddushei Harim went on in this vein for another few minutes, but the Sfas Emes did not say one word in his own defense. He could have argued that it had been an accident, that he had stayed up all night learning Torah and that sleep had overcome him at the end for just a few minutes. But he remained silent.

A little while later, the *chavrusa* of the Sfas Emes asked him, "Why didn't you say anything to defend yourself? You were innocent! Why were you silent?"

"When a great man gives you *Mussar*," said the Sfas Emes, "it is worthwhile to listen, even if you don't deserve it, even if you are completely innocent. I wanted to hear my grandfather's *Mussar*. I have a proof to this from the Torah. Moshe Rabbeinu gave the tribes of Gad and Reuven a strong tongue-lashing. He accused them of cowardice. He told them they were demoralizing the people just like the *Meraglim* did. He went on and on for nine verses, and they remained silent. They never mentioned that they had intended all along to participate in the conquest. Why? Because it is always worthwhile to hear the *Mussar* of a great man."

Money and the Kids

וַיֹּאמְרוּ גִּדְרֹת צֹאן נִבְנֶה לְמִקְנֵנוּ פֹּה וְעָרִים לְטַפֵּנוּ

And they said, "We will build sheep pens for our livestock here and cities for our children." (32:16)

THE JEWISH PEOPLE REACHED THE PLAINS OF MOAV, the jumping-off point for the invasion of Canaan, which was imminent. But the tribes of Gad and Reuven, rich in livestock, preferred the lush pasturelands of the Trans-Jordan to shares in Eretz Yisrael proper. They asked Moshe for permission to take their share in the Trans-Jordan.

Moshe berated them for letting the others fight to conquer Canaan while they settled down in their ranches. Furthermore, their reluctance to cross would have a demoralizing effect on the others, just as the report of the *Meraglim* had demoralized the people thirty-eight years earlier.

"This is what we want to do," they said to Moshe. "We want to build sheep pens for our livestock here and towns for our children. Then we will go quickly at the head of the army and fight until the land is conquered and apportioned. Only then will we return to our homes."

"All right," said Moshe (32:24), "build towns for your children and pens for your sheep. And make sure you keep your word."

Notice that Moshe reversed the order of their priorities. They wanted to "build sheep pens for our livestock here and towns for our children." First let us take care of the livestock. Let us make sure we have pens in which to keep them so they don't wander off into the hills and get lost or stolen. Cows and sheep are valuable assets, and we have to take good care of them. Then they spoke about building "towns for our children." Then we will provide our children with a place to live while we are at war.

Oh no, Moshe replied. You have it backwards. First of all, "build towns for your children." Make sure you have attended to the needs of your children. Afterwards, you can also build "pens for your sheep." First you take care of your children, then you worry about your cattle.

The Midrash sums up the exchange with the verse (*Koheles* 10:2), "The heart of the wise man is on his right, and the heart of the fool is on his left." Moshe's heart was on the right. He had his priorities right. Their hearts were on the left. They gave precedence to secondary considerations. They were more worried about their money than their children.

When we look at this incident, we say to ourselves, "How foolish can people be? How warped can their values be? How can anyone put the welfare of his cattle before the welfare of his children?"

Unfortunately, this is not an isolated incident, something bizarre that happened thousands of years ago. It is an everyday phenomenon. People become focused on their livelihood, on developing a business, on advancing professionally, on building a practice, and their kids get lost in the shuffle. They don't realize that they are making the exact same mistake as the tribes of Gad and Reuven. But it is true. It happens all too often.

Rashi writes (32:24) that the tribes of Gad and Reuven did not return home to the Trans-Jordan until after the seven years of conquest and the seven years of apportionment. They remained in Eretz Yisrael for a full fourteen years. Those little children they left behind — let's assume they were 3 or 4 years old — how old were they when their fathers returned home? Teenagers! Practically adults. The Midrash tells us that their fathers were shocked to find that their sons had long hair, that they were indistinguishable from their pagan neighbors.

This is what happens when parents give priority to their wealth over their children.

The Ksav Sofer raises a question with the latter part of Moshe's words. After helping the tribes of Gad and Reuven get their priorities straight, he told them, "Make sure you keep your word." Why was this necessary?

The answer, says the Ksav Sofer, is that Moshe knew with whom he was dealing. People who could even think of protecting their money before they protect their children cannot be trusted. They are so intent on their wealth that they can do anything. Therefore, Moshe had to exhort them to keep their word.

Rav Tzaddok Hakohein explains that the desire for money is greater than any other material drive, since it is the only one that is insatiable. There is a limit to how much a person can eat, to how many times he can commit adultery, but there is no limit to how much money he can accumulate. The quest for wealth can become more obsessive than any other quest. All too often, the children are the price of the wealth.

Devarim

Parashas Devarim
פרשת דברים

Children are a Gift

ד' אֱלֹקֵי אֲבוֹתֵכֶם יֹסֵף עֲלֵיכֶם כָּכֶם אֶלֶף פְּעָמִים וִיבָרֵךְ
אֶתְכֶם כַּאֲשֶׁר דִּבֶּר לָכֶם

May God, the Lord of your fathers,
add a thousandfold more like you
and bless you, as He spoke to you. (1:11)

THE JEWISH PEOPLE, RASHI INFORMS US, WERE NOT very
happy with the blessing Moshe gave them. "May God,
the Lord of your fathers," he had said, "add a thousandfold more like you and bless you as He spoke to you."

"Only that and no more?" the people responded. "Is that
the full extent of your blessing? Hashem blessed us
(*Bereishis* 32:13) to be 'like the dust of the earth that is too
numerous to count.'"

"You will surely get the blessing Hashem gave you,"
Moshe replied. "This is just my own personal blessing to you."

What exactly was Moshe's reply? What additional benefit
would the Jewish people derive from his blessing of a thousandfold increase if they were already receiving Hashem's
blessing of virtually limitless increase?

The Chasam Sofer explains that Moshe was testing them. Why did they want children? Was it because children were useful, because they help carry the household burden, provide companionship and are a source of security in old age? Or is it because each child is a spark of the Divine, a priceless gift from Heaven, a piece of the World to Come?

So Moshe gave the Jewish people a test. He blessed them with a "thousandfold" increase in their population. If they had wanted children for their usefulness alone, they would have said, "Thank you, but that's enough already! A thousandfold will suit our purposes just fine. We have no use for any more right now." But that was not what they said. They wanted more children. They wanted children "too numerous to count." Obviously, they were not thinking about their own material and emotional needs, but about the transcendent blessing that each child represents, and so, they proved themselves worthy of Hashem's blessing.

Hundreds of years earlier, these two conflicting attitudes toward children had already become an issue. Yaakov and Eisav had made a division. Eisav was to take this world, and Yaakov was to take the World to Come. When Yaakov came back from Aram, Eisav welcomed him at the head of an army four hundred men strong. In the tense early minutes of the confrontation, Eisav noticed Yaakov's many children.

"Who are these children?" Eisav asked.

"These are the children," Yaakov replied, "that Hashem graciously gave to your servant."

The *Pirkei d'Rabbi Eliezer* expands the dialogue between Yaakov and Eisav and reveals the underlying argument.

"What are you doing with all these children?" Eisav asked. "I thought we made a division, that I would take this world and you would take the World to Come. So why do you have so many children? What do children have to do with the World to Come? Children are a boon in this world!"

"Not so," Yaakov responded. "Children are sparks of the Divine. The opportunity to raise a child, to develop a Divine soul to the point where it can enter the World to Come, is a privilege of the highest spiritual worth. That is why I have children."

Yaakov wants children for their own sake, but Eisav views them as an asset in this world. Children are an extra pair of hands on the farm. They can milk the cows and help with many other chores that need to be done in agrarian societies.

Modern man has progressed beyond agrarian life. He has moved off the farm and does not have such a need for children anymore. In fact, he has made a startling discovery. Children are a tremendous burden. They are expensive, time consuming and exasperating. Who needs children?

But what about companionship? Loneliness? No problem. Modern man can get a dog. Dogs are wonderful. Instead of coming home to a house full of clamoring, demanding, frustrating children, he can come home to an adoring, tail-wagging dog who will run to bring him his slippers and newspaper. So why does he need children? This is the attitude of Eisav adapted to modern times.

Yaakov, on the other hand, understands that the purpose of children is not for enjoying this world or for making our lives easier. Each child represents a spiritual mission, a spark of the Divine entrusted to our care and our guidance, an opportunity to fulfill Hashem's desire to have this soul brought to the World to Come.

Don't Flaunt It

רַב לָכֶם סֹב אֶת הָהָר הַזֶּה פְּנוּ לָכֶם צָפֹנָה

*You have enough, circle the mountain,
and turn to the north (tzafonah). (2:3)*

THE KLI YAKAR LIVED DURING A TIME WHEN THE JEWS enjoyed prosperity, and he did not approve of the way they dealt with it. He urged them to be more discreet, to keep a low profile and not draw attention to themselves with ostentatious lifestyles.

He supported his exhortation with a homiletic interpretation of Moshe's words to the Jewish people. "You have enough, circle the mountain, and turn to the north (*tzafonah*)." The word *tzafonah* can alternatively be translated as "the hidden." In other words, you have enough material things. Now hide them! If you've got it, you don't have to flaunt it!

Eisav has a long memory, writes the Kli Yakar. Whenever he sees Yaakov prosper, he believes with all his heart that it is only because of the blessings he stole, the blessing that should have gone to Eisav.

Yaakov himself was already worried about this. When famine struck all of the Middle East, everyone was forced to run to Egypt, the only place where large stockpiles of food existed. It was the only way to avoid starvation. Yaakov's pantry, however, was well stocked with food, and his family could have gone a long time without a trip to Egypt. Nonetheless, Yaakov sent them to buy food. "*Lamah tisra'u?*" he said. "Why should you show off?" According to Rashi, Yaakov was concerned about the children of Eisav and Yishmael. Why should they see that you have plenty of food while they are starving? That would be a foolish thing to do.

Living in the United States, which is so liberal, so tolerant, we tend to forget this important lesson. Regardless of how benign American society is, it is still exile. We still live among the gentiles, and we still need to watch our step. If we have been blessed with prosperity — money, real estate, nice homes, automobiles and clothing — there is no need to flaunt our wealth.

"Why do you show off?" said Yaakov. It is impolite. It is unwise. It is even dangerous.

Parashas Vaes'chanan
פרשת ואתחנן

The Easy Commandment

כַּבֵּד אֶת אָבִיךָ וְאֶת אִמֶּךָ כַּאֲשֶׁר צִוְּךָ ד' אֱלֹקֶיךָ לְמַעַן
יַאֲרִיכֻן יָמֶיךָ

Honor your father and mother,
as God your Lord has commanded you,
so that you may live long. (5:16)

WHY SHOULD WE HONOR OUR FATHERS AND mothers? The Torah gives us one reason in *Parashas Shemos* (20:12), "So that you may live long." In *Parashas Vaes'chanan*, however, the Torah gives an additional reason, "As God your Lord has commanded you." What is the significance of this additional phrase?

The *Meshech Chachmah* refers to the *Talmud Yerushalmi* that considers honoring parents an "easy commandment." Every person understands that debts have to be repaid. If someone lends you $100,000 when you need it, you would be only too happy to repay the money once you have enough of your own. It would not be a hard thing to do.

By the same token, every person also understands that he has a moral obligation to repay his debt of gratitude to his parents. After all, the cost of raising a child must be at least between $100,000 and $200,000. Not to mention the time, effort and energy parents invest in their children. Therefore, the least people can do is honor their parents. It is not a hard thing to make such a small payment on such a large debt.

The Torah tells us here that this is not the proper motivation for honoring parents. It is not a self-evident obligation to make at least a small payment on a debt owed the parents. It is an obligation incumbent on us solely because "God your Lord has commanded you" to do so.

The Torah waited until *Parashas Vaes'chanan* to make this point, because it becomes most clear after forty years in the desert. During those years, raising children was easier than it ever was, before or since. They did not have to be fed. There was *manna* from heaven. They did not need to be given to drink. There was water from Miriam's Well. They did not need new shoes and clothing all the time. Nothing ever wore out. Most likely they didn't need orthodontic braces either, because life in the desert was paradise. And still, the Torah demanded that parents be honored. Clearly, the obligation was to obey Hashem's commandment rather than repay a debt of gratitude. By the time the Jewish people had lived through the era of the desert, they could relate to the *mitzvah* of honoring parents as an independent obligation.

How far does this go? How much do you have to do for your parents? The Talmud responds (*Kiddushin* 31a) to this question with the famous story about a gentile from Ashkelon by the name of Dama bar Nesinah.

The Sages once needed a stone for the *Urim v'Tumim*, and they heard that Dama had exactly the stone they needed. A delegation came to see him and offer to pay him a princely sum for the stone. The stone was in a strongbox, with the key under his father's pillow. Dama did not disturb him.

"I cannot help you," he told the Sages. "My father is sleeping, and I wouldn't disturb his sleep."

The Sages left.

A year later, a perfect red heifer, suitable for a *parah adumah*, was born in Dama's herd. The Sages came to purchase it.

"How much do you want for it?"

"I know that you would give me any price I ask," he replied. "But I only want the amount of money I lost by not waking my father last year."

This story establishes the parameters of the *mitzvah* of honoring parents.

At first glance, the Talmud seems to be deriving *halachos*, laws, from the conduct of a gentile. But this cannot be. Rather, the Talmud uses this story to establish the parameters of human nature.

As parents get older, they can become querulous and demanding. They can test the patience of their children. Sometimes, honoring parents under such circumstances can take a lot of patience and forbearance. Is there a limit to such patience? How much patience can be expected of a person? Is there a point where a person is allowed to run out of patience and be exempt from this *mitzvah*?

This is what the story about Dama bar Nesinah teaches us. The Sages were offering him a huge sum of money for the single stone they needed for the *Urim v'Tumim*. He knew that if he could only get the key, the money would be his. What thoughts must have gone through his mind. Maybe I'll make a little noise and he'll wake up. Maybe I'll slide my hand under the pillow very slowly so that I'll be able to get the key without waking him up. He must have been very tempted. But he didn't give in. He was able to honor his father even under such circumstances. This was the extent of what human nature is capable.

It follows, therefore, that if a gentile could have the forbearance to forgo such a huge sum of money and allow his father to sleep, certainly a Jewish person, descended from Avraham, Yitzchak and Yaakov, can find it in himself to honor his parents under any and all circumstances.

Parashas Eikev
פרשת עקב

Manna From Heaven

הַמַּאֲכִלְךָ מָן בַּמִּדְבָּר . . . וּלְמַעַן נַסֹּתֶךָ

*The One Who feeds you manna in
the desert . . . in order to test you. (8:16)*

EVERYONE KNOWS THAT LIFE IS A TEST. WE STRUGGLE TO
make a living, to raise our children, to build up our communities. Nothing comes easy, and our test is to deal
with the hardships and frustrations in the best way possible.

But what if our livelihood were served up to us on a silver
platter? How wonderful that would be! No more worries
about how to pay for the children's tuition or the new roof.
What if everything we needed came to us like manna from
heaven? Would we consider this a test? Hardly. We would
consider it a blessing. The Torah, however, seems to say otherwise.

No sooner had the Jewish people come forth from Egypt
that they complained (*Shemos* 16:3), "If only we had died by
the hand of God in the land of Egypt when we were sitting
beside the fleshpots, when we ate our fill of bread; now you
have brought us out into the desert to let the entire congregation starve to death."

"Behold, I will rain down bread from the heavens on you," Hashem replied (*ibid.* 16:4). "The people shall go out to collect their daily portion every day, in order to test whether or not they will follow My Torah."

The commentators wonder what kind of test this is. What could be better than having everything you need delivered to your doorstep every day? This is a test? This is a blessing!

Rashi explains that Hashem was referring to the laws that govern the manna. One could not store away any manna for the next day. One had to collect a double portion on Friday. And so forth. This was the test. Would the Jewish people observe the laws of the manna scrupulously?

This test is also mentioned in *Parashas Eikev*, "The One Who feeds you manna in the desert . . . in order to test you." Sforno explains that the test is to see if the Jews would still follow the Torah when they do not have to worry about their livelihood.

Yes, there is a great test in "bread raining down from heaven." Affluence without effort is a dangerous thing. It comes with a great amount of leisure time and freedom of action. What do we do with that leisure time and that freedom of action? Do we use our leisure time and freedom of action to taste the forbidden? This is the great test of the manna.

We are all aware of the test of poverty. We are all aware of the trials and tribulations of being poor. However, says Sforno, affluence also comes with great temptations. It puts a tremendous responsibility on a person. This is the test of the manna, and it is the test for many Jews in these affluent times.

The *Chovos Halevavos* writes in *Shaar Habitachon* that one of the reasons people, unlike birds and animals, must make a great effort to earn their livelihood is to control the *yetzer hara*. If we had too much time on our hands, we would be unable to resist the temptations he puts before us. As it is, we are either too busy or too tired most of the time. And even then it is a struggle to resist temptation.

The Maggid of Mezritch once said that when people face troubles, sickness or mortal danger, Heaven forbid, they all become religious. They all come to *shul*. They pray fervently. They say *Tehillim* with tears streaming down their cheeks. They give charity generously. But when things are going well, when they are going wonderfully, do they give much thought to the Almighty? This is the test of the manna.

The Silent Witness

וּכְתַבְתָּם עַל מְזוּזוֹת בֵּיתֶךָ וּבִשְׁעָרֶיךָ

*And you shall write them on the doorposts
of your homes and your gates. (11:20)*

THE *MEZUZAH* STANDS LIKE A SENTINEL AT THE DOOR; we pass it whenever we enter or leave the room. What are we to think as we look upon the *mezuzah*? What are we to contemplate when we see the letter *shin* on the case and are reminded of the holy scrolls within?

The Rambam, at the end of his presentation of the laws of *mezuzah*, tells us to think about the eternal nature of the Almighty. This will inspire us to awaken from our slumber and come to the realization that nothing in this world is permanent other than the Almighty, His Torah.

Why does the *mezuzah* remind us of these concepts?

Perhaps it is because the *mezuzah* is a silent witness to the ebb and flow of history and human events. Think about the *mezuzah* of an old *shul* or some other venerable edifice. It has been hanging there for decades if not centuries. It has seen infants brought into the *shul* to be circumcised, and it has seen these same people grown old brought into the *shul* to be eulogized and buried. It has seen generations come and go. It has seen empires rise and fall. It has seen the birth of ideologies and their demise.

In the last century alone, our hypothetical *mezuzah* would have seen humanism, capitalism, materialism, existentialism, each embraced as life philosophies and then discredited. It would have seen the rise of the Soviet Union and Communism and their ignominious collapse. It would have seen the creation of the Third Reich, the Thousand-Year Reich, its perpetration of the Holocaust against the Jewish people and its ultimate defeat and destruction. It would have seen the birth of Israel and it growth to maturity.

When the railroads were introduced in the 19th century, people thought the new technology was so perfect that it would never change. The railroad companies sold corporate bonds for centuries in advance. And where are they all today? On the scrap heap, along with their rusting trains.

Human beings are always seeking immortality. This invention, this idea, this building, this book, this one will capture that elusive immortality, this one will stand the test of time, this is one for the ages, this one will make me immortal. But it doesn't work.

The Torah tells us (*Bamidbar* 32:42), "And Novach went and captured Kenas and its suburbs, and he named it (*lah*) Novach in his name." According to the rules of Hebrew grammar, the word *lah* should end with a *mappik heh*, a mark of emphasis, but it doesn't. It ends with a weak *heh*. The Midrash tells us that the weak *heh* lets us know that the city did not last. It was eventually destroyed.

Why does the Torah consider it important to let us know this information? It is meant to teach us the futility of immortalization. Novach wanted to immortalize himself by creating something permanent — an entire city, no less! — and crowning it with his own name. But he failed. The city was destroyed, and his name would be forgotten if it were not mentioned in the Torah.

Everything constantly changes. Nothing is permanent. Only the Almighty and His Torah. The *mezuzah* can bear witness.

Parashas Re'eh
פרשת ראה

Seeing Is Believing

רְאֵה אָנֹכִי נֹתֵן לִפְנֵיכֶם הַיּוֹם בְּרָכָה וּקְלָלָה

See, I am setting before you, on this day, blessings and curses. (11:26)

QUIRKS IN THE GRAMMAR OF THE TORAH'S VERSES hold many lessons for us. Hashem tells the Jewish people, "See (*re'eh*), I am setting before you (*lifneichem*), on this day, blessings and curses." The word *re'eh* is the singular form of the verb, but the preposition *lifneichem* is plural. Why the discrepancy?

Furthermore, why was it necessary to preface the gift with the word "see"? If you give someone a present, is it necessary to tell him, "Look, I am giving you a present"? Is it necessary to point out the obvious?

The answer is that blessings are not always so obvious. If we don't make an effort to "see" them, to perceive them, we may not even be aware that we have been blessed. If we think about it, life is full of blessings. In fact, life itself is the greatest blessing. But we take all these thing for granted and do not realize how blessed we are. Therefore, Hashem reminds us to "see" the blessing He has given us.

The Kotzker Rebbe points out that blessings can be given collectively to many people, but each individual will perceive it in his own way, depending on his own particular personality and outlook. Blessings can be universal, but the perception of them is always individual. Therefore, when Hashem tells us to "see" He uses the singular form, but the placement of the blessing is expressed in the plural.

The Talmud tells us (*Taanis* 30b), "Whoever mourns the destruction of Yerushalayim will eventually merit to see its joy." Rav Avraham Yitzchak Hakohein Kook asks a simple question. If we are talking about someone who mourns the "destruction of Yerushalayim," then his reward should be to see it rebuilt. Why do the Sages speak about its "joy"?

Rav Kook explains that even when Yerushalayim will be rebuilt not everyone will "see" the profound depths of its joy; that will take a special blessing. The Sages are telling us that if one truly mourns the destruction of Yerushalayim, not only will he see the physical rebuilding of it, he will also be deemed worthy of seeing "joy."

A Spoon and a Handle

כִּי פָתֹחַ תִּפְתַּח אֶת יָדְךָ לוֹ

For you shall surely open your hand to him. (15:8)

IRST, THE TORAH TELLS US (15:7), "IF THERE BE A PAUPER among you, one of your brethren, in one of your gateways in your land that God your Lord has given you, do not harden your heart nor close your hand tight against your impoverished brother." This is clearly telling us to give charity to the poor person. Then the Torah goes on, "For you shall surely open your hand to him and provide him with the necessities he is missing." This seems to call for a higher level of charity not covered by the first commandment.

There was once a Jew in Vilna who took a great interest in local history. In the course of his research, he would often go out to the old cemetery and read the inscriptions on the tombstones. He was able to gather a surprising amount of information in this fashion.

One day, he came across two adjacent graves. According to the inscriptions, the two men were brothers, both *talmidei chachamim*, both extraordinary *baalei tzedakah*, philanthropists. Strangely, the two tombstones shared an inscription from *Eishes Chayil*, the last chapter of *Mishlei* (31:20). The inscription began on one tombstone with "she extended her palm (*kappah*) to the poor" and was completed on the other with "and she stretched out her hand (*yadeha*) to the pauper."

The man was puzzled. First of all, he had never seen an inscription shared by two tombstones. Second, inscriptions from *Eishes Chayil* were used almost exclusively for women.

There was obviously a story behind all this, and by all appearances, an interesting story. The man sought out one of the oldest men in the Vilna community and asked him about the inscription. The old man indeed had a story to tell.

These two brothers were Torah scholars of the highest order, and they were also wealthy and extremely generous in their charities. They were much respected and admired in the community.

Suddenly, their fortunes took a turn for the worse. Some of their businesses failed. Their investments stagnated. People began to wonder and whisper. Why would such a thing happen to such sterling people?

The Rabbinical Court of Vilna also heard the stories and took the matter under advisement. "How can this be," declared one of the judges, "that two such exemplary *talmidei chachamim* should be going bankrupt? It is a *chillul Hashem*! We have to do something about it."

"But what can we do about it?" asked another judge. "Should we give them a loan?"

"No, of course not," said the first judge. "We have to get to the bottom of this and correct it."

"But how?" said the second judge.

"There is a simple way," offered a third judge. "We have to summon the brothers to court and interrogate them about everything they've done for the past few years. I have no doubt they will answer our questions truthfully."

The Rabbinical Court questioned the brothers for hours and discovered only one instance of wrongdoing. The Halachah demands (*Kesubos* 50a) that a person should not give away more than a fifth of his wealth to charity, but the brothers often exceeded this limit. Their only crime was that they gave too much charity!

What was to be done about this? The Rabbinical Court decided that the brothers could not be trusted to stay within the prescribed limits. Therefore, they themselves took control of the finances and decreed that anyone approaching the brothers for charitable donations should come to the Rabbinical Court's appointed administrator of the brothers' accounts.

The poor appeared on the doorstep of the brothers, and they duly directed them to the court-appointed administrator of their accounts.

"We've been to him already," they protested, "and he is not nearly as generous as you've always been. We'll never feed our children on what the administrator gives us."

The brothers' hearts melted, but what could they do? They didn't have control of their money. So they began to give away the silver in their cabinets to the poor. Eventually, this trove was also depleted, and they were left with one silver spoon between them.

The next day, when a beggar approached each of the brothers, they broke the last spoon in half. One took the spoon part and gave it to a beggar, and the other took the handle and gave it to a beggar.

This wonderful act of charity was memorialized on their tombstones, relying on a wordplay. The beginning of the verse, "She extended her palm (*kappah*) to the poor" — *kappah* also meaning "her spoon" — appeared on the first tombstone. The completion of the verse, "And she stretched out her hand (*yadeha*) to the pauper" — *yadeha* also meaning "her handle" — appeared on the other.

This is an example of "opening the hand" of the highest order.

Parashas Shoftim
פרשת שופטים

The Judge in Your Times

וּבָאתָ אֶל . . . הַשֹּׁפֵט אֲשֶׁר יִהְיֶה בַּיָּמִים הָהֵם

*And you shall come to . . . the judge
that shall be in those days. (17:9)*

IF YOU HAVE TO GO TO COURT, IT SHOULD BE FAIRLY OBVIOUS that your case will be tried by a judge from your own times. Much as you would prefer to have a distinguished jurist from an earlier time adjudicate your case, it just won't happen. Why then does the Torah have to speak about going to "the judge that shall be in those days"?

Rashi explains that the Torah is telling us to accept the judges of our times even if they don't measure up to the judges of earlier times. These are our judges. These are the ones who are entrusted with the authority to rule on questions of Halachah in this generation. These are the judges we must respect and obey.

There are people alive today who saw the Chafetz Chaim, who saw Rav Chaim Ozer Grodzinski, who saw the Brisker Rav and the Chazon Ish. No one would argue that our *gedolim* today measure up to those giants of the past. Nonetheless, we must accept the authority and leadership of our own *gedolim*, because they are all we have.

Earlier generations undoubtedly struggled with similar perceptions, comparing their *gedolim*, such as Rav Chaim Ozer, with even greater *gedolim* of yet earlier times, such as Rav Akiva Eiger. There is no end. The Torah is speaking to each generation. Look up to the judges in your times; do not measure them against the judges of earlier times.

Rav Avraham Pam contends that the inclination to compare our own *gedolim* to those of earlier generations is the work of the *yetzer hara*. What kind of comments do such comparisons elicit? "Who are today's leaders? C'mon, these you call *gedolim*? I'll tell you what *gedolim* are. I'm from the old country. I saw real *gedolim*. These people are a joke, a farce. Don't make me laugh." This is the language of the *yetzer hara*. These are his trademark expressions!

When the great Rav Chaim Soloveitchik became a *maggid shiur*, a Torah lecturer, in the Volozhin Yeshivah, the students complained about him to the administration. Who was this "Rav Chaim" anyway? After all, he only got this position because he had married the granddaughter of Rav Naftali Tzvi Yehudah Berlin, the *Rosh Yeshivah* of Volozhin, known as the Netziv. They, too, fell into the trap of saying, "Who are today's leaders?"

The end of the story is somewhat tangential to our discussion, but it is too good to omit. The resolution of this minor uprising was to bring in three of the greatest *gedolim* of the generation to come observe Rav Chaim and decide if he was worthy of giving a *shiur* in the Volozhin Yeshivah.

On that day, Rav Chaim gave a *shiur* on a very challenging and complex part of Tractate *Yevamos*. He presented a brilliant solution to a difficult passage of the Rambam in his *Yad Hachazakah*, and he could see that the students and the visiting rabbis as well were amazed at his originality. Suddenly, Rav Chaim recalled a particular phrasing in the Rambam's commentary to the Mishneh that did not fit well with the solution he was proposing. His *shiur* didn't work.

Rav Chaim slapped his lectern and said, "The *shiur* I prepared is not true. The Rambam's words in his Mishneh Commentary contradict my hypothesis. It is wrong."

Rav Chaim then sat down.

The three great rabbis conferred quickly and rendered their decision. "He is worthy to say a *shiur* in the Volozhin Yeshivah. Anyone who cares so much about the truth that he is willing to suffer the embarrassment of admitting his own mistake in public, even when no one else has noticed it, definitely deserves this position in the Volozhin Yeshivah."

Rav Yosef Henkin's grandson, writing in his *Sheilos Uteshuvos Bnei Banim*, discusses the greatness of his illustrious grandfather. He raises another question with the words "the judge that shall be in those days." It would have been sufficient to say "the judge in your days." What do the words "that shall be" add? These words, he explains, are an instruction to the judges themselves.

An effective judge cannot live in the past either; he cannot be above his generation. On the contrary, he must be closely attuned to the feelings and attitudes of the generation in which he lives. He must understand the mindset of his generation. He must be "in touch" with his generation's youth, its problems, its fears, its aspirations. The Mishneh says in *Avos* (2:5), "Do not judge your friend until you arrive in his place." The Mishneh may be making this very point. Do not judge your friend until you have an appreciation for his situation. Rav Henkin, he concludes, lived to a very old age. He was a representative of an earlier generation. But he always had an appreciation for the younger generation, and therefore, he was such an effective interpreter of the Halachah.

Reb Levi Yitzchak of Berditchev makes a similar point. The Talmud often leaves a question unresolved, adding the comment *teiku*. The word *teiku* is really an acronym for *Tishbi yetaretz kushios ve'abaios*, the prophet Eliahu will resolve difficulties and questions. With all due respect to Eliahu, says Rav Levi Yitzchak, why is he the one who will resolve all questions? Why not Moshe? Why not Shmuel?

The answer, says Rav Levi Yitzchak, is that Eliahu never died. He lived through every generation, and he understands all of them. Therefore, no one is better qualified to issue final rulings.

A Personal Torah Scroll

וְהָיָה כְשִׁבְתּוֹ עַל כִּסֵּא מַמְלַכְתּוֹ וְכָתַב לוֹ אֶת מִשְׁנֵה הַתּוֹרָה הַזֹּאת

And when he sits on his throne, he shall write two copies of this Torah for himself. (17:18)

EVERY JEW HAS A *MITZVAH* TO WRITE A *SEFER TORAH*, but a Jewish king has a *mitzvah* to write two of them, one to keep at home and one to carry with him wherever he goes. "And it shall be with him, and he shall read from it all the days of his life, in order that he learn to fear God his Lord, to observe all the words of this Torah."

Some commentators contend that the king has to do more than read from the Torah each day. He has to find the pathways and threads of his own life in the Torah and seek his guidance there. Whenever he has a personal question, he should be able to look in the Torah and find his answer. The Talmud considers (*Shabbos* 67a) all Jews to be princes.

Therefore, like the king, all Jews should also seek personal guidance in the Torah.

When Rav Yaakov Kamenetsky first came to the United States he was a *rav* in Seattle, Washington, for a short time and then in Toronto, Canada, which did not have much of a Torah community at the time. About fifty years ago, while still in Toronto, he was walking back from *shul* with a companion on Shavuos, having just heard *Megillas Rus*. He was disturbed.

"I am no better than Elimelech," he told his companion. "Elimelech left Eretz Yisrael for financial reasons. He went from a Jewish place to the fields of Moab, a place without Jews. He was prepared to sacrifice the education and environment of his children, just so he could escape the famine in Eretz Yisrael. Why am I here in Toronto? It does not provide the best environment. It is because I have a job in Toronto, and I don't have a job anywhere else. I'm wrong! This is why Elimelech was punished. I must move to a more Jewish environment."

He had made his decision. Shortly afterward, he moved to New York, where he eventually became the *Rosh Yeshivah* of Torah Vodaath.

Rav Yaakov related to the Torah on a personal level. He saw his own life story in its pages, his own biography, and he also found in it the guidance for all the decisions that would determine the future trajectory of his life.

The Value of Life

כִּי יִמָּצֵא חָלָל בָּאֲדָמָה אֲשֶׁר ד' אֱלֹקֶיךָ נֹתֵן לְךָ
לְרִשְׁתָּהּ נֹפֵל בַּשָּׂדֶה לֹא נוֹדַע מִי הִכָּהוּ

*If you find a murdered person fallen on the field
on the ground God your Lord grants you as a heritage
and no one knows who struck him down. (21:1)*

MURDER VICTIM IS FOUND IN A FIELD OUT IN THE OPEN country between two cities. There are no witnesses and no clues to the identity of his assailant. The Torah demands an exact measurement to determine the closest city. The elders of that city have to declare, "We were not derelict in our responsibilities to this traveler. Our hands did not spill this innocent blood." Then they go through a process of atonement called the *eglah arufah*.

These laws seem to be incongruously wedged in between two chapters that talk about going out to war. What is it doing there?

Rav Yaakov Yitzchak Ruderman, my *Rosh Yeshivah*, explains that the Torah is teaching us a lesson. In times of war, life becomes incredibly cheap. People are dying left and right, men, women, children, soldiers, civilians. Life somehow loses it value.

Therefore, right in the middle of the discussion of war, the Torah interrupts to present the laws of *eglah arufah*, laws that underscore the extreme preciousness of each individual life. An entire city must bring atonement for the loss of one unidentified person who may or may not have passed through unnoticed.

The *Shemen Hatov* suggests that this may be why Yaakov learned the laws of *eglah arufah* with Yosef on their last day together. Perhaps Yaakov's soul felt intuitively that Yosef would become the leader of a huge and powerful nation, that he would have the power of life and death over millions and millions of people. Therefore, it was important to teach him about *eglah arufah* to impress on him the importance of every single human life.

Rav Chaim Soloveitchik, the *rav* of Brisk, once called a special meeting in the *shul*. "My dear friends, we have a serious problem. The Czar's police have arrested a young Jewish boy."

"What did he do?" asked a congregant.

"He burned the Czar in effigy."

The man slapped his forehead in frustration.

"Regardless of what he has done," Rav Chaim continued, "the boy is in danger. We must get him out immediately. It is a question of money. Just money."

"How much money?"

Rav Chaim mentioned the sum. It was an exorbitant amount, and people gasped audibly.

"We are faced with a great *mitzvah*," said Rav Chaim. "This is true *pidyon shevuyim*, ransoming captives."

"Who is the boy?" one man wanted to know. "Is he a *yeshivah* boy?"

"No," said Rav Chaim.

"Is he a member of our *shul*? Is he someone we know?"

"No."

"Is he religious?"

"I'm afraid not. At least not yet. He is from a secular family."

One of the men threw up his hands in frustration. "How will we raise money for a boy like that? And such a large sum!"

"I don't know," said Reb Chaim said, "but somehow it must be done. I am not coming to *shul* on Yom Kippur until the money is collected."

Time passed, and only a small amount of money was raised.

Yom Kippur came. It was time for *Kol Nidrei*, and Rav Chaim still had not come to *shul*. The elders of the community went to his house.

"I told you," he said. "I am not coming until you raise the money. It doesn't matter if the boy is religious or not. A Jewish soul is a Jewish soul!"

The community raised the money to ransom the boy.

Every life is precious.

Parashas Ki Seitzei
פרשת כי תצא

A Month of Days

וְיָשְׁבָה בְּבֵיתֶךָ וּבָכְתָה אֶת אָבִיהָ וְאֶת אִמָּהּ יֶרַח יָמִים

And she shall sit in your house
and bewail her father and mother
for a month (yerach) of days. (21:13)

I N SPECIAL CONSIDERATION OF THE PASSIONS STIRRED BY war, the Torah allows a Jewish soldier to take as a wife a captive gentile woman, called a *yefas to'ar*, provided she converts to Judaism. She is brought into his house, her head is shaved, her clothes of captivity are removed, and she mourns for her parents for thirty days. Afterwards, the soldier is allowed to marry her.

The *Zohar* compares this thirty-day period during which she bewails her parents to the month of Elul that precedes Rosh Hashanah. What is the connection?

There is an oddity in the language of the verse, which refers to the month-long waiting period by the unusual term *yerach* rather than the more common *chodesh*. Why is this so?

We may find a clue in the respective language of a *kesubah*, a prenuptial marriage agreement, and a *get*, a bill of divorce. The date of the *kesubah* refers to a month as *chodesh*, whereas the date of the *get* refers to it as *yerach*. The word *chodesh* is related to the word *chadash*, new. It views the month from the perspective of renewal. It is the time of a new marriage, the beginning of a marital relationship. But the *get* views the month from the perspective of closure, the marital relationship coming to an end. Therefore, it uses the word *yerach*.

The role of the month of Elul is to prepare for Rosh Hashanah, Yom Kippur and the new year. It is a time for contemplation, for reflection, for taking stock, for repentance, a time to look back and ask ourselves, "Where did we go wrong? Where did that year go? How did we let it get away from us?" It is a time for closure, for wrapping up the year and preparing for a brand-new year. It is a month that is essentially a *yerach*, an end to the past that paves the way for a new beginning.

This, according to the *Zohar*, is how the *yefas to'ar* is to spend her month of waiting. She must "bewail her father and mother," which the *Zohar* identifies as turning away from the idolatrous practices of her youth. This month must be a *yerach* for her, a time for closure. In her own mind, she must sever her association with her past. She must close this chapter in her life and begin a new chapter as a loyal Jewish woman.

Mother Birds

שַׁלֵּחַ תְּשַׁלַּח אֶת הָאֵם וְאֶת הַבָּנִים תִּקַּח לָךְ לְמַעַן
יִיטַב לָךְ וְהַאֲרַכְתָּ יָמִים

*Send away the mother bird and take the fledglings
to you in order that it be good for you
and that you will live long. (22:7)*

ONLY TWO OF THE *MITZVOS* IN THE TORAH COME WITH a promise of long life, *kibud av va'eim*, honoring parents, and *sheluach hakan*, sending off the mother bird before taking the fledglings. At first glance, these seem totally dissimilar and unrelated, but intuitively it seems there must be some sort of a common denominator. What can it be?

Rav Yaakov Weinberg, my *Rosh Yeshivah*, suggests that the common denominator may be that both *mitzvos* acknowledge *mesiras nefesh*, self-sacrifice. The Torah tells us to honor our parents because of all the *mesiras nefesh* they have for their children. They sacrifice their time, their energy, their wealth, their hearts and souls for their children, and we must show our appreciation.

A new father once said, "When I was younger, I thought my parents did many things for me, but now that I am a father myself, I realize they did only one thing for me. They gave me their lives." That is *mesiras nefesh*.

We find the same concept of *mesiras nefesh* in the *mitzvah* of *sheluach hakan*. Anyone who has ever tried to catch a bird knows it is virtually impossible to do so. So why does the Torah have to tell us not to take the mother bird? How would we be able to take her if we wanted to? Wouldn't she fly away?

The answer is that the bird would not fly away when her nest is full of fledglings. She is a mother, and she is prepared to sacrifice freedom and even her life in order to remain with her children. For a person to capture that bird is prohibited, because it takes advantage of the *mesiras nefesh* of the maternal instinct and disrespects it. By sending away the mother first, he shows his appreciation for *mesiras nefesh*. In this sense, it is like honoring parents.

The Midrash comments that the two *mitzvos* of honoring parents and sending away the mother bird are the "easiest of the easy" and the "most difficult of the difficult," yet they share the same reward — long life. Apparently, we cannot really know the reward of the *mitzvos*.

Why is sending away of the mother bird referred to as "the easiest of the easy" and honoring parents as "the most difficult of the difficult"?

The *Shemen Hatov* suggests that these *mitzvos* span the spectrum of human nature. According to the Ramban, the Torah wants us to perform the merciful act of sending away the mother bird before taking the fledglings, because this will condition us to become more merciful toward people. Mercy is a common human emotion. People instinctively feel a surge of mercy when they see an animal in distress. We should feel the same instinctive mercy when we see a person in distress, but with other people, all sorts of complicated feelings and prejudices come into play. Therefore, when we develop and reinforce our natural faculty of mercy through a compassionate act toward a mother bird, we will feel a stronger impulse to be merciful when we see a person suffering. This then is the "easiest of the easy" *mitzvos*, because it taps into a natural tendency in human nature.

Honoring parents, on the other hand, goes against human nature. It requires us to acknowledge all they've done for us and show gratitude. It requires us to admit that we needed them, that we could not have done it ourselves. This is a difficult thing for the human ego. The ego would have us view ourselves as independent, self-sufficient and invincible. We can bring ourselves to thank strangers who do small things for us now and then, because this does not really affect our egotistical self-image. But when it comes to our parents, if we admit they did anything, we also have to admit they did everything for us. Our egos do not allow us to say, "I owe you everything." This then is the "most difficult of the difficult" *mitzvos*.

The Tears of the Altar

וְכָתַב לָהּ סֵפֶר כְּרִיתֻת

And he shall write for her a bill of divorce. (24:1)

DIVORCE IS A TERRIBLE THING, BUT THE TORAH recognizes that it is sometimes inevitable, that the differences are sometimes irreconcilable. Nonetheless, comments the Talmud (*Gittin* 90b), "When a first marriage ends in divorce, the Altar [in the *Beis Hamikdash*] sheds tears." Why the Altar of all things?

Some commentators find the connection in the concept of sacrifice. The Altar is the place of sacrifice, the process that brings people closer to the Almighty. Sacrifice is also required in human relationships, especially the marital relationship. When the parties to the marriage are "into themselves" and not willing to give, when eager sacrifice plays no role in the marriage, it cannot remain healthy and vigorous. The Altar, the symbol of sacrifice, weeps for the people who are unable to sacrifice.

Parashas Ki Savo
פָּרָשַׁת כִּי תָבוֹא

They Will Reach You

וּבָאוּ עָלֶיךָ כָּל הַבְּרָכוֹת הָאֵלֶּה וְהִשִּׂיגֻךָ

*And all these blessings will come
upon you, and they will reach you. (28:2)*

THE BLESSINGS OF THE TORAH SEEM TO DO TWO THINGS.
They come upon you, and they also reach you.
Further along (28:15), we find similar language
regarding curses, "And all these curses will come upon you,
and they will reach you." The commentators wonder what
the Torah adds by telling us that the blessings or the curses
"will reach you." How is this different from they "will come
upon you"?

The Torah tells us (*Vayikra* 26:5), "And you will eat your
bread and be satisfied." Rashi, quoting the *Toras Kohanim*,
explains that "you will eat only a small piece of bread and it
will be blessed within you." That little piece of bread will provide an enormous amount of nourishment. In this way, you
will "be satisfied."

The *Beis Av* points out that the blessing is "you will be
satisfied"; you will appreciate the blessing of the bread, and
it will satisfy your mind. That is the ultimate blessing — to

receive the benefit and be aware of it. Sometimes, Hashem showers a person with all manner of blessing — health, a fine family, abundant wealth — and still the person is not satisfied. What good are these blessings to him if they do not satisfy him? Rashi writes (*Avos* 4:1) that a person can be the richest of the rich, but if he is dissatisfied he is no better off than the poorest of the poor. On the other hand, a person can have just a little bit, but if he is satisfied with it, he is blessed.

This is what the Torah means by the words "they will reach you." Even if all the blessings "come upon you," you will not be truly blessed if you are dissatisfied, if you do not appreciate what Hashem has done for you. Only if they penetrate, if "they reach you," will you be considered truly blessed.

The *Beis Av* applies this line of reasoning to curses as well. What good does it do if Hashem sends a person hardships or difficulties to gain his attention and the message goes right by him? What if his car keeps breaking down every other day and it never occurs to him that Hashem is gently reminding him to do some soul-searching? If he does not hear the message, Hashem may need to send him a more explicit one, such as illness in the family. It is much better if "they reach him" right away.

Rav Noach Weinberg once met a longhaired Jewish boy and invited him to his *yeshivah*.

"I don't need a *yeshivah*," the boy said. "The Lord and I are real tight. Like this!" He twisted his index and middle fingers together.

"How do you know that you and the Lord are 'like this,' as you say?" asked Rav Noach.

"Hey, it's clear as the day. The Lord loves me and takes care of me. We're like buddies. You see, here I was riding down this mountain road on my Harley Davidson and this monster truck comes around a hairpin turn — in my lane! — heading right at me. I spun my bike to the left, and next thing you know I was over the cliff. There was nothing in front of me but empty space. I was looking at death, man. They say your whole life passes in front of your eyes at a time like that, but I was too scared to notice. Hey, I was going to die! And as I'm falling down the cliff, I see a branch sticking out of the mountainside. I grabbed it and hung on for dear life. My bike crashed all the way down and exploded in a big ball of fire, but I walked away without a scratch. That's how I know," he concluded, "that me and the Lord are real tight, if you know what I mean."

Rav Noach nodded gravely. "Terrific story, my friend," he said. "The Lord definitely put that tree branch right there to save you. But tell me, who sent that monster truck that drove you off the road? Maybe the Lord was trying to tell you something. May be He was sending you a message."

Expanded Borders

וְהָיִיתָ רַק לְמַעְלָה וְלֹא תִהְיֶה לְמָטָּה

*And you will be only on top
and not on the bottom. (28:13)*

YOU CAN'T BE ON TOP AND ON THE BOTTOM AT THE same time. If you're on top, you're obviously not on the bottom, and vice versa. Why then does the Torah have to tell us that "you will be only on top and not on the bottom"?

Rav Tzaddok Hakohein of Lublin draws our attention to the prayer of Yaavetz (*Divrei Hayamim* I 4:10), "If You will bless me and extend my borders." Why does he ask for both a blessing and an extension? Rav Tzaddok explains that people may be given tremendous bounty, but if they are not properly equipped to handle it, it can destroy their lives. Yaavetz asked Hashem for a blessing, but prudently, he also asked Hashem to extend his borders. He asked to become a bigger, better and wiser person, a man of deep understanding and broad horizons, a man who would be the master of his blessings.

There are classic examples in today's society of people who receive blessings but are not equipped to handle it. We see actors become overnight sensations. They become instant multimillionaires. They buy huge mansions and expensive cars, and they take on the ultra-affluent, high-profile lifestyle of a celebrity. But they don't know how to do it, because after all, they are only ordinary people. And so they have higher rates of divorce, drug abuse, alcoholism and mental breakdown than in any other sector of society. Their blessings turn out to be a curse.

The same holds true with athletes. A fellow can throw a ninety-five miles per hour fastball and has control of his curve ball, and all of a sudden, he's making $10 Million a year. People are hanging on his every word.

"What did you think of this? What did you think of that?"

"Think? What does that mean?"

The guy is a millionaire, his picture is on magazines everywhere, and kids are asking him for autographs. He thinks he is someone, but he is nothing. He received a blessing, but he is not equipped to handle it.

Ordinary people win the lottery. One day they're stuffing bags in the post office, and the next they're multimillionaires. How are they affected? Their lives fall apart. Often, they get divorced or commit suicide. The man hasn't changed. He is still the same insignificant postal worker. He doesn't know how to deal with a million dollars, and so, it destroys his life.

How does one become a bigger person? The Talmud elaborates (*Temurah* 16a) on the prayer of Yaavetz, "If you will bless me with Torah and expand my borders with disciples." We become bigger, expanded people by giving to others. If you give me Torah, Yaavetz prayed, give me disciples with whom to share it.

We grow by being parents. We grow by becoming community-minded individuals. We grow by helping the poor. When we give to others, we go beyond the narrow borders of our own existence. We become broader, more sensitive, people with expanded horizons.

The Talmud states (*Taanis* 9a), "*Asser bishvil she'tis'asher.* Tithe in order to become rich." At first glance, this may seem like some sort of *segulah*, a charm, but it is nothing of the sort. Rav Tzaddok says that this is a logical mechanism. The more money you give away, the more people become dependent on you, the bigger you will become. The more your needs grow, the more Hashem will give you, the more your spheres of influence will expand, the bigger you will become. And so on."

This is the nature of things. The more one makes oneself indispensable to others, the more one grows. The more one grows, the more one is capable of handling it.

Perhaps this is what the Torah meant by the double blessing of "you will be on top" and "you will not be on bottom." Hashem will give us so much blessing that we will be "on top." And at the same time, He will make sure that we don't remain "on bottom," little people with blessings too big to handle. He will help us grow and expand to receive the blessings properly.

Parashas Nitzavim-Vayelech
פרשת נצבים-וילך

Do Not Despair

אַתֶּם נִצָּבִים הַיּוֹם כֻּלְּכֶם

You are all standing here today. (29:9)

IMMEDIATELY AFTER ENUMERATING THE LONG LITANY OF
ninety-eight curses they would face if they disobeyed
Hashem, Moshe called together the Jewish people and
said, "You are all standing here today." What is the significance of this sequence of events?

The Midrash, quoted by Rashi, explains that when the
Jewish people heard the curses they turned green. "Who can
withstand all these curses?" they moaned despondently.
"What will become of us?"

Therefore, Moshe called them together to calm them
down. "Don't be so worried," he said. "You are all standing
here today. After forty turbulent years in the desert, after
angering Hashem so many times — with the Golden Calf, the
Meraglim, the complainers — you are still here today.
Hashem has not destroyed you. So you see, you do not need
to despair."

The commentators are puzzled. Moshe seems to be taking the wind out of his own sails. First, he read off all the horrible curses to scare the Jewish people into obedience, to put "the fear of the Lord" into them. The threat of the curses accomplished their purpose. The people were terrified. Then all of sudden, he relented and told them that it's not so bad. They don't have to be so terrified. Wasn't he defeating his whole purpose by taking the sting out of the *Tochachah*?

The answer is that there is a vast difference between healthy fear and hopelessness. It is a good thing to be realistically apprehensive about the future. It is unhealthy to live in a fool's paradise, believing you can do as you please without suffering any consequences. But hopelessness is destructive. It demoralizes, debilitates and reduces a person to a bowl of quaking jelly.

Moshe saw that the Jewish people had gone beyond fear when they heard the curses. They lost hope and threw in the towel. Therefore, he had to calm them down until they recovered their hope and all they felt was a healthy fear.

Our Sages tell us (*Bava Metzia* 59a) that after the destruction of the Temple "all the gates of prayer were closed, except for the Gates of Tears." The Gates of Tears are the channel of last resort for prayers, and they are never closed.

But if they are never closed, asks the Kotzker Rebbe, why is there a need for gates at all? Why not remove the gates and leave the entranceway wide open?

There are some tears that do not get through, says the Kotzker Rebbe. The gates screen out tears of desperation and hopelessness. Despair is not considered a prayer to the Almighty. If a person is in a state of helplessness and desperation, if he feels backed into a corner so that Hashem is his only hope of salvation, if he calls forth his innermost feelings and thoughts, if he wrings out the perspiration of his heart and soul and sends his hope-laden tears heavenward, there are no barriers in Heaven to a prayer of this sort. It travels directly to the Heavenly Throne.

The Izhbitzer Rebbe connects this concept with the very essence of Jewish identity. The name Jew is derived from the tribe of Judah, as is the Hebrew name Yehudi. Why are all Jews known by the name of one tribe? Because when the brothers stood accused of theft before Yosef in Egypt, the Torah tells us (*Bereishis* 44:18) that Yehudah "stepped up" to argue in their defense. When all seemed to be lost, when faced with the overwhelming weight of evidence against them, Yehudah never gave up hope. That is the definition of a Jew, a person who knows that the Almighty will never abandon him. A person who never gives up hope.

Choose Life

רְאֵה נָתַתִּי לְפָנֶיךָ הַיּוֹם אֶת הַחַיִּים וְאֶת הַטּוֹב וְאֶת
הַמָּוֶת וְאֶת הָרָע

*Behold, I have placed before you today
life and goodness, death and adversity. (30:15)*

SOMETIMES THE CHOICES WE FACE ARE SO CLEARLY defined that we can choose easily. We don't need to be prompted. Near the end of the Torah, Hashem presents the Jewish people with a choice, "Behold, I have placed before you today life and goodness, death and adversity." The correct choice is rather clear, one would think. And then, for good measure, Hashem goes on to tell them, "And you shall choose life in order that you and your children shall live."

The Midrash, however, seems to understand these verses somewhat differently, "I have shown you two paths, and I have gone above and beyond the call of duty by telling you which path to take." What does this mean? How is giving this last piece of seemingly self-evident advice considered going "above and beyond the call of duty"?

Rav Yosef Chaim Sonnenfeld offers an explanation based on another statement in the Midrash in *Parashas Bechukosai*. The Torah tells us (*Vayikra* 26:3), "If you go according to My statutes, safeguard My commandments and do them." What is the difference between "safeguarding" and "doing"? The Midrash comments that "if you safeguard the commandments, I will consider it as if you have done them." As long as a person undertakes to safeguard the commandments, as long as he embraces them and agrees in principle that they should be done — although he has not yet had the opportunity to actualy perform them — he is considered to have done them.

This is precisely what the Midrash is telling us here. Hashem tells the Jewish people that they have a choice — life and goodness or death and adversity. And then, going above and beyond the call of duty, Hashem sweetens the pot. "Choose life," He says. "All you have to do is make the right choice and I will immediately consider it as if you have kept all the *mitzvos*. Just make the choice, and you and your children shall live."

Hopeless and Fearless

וְאָמַר בַּיּוֹם הַהוּא הֲלֹא עַל כִּי אֵין אֱלֹהַי בְּקִרְבִּי
מְצָאוּנִי הָרָעוֹת הָאֵלֶּה

And they will say on that day,
"It is because the Lord is not among us
that all these evils have found us." (31:17)

RECOGNIZING THE ERROR OF ONE'S WAYS IS THE CRITICAL first step toward repentance. It seems, therefore, that the Jewish people would be well on their way to repentance if they should say, "It is because the Lord is not among us that all these evils have found us." But Hashem responds to this admission by saying, "And I will hide My face on that day because of all the evil they have done, for they turned to other gods." Why does Hashem respond so harshly? Aren't the words of the Jewish people an appropriate expression of contrition and remorse?

We read in *Tehillim* (130:4), "Forgiveness is with You so that You shall be feared." Why does the power of forgiveness inspire fear? Wouldn't we fear Him even more if He was unforgiving? Rav Eliahu Dessler explains that people who lose all hope and succumb to despair no longer have any fear. Soldiers are afraid on the eve of battle, but in the heat of the battle, when they are certain they will die, they are no longer afraid. If Hashem did not forgive, we would all be lost. There would be no hope for us, and therefore, we would not fear Him. It is only because He forgives that we are capable of fearing Him.

The Sfas Emes explains that repentance flows from a feeling of hope, from a profound belief that amends can be made and the relationship repaired. Despair is not repentance. When the Jewish people say, "It is because the Lord is not among us that all these evils have found us," this is despair, hopelessness. To feel so unworthy that Hashem has departed from them and abandoned them completely is in itself a further turning away from Him. It just compounds their earlier sins and elicits a further hiding of His face.

Parashas Haazinu
פרשת האזינו

Consider the Changes

זְכֹר יְמוֹת עוֹלָם בִּינוּ שְׁנוֹת דֹּר וָדֹר

*Remember the days of old, consider
the years of each generation. (32:7)*

ISTORY IS AN INTEGRAL PART OF JEWISH LIFE. THE
Torah tells us, "Remember the days of old, consider
the years (*shenos*) of each generation; ask your
father and he will tell you, your grandfather and he will say it
to you." A Jew must always remember the Exodus, the
Giving of the Torah at Mount Sinai, the forty years in the
desert and all the other seminal events of our history that
form the foundation of our faith and our observances. A Jew
must see Hashem's hand in the events of the past and their
consequences. As a secular philosopher once said, "Those
who cannot remember the past are doomed to repeat it."

This we all know and understand. But what is the significance of the repetitive language of the verse? How does
"remember the days of old" differ from "consider the years
of each generation"?

The *Menachem Tzion* resolves this question homiletically.
The word for "years" used here, *shenos*, can also be trans-

lated as "the changes." Consider the changes of each generation. Understand that the lessons of the past must be applied to the present with wisdom and discernment. Times change, people change, circumstances change. Not everything that worked in the past will work today, and not everything that failed in the past would fail today. The Torah can never be changed but it has enough built-in flexibility to allow it to adapt perfectly to all times and places. We have to think and consider hard before we make the application.

The Divine Protectorate

זְכֹר יְמוֹת עוֹלָם בִּינוּ שְׁנוֹת דֹּר וָדֹר

Remember the days of old, consider the years of each generation. (32:7)

WITH BROAD STROKES MOSHE PRESENTS THE SWEEP of history, "Remember the days of old, consider the years of each generation; ask your father and he will tell you, your grandfather and he will say it to you. When the Supreme One gave nations their portion, when He separated the children of man, He set the borders of peoples according to the number of the people of Israel."

Rashi gives a Midrashic interpretation of the references. "Remember the days of old" is a general admonition to recall what happened to our predecessors who angered Hashem. "Consider the years of each generation" refers to the generation of Enosh who were inundated by ocean waters and the generation of the Great Flood. "When the Supreme One gave nations their portion, when He separated the children of man" refers to the generation of the Dispersion when people tried to build the Tower of Babel.

We have a rule, however, that the plain meaning of the verse is always significant. The simple interpretation of these verses is an admonition to us to understand history and learn its lessons.

As Jews, we believe that the Almighty is not only the Creator but that He is also the Guide of history. We see His hand in the historical events that we witness. And the Torah is telling us that "He set the borders of peoples according to the number of the people of Israel." The ultimate purpose of the wars and conflicts that shape the world, the shifting borders of the globe, all of these are determined by the Divine plan for the Jewish people. We may not see it immediately. We may never see it at all. But in some way, the destiny of the Jewish people turns the intricate wheels of history.

Rav Elchanan Wasserman, whom the Nazis murdered at the beginning of the Second World War, quotes these verses as proof that all world history revolves around the Jewish people. "When the Treaty of Versailles drew a new map of Europe [at the end of the First World War]," he writes, "the borders were already drawn in Heaven."

One does not have to be a politically astute individual to appreciate the impact of the breakup of the Soviet Union on the Jewish people. But we sometimes think the smaller details do not really affect us. What difference is it to us whether or not Azerbaijan goes its own way? What difference is it to us if Chechnya declares its independence? But this is a mistake. It makes a difference — even if we don't see it.

What difference did it make if the Ottoman Empire sided with the Allies or the Germans during the First World War? Who at the time gave it a second thought from the perspective of the Jewish people? But in retrospect, it was a critical decision. By choosing the wrong side, the Ottoman Turks were forced to surrender their possessions in the Middle East, among these a dusty strip of land called Palestine. Great Britain received the mandate for Palestine, which opened the way for the establishment of modern-day Israel.

When we see maps changing, we need to hold our breaths. Somehow or another, this will affect us, either for the good or, Heaven forbid, otherwise. Sometimes it is for our benefit. Sometimes, G-d forbid, it is for our punishment. We are always on center stage, because we are the protectorate of the Master of the Universe.

Parashas Vezos Haberachah
פרשת וזאת הברכה

The National Heirloom

תּוֹרָה צִוָּה לָנוּ מֹשֶׁה מוֹרָשָׁה קְהִלַּת יַעֲקֹב

The Torah Moshe commanded us is an heirloom
for the congregation of Yaakov. (33:4)

EVERY LITTLE JEWISH CHILD LEARNS THIS VERSE. "*TORAH tzivah lanu Moshe morashah kehillas Yaakov*. The Torah Moshe commanded us is an heirloom for the congregation of Yaakov." Sometimes the word *morashah* is translated as an inheritance or a heritage, but this is not precise. The exact translation of the word *morashah* is heirloom.

An heirloom is something we hold precious and dear, something we cherish because it connects us to the treasured past, something we want to pass along to future generations, just as we have received it ourselves from earlier generations.

The Torah is the heirloom of the Jewish people. It is the sublime heirloom, our eternal connection to the Almighty. In the words of the Psalmist (*Tehillim* 144:15), "Fortunate is the nation that has it so, fortunate is the nation that God is their Lord."

What is an heirloom to the gentile world? I would like to recount a story I once read about a woman who went on her first deer hunt and shot her first deer. She made laborious preparations for this momentous event. She studied a stack of books about deer hunting, and she learned how to shoot a 30-30 Model 94 Winchester rifle that had been handed down in the family for generations.

So what was her heirloom? A 30-30 Model 94 Winchester rifle. Her great-grandfather passed it on lovingly to her grandfather, and her grandfather gave it to her. On the morning of the hunt, she took the rifle apart and lovingly cleaned and oiled it until it gleamed. And then she went out and shot her first deer. A thrilling moment.

How fortunate are we that the Torah is our heirloom! How fortunate are the Jewish people that God is their Lord!

His Finest Moment

וּלְכֹל הַיָּד הַחֲזָקָה וּלְכֹל הַמּוֹרָא הַגָּדוֹל אֲשֶׁר
עָשָׂה מֹשֶׁה לְעֵינֵי כָּל יִשְׂרָאֵל

*For all the strong hands and great awesome deeds
Moshe displayed before the eyes of all Israel. (34:12)*

The Torah concludes with a stirring eulogy for Moshe, the lawgiver of the Jewish people, "Never again has there arisen in Israel a prophet like Moshe, whom God knew face to face; all the signs and wonders that God sent him to perform in the land of Egypt against Pharaoh, all his servants and all his land; all the strong hands and great awesome deeds Moshe displayed before the eyes of all Israel."

Each of these phrases, as interpreted by Rashi, recalls a specific aspect of Moshe's greatness, leading step by step to the climax of his epitaph: "before the eyes of all Israel," that he had the courage to smash the *Luchos*, Tablets of the Ten Commandments, in full view of the Jewish people. When all was said and done, this was the ultimate expression of Moshe's greatness, the most superb act he ever performed.

What was so magnificent about this act that it transcended his Torah and all the great miracles he performed?

The *Ateres Mordechai* offers a profound insight. Before we begin a project, whether it is a book or a building or anything else, we can consider it critically and objectively. But once the project gets underway, we are no longer so objective. And as the project progresses, our objectivity progressively shrinks — until it completely disappears. After we have written our book, we are so invested that we no longer want to entertain any critical thoughts. We don't want to hear that we made a mistake in this or that we shouldn't have written that. We go to extremes to defend against our critics, although we might have made the same arguments ourselves before the fact.

And what if we publish a work on the Torah or even a single *shtickel Torah*, an original Torah homily? We are so proud and pleased with ourselves that we will twist and turn and squirm and contort ourselves every which way to make the unworkable work.

Can we imagine then how Moshe must have felt when he came down the mountain with the Ten Commandments? This was what he had been working toward for years. He had sacrificed for these Tablets. He had spent forty days in Heaven without food or drink fending off the angels and securing the Tablets for the Jewish people. This was his magnum opus, his life's work.

Now he comes down the mountain and sees the people worshiping the Golden Calf. He knows instinctively what he must do. He knows that the people are unworthy and that he must smash the Tablets.

And what about all the toil and effort he had invested in them?

He could easily have rationalized to himself, "All right, the people clearly don't deserve the Tablets now, but maybe things will change. What's the point of breaking the *Luchos* if I might need them again in a day or two? Perhaps I should just put them aside without showing them to the people until they are again deserving. Why ruin a good pair of Tablets?"

But Moshe did not do this. He had absolute integrity. He disregarded all the efforts he had invested in the Tablets. He did not consider that his life's work was going to waste. Truth demanded that he break them, and he did not hesitate to do so.

This was the ultimate virtue the Torah could ascribe to Moshe. The truth, the integrity, the honesty, the clarity of vision uncolored by personal considerations. This was his greatest accomplishment.

I heard a beautiful comment along these lines from Rav Mordechai Gifter. The Talmud tells us (*Kiddushin* 57a) that Shimon the Amsonite used to develop a secondary meaning from every single occurrence of the Hebrew particle *es* in the Torah. For instance, in the commandment of honoring parents there is an *es*, from which he derived the inclusion of older siblings.

One day, he turned his attention to the verse (*Devarim* 6:13), "*Es Hashem Elokecha tira.* You shall fear God your Lord." All of a sudden, he said, "This cannot be. There is no secondary recipient of the fear we must feel for Hashem." Therefore, he recanted on all his original derivations, thousand and thousands of insights, because his rule could not be applied consistently to the entire Torah.

And then Rabbi Akiva came along and taught that even in this there could be secondary recipients — Torah scholars! They are worthy of sharing the reverence for the Divine.

Wonderful.

But why, asks Rav Gifter, couldn't Shimon the Amsonite think of this solution? Why was this specialist on the *es* particle stumped while Rabbi Akiva was able to figure it out?

The answer, says Rav Gifter, is that Rabbi Akiva saw the way Shimon the Amsonite dealt with this problem. He saw the tremendous devotion to truth, the inviolable intellectual integrity, the willingness to forfeit many years of effort and creativity if there was a problem with the reasoning. When Rabbi Akiva saw that a Torah scholar could reach such a level of integrity and honesty in defense of the truth of Torah, he realized that Torah scholars too can share in the reverence for the Divine. They can be included in *"Es Hashem Elokecha tira."*

Customarily, a glass is broken at a Jewish wedding. What is the reason for this custom? The reason most commonly given is to recall the destruction of Yerushalayim during times of rejoicing. One commentator connects this custom to the breaking of the Tablets of the Commandments. Why do we need to be reminded of this event during a wedding?

Perhaps it is because the breaking of the Tablets was such an act of profound honesty and integrity on the part of Moshe. In order for a marriage to work, there is also a need for extraordinary honesty and integrity on the part of both husband and wife. In case of discussion or disagreement, both have to speak and act with absolute honesty and integrity, to be straight and aboveboard, to do what is right rather than what is comfortable and convenient. Both have to be ready to admit their mistakes rather than stand on their pride. Both need to be prepared to let go of their preconceived notions and prejudices and work toward the common good. Both have to be willing to face the truth.

These are not easy demands, but if husband and wife want to gain the most happiness possible from their marriage, they have to find the strength of character in themselves to do these things. The reminder of the breaking of the Tablets is meant to give them courage. If Moshe was ready to break them and let go of all his hopes and dreams for the sake of truth, these two people can find a way to build their marriage on a foundation of truth.

4401 Second Avenue
Brooklyn, New York 11232
(718) 921-9000
www.artscroll.com